Thanks, but This Isn't for Us

Thanks, but This Isn't for Us

A (Sort of) Compassionate Guide to Why Your Writing Is Being Rejected

JESSICA PAGE MORRELL

JEREMY P. TARCHER/PENGUIN
a member of Penguin Group (USA) Inc.
New York

JEREMY P. TARCHER/PENGUIN
Published by the Penguin Group
Penguin Group (USA) Inc., 375 Hudson Street, New York, New York 10014, USA • Penguin Group (Canada), 90 Eglinton Avenue East, Suite 700, Toronto, Ontario M4P 2Y3, Canada (a division of Pearson Canada Inc.) • Penguin Books Ltd, 80 Strand, London WC2R 0RL, England • Penguin Ireland, 25 St Stephen's Green, Dublin 2, Ireland (a division of Penguin Books Ltd) • Penguin Group (Australia), 250 Camberwell Road, Camberwell, Victoria 3124, Australia (a division of Pearson Australia Group Pty Ltd) • Penguin Books India Pvt Ltd, 11 Community Centre, Panchsheel Park, New Delhi–110 017, India • Penguin Group (NZ), 67 Apollo Drive, Rosedale, North Shore 0632, New Zealand (a division of Pearson New Zealand Ltd) • Penguin Books (South Africa) (Pty) Ltd, 24 Sturdee Avenue, Rosebank, Johannesburg 2196, South Africa

Penguin Books Ltd, Registered Offices: 80 Strand, London WC2R 0RL, England

Published simultaneously in Canada

Most Tarcher/Penguin books are available at special quantity discounts for bulk purchase for sales promotions, premiums, fund-raising, and educational needs. Special books or book excerpts also can be created to fit specific needs. For details, write Penguin Group (USA) Inc. Special Markets, 375 Hudson Street, New York, NY 10014.

Library of Congress Cataloging-in-Publication Data

Morrell, Jessica Page, (date).
Thanks, but this isn't for us : a (sort of) compassionate guide to why your writing is being rejected / Jessica Page Morrell.
p. cm.
ISBN 978-1-58542-721-5
1. Fiction—Authorship. 2. Autobiography—Authorship. 3. Authorship. I. Title.
PN3355.M675 2009 2009023252
808.3—dc22

Printed in the United States of America
10 9 8 7 6 5 4 3 2 1

BOOK DESIGN BY MEIGHAN CAVANAUGH

Contents

Being a writer is like having homework

every night for the rest of your life.

—Lawrence Kasdan

Preface

A naked truth about the publishing industry is that far more manuscripts are rejected than are published. No one knows the exact statistic that reveals the proportion of acceptances to rejections, but it's less than 1 percent, a depressing and daunting number. Because rejection stings, shakes our confidence, and makes us question our sanity, this is a book about avoiding rejection. In these pages I hope to transform your manuscript into a marketable product and help you realize your elusive dream of getting published.

Yes, I just wrote that sadly unromantic word *product.* But I'm getting ahead of myself. I work as a developmental editor, and the feedback that writers receive from someone like me, who wields a pen as sharp as a scalpel, can also be painful. I want to spare you months of toil and large doses of humiliation. I want to give you an insider's view in the hope that you can apply these insights to your manuscript *before* you show it to another person.

The idea for this book began because of one of my biggest fears. It goes like this: after I die at a ripe old age, I'm restless and I cannot adjust to the afterlife, whatever that may be. I imagine death to be like wearing a permanent invisibility cloak like in the Harry Potter books. So, knowing I cannot be spotted, I return to the place I once lived and wander around town, visiting friends and family and old haunts. Well, to tell the truth, I'm snooping the way I did when I was twelve and would babysit for my neighbors and poke around in their closets, cupboards, and—God slap some decency into me but it's already too late—dresser drawers.

Then on a lark—if you can call ideas that occur when you're dead a lark—I decide to visit my grave. Perhaps it's morbid curiosity, or maybe right after I died I was too busy making the transition to the dead zone to notice details of my final resting place.

During these wanderings I find my grave, check out the view, and notice there's a bouquet near the headstone. I'm cheered by this little detail because while alive I always had fresh flowers around. Then I bend down and read the inscription on the headstone: "Children and dogs loved her, but writers called her the Angel of Death."

And if I weren't already dead, I'd keel over.

Because, of course, being compared to this sword-wielding creature is not exactly a compliment. If you're not up on biblical lore, this angel was referred to in both testaments and killed the Egyptians' firstborn children before the Jews were set free to wander around clueless in the desert for forty years.

In my defense, let me explain how I received this name from a student attending one of my critique groups. I started teaching writers in 1991, and for the past twelve years or so I've also made my living by breaking writers' hearts. This bit of cruelty stems from my gig as a developmental editor, although there has also been plenty of heartbreak to go around in my critique groups over the years. I also teach at writing conferences around North America and in this capacity am usually critiquing the manuscripts of hopefuls.

I've read hundreds of manuscripts and have taught thousands of writers over the years and I usually dole out a lot of bad news for these writers, although praise is also given when due. So here's the irony: in order for writers to turn over their precious manuscripts for my opinion, they must trust me. If they've attended my workshops or classes, they recognize that I'm the real deal and know a lot about writing. Likewise if they've read my books.

So because of this trust and because writing is simply a difficult undertaking, when I'm sending a critique to a writer whose manuscript I've edited, I often feel like Simon Cowell meets the Grinch. Like many writers, I know what it's like to have a stranger scrutinize my words. As author Elizabeth Berg said so aptly, having your writing critiqued is like handing over your naked baby to strangers armed with rocks. So I don't take this trust lightly and I feel your pain. Really. But tough critiquing is a basic and essential part of the writing process. It's not only a fact that beginning writers need to accept; it's likely the only way your writing will improve.

It amazes me how many good ideas I've seen in manuscripts over the years and how few of those ideas are ready for the cold gimlet eyes of the publishing industry. Talk about naked babies—most of these stories (and by this I'm referring broadly to book-length manuscripts, including novels, memoirs, how-to books, and screenplays) will be chewed up and spit out faster than you can say "fuhgettaboutit."

The reason is simple: too many beginning writers are bad writers. Too many don't understand the underpinnings of fiction or how to craft a scene based on opposition or cannot fathom why their childhood in Sheboygan with a father who didn't laugh at their knock-knock jokes is not the stuff from which memoirs are made. Too many cannot write with poetry and resonance, and too many know too little about the publishing biz.

It also puzzles me how seemingly bright people write stuff so overwrought, anemic, pointless, or just plain crappy that I have longed to tack on extra charges for pain and suffering. While I've read manuscripts that prove the writer is brilliant, steeped in craft, I've also read manuscripts by writers who can barely manage to string together sentences, and some who are clearly a few sandwiches short of a picnic.

Now I know this sounds cruel and, like, well, just maybe I've earned my reputation as the Angel of Death, but if you sat in my chair, you might be tempted to write this book, too.

In my work as a developmental editor I write my clients long memos after I've read and analyzed their manuscripts. When I send off a memo about a story that isn't working most of the time, I feel a little queasy. Well, actually sometimes I'm nearly ready to throw up because I know how much pain it might cause the person receiving it. I realize that the writer has worked on the manuscript for months or years and sometimes has rewritten it three or four times. The writer toiled away at his computer while friends were at parties or ball games or movies or picnics.

I'm the person telling him his belief in his story is misplaced, and this breaks my heart. And I know that reading my memo will be about as much fun as undergoing surgery and when you awake, dazed and nauseous from the anesthesia and reeling from pain, your true love dumps you.

Surprisingly, many of my clients, especially those who are published authors, are remarkably good sports about my critiques. I have received gracious thank-yous, and heard sighs of relief because the writer now understands what is missing from his story, and good-natured laughs over mistakes now explained. We often chat on the phone or meet in person after they've read my memo. This is when we brainstorm solutions—perhaps tighten the opening, intensify or change the locale of the ending, or develop the protagonist's backstory or motivations.

A number of my clients buckle down and crank out a much better version of their story. A number go on to receive publishing contracts. On the other hand, I suspect some never quite recover, although I hope their scars fade with the years.

The hardest part of writing these memos is being diplomatic and encouraging while pointing out the manuscript's problems. Obviously I cannot come out and tell the writer that his or her story sucks and he or she should take up breeding long-haired dachshunds. But there have been times when I've wanted to suggest a change of occupation even as I felt so much sympathy for the writer that I could have wept.

I conceived the idea for this book in 2007, began writing it in the spring of 2008, and completed it in the spring of 2009. During that time the country underwent a huge economic downturn, banks failed, the mortgage bubble burst, and the world of book publishing as we knew it disappeared. Publishers now operate in a more corporate culture than in previous times, only best-selling authors receive major support for marketing their books, and mega stores and big box stores call the shots on which authors are granted shelf space and which are not.

Book sales are down, publishing companies are trimming staffs, and independent presses are closing their doors. This means writers without platforms often have difficulties finding agents willing to represent them. This means we need to weather this publishing downturn, and if you're a good writer, it's time to become an amazing writer.

This is my memo from the trenches to help you become an amazing writer. It includes the main screwups and weaknesses I've seen in manuscripts and advice for heading in a more publishable direction. I start with making a rollicking first impression by writing a powerful beginning, then move on to the basics of structure and plot. The book also explains how suspense works, why we need sensory details in our writing, how language can sink a story, and how to craft effective dialogue. Chapters also cover how conflict fuels all storytelling, how to make readers care about your characters, how to write in scenes, and how to stir emotions in the reader. I also include a chapter on writing memoirs because I've read so many by writers who are simply clueless about this genre. There is also a chapter on editing that is based on the process I use in working on my clients' manuscripts. Finally, I include tips about living the writing life, because if you can't keep it together while writing, the work will never get done.

In these pages I use deal breakers that have sunk stories I've worked on, but I have disguised details to protect the guilty. These examples aren't used to embarrass anyone but rather to demonstrate that while all great writing is unique, all bad writing shares common traits. But first you need to recognize your mistakes, then you can use the instruction in these chapters to fix them.

If I sound like a badass on these pages, keep in mind that I'm a pussycat compared to the suits in the publishing world. You know, the folks who send out the rejection letters. So let's get started on filling your mailbox with good news.

One

First Impressions: How to Write Dynamic, Evocative, and Potent Beginnings

> Remember, begin with tension and immediacy. Make readers feel the story has started. They want to be in your world, not be told about it. Don't preface—plunge in.
>
> —JEROME STERN, *Making Shapely Fiction*

Dear Wanna Be a Published Writer:

This isn't a book about false promises or cheery rah-rahs. This book never claims that anyone can write a best seller or become a billionaire just by typing away, or even that writing is the greatest joy because, after all, we cannot forget about dancing, chocolate, and sex. Rather, it's written by a Demon of Harsh Reality and meant as a hefty dose of reality along with encouragement to keep trying, to keep learning. Because writing is a craft, and it can be learned. And as for any craft, we need to recognize our weaknesses before we can succeed, and often the period of mastery is preceded by some truly awful attempts.

Let's start at the beginning of your tale and talk about making a kick-ass first impression. Story openings are like job interviews, and if the words on the page entertain, you get the job. If they don't, somebody who writes better gets the job.

The best openings of a story, novel, or memoir are contagious—they make the reader yearn for more because you chose the best words at the best moment to launch the events that follow while raising questions that demand answers. After all, you're writing for an editor, a highly discerning reader. Editors are word people. They are connoisseurs who love the written word and appreciate delicate language, carefully crafted sentences, and refinement.

Along with a knack for crafting beautiful language, your first paragraphs need to set the tone for the story to come. Especially in these days of blogging, dashed-off e-mails, and self-publishing, it's important to strive for perfection. As in strutting-the-red-carpet-at-the-Academy-Awards first impression. And your opening needs to have the impact of a starlet draped in a strapless gown and diamonds or a debonair actor in a crisp and oh-so-sexy tux. It needs to dazzle and assure the reader that you can handle what follows. It needs to make a promise about the kind of story that follows.

Promises, Promises

So your opening words contain a promise to your reader: *Read these pages, and I'll transport you to a world based on your expectations, where the story events deliver an emotionally satisfying experience.* And the unfolding events in your novel must be appropriate for the genre or type of story that you're writing.

This works for memoir, also. When a reader opens the first

page of a memoir, he wants to read the truth about the author's dramatic experiences. Your opening promises that the true events of a life are fascinating and possibly horrifying. Now, your story might be a bare-assed exposé of squalor and debauchery with your skinny-necked stepfather starring as the true-life villain. Or it might be a luminous and uplifting tale of endurance, or a life story that lies somewhere in between. No matter your approach, your first words telegraph that this story will make a reader laugh, cry, and ponder truths about the human experience.

On the other hand, when a reader opens a novel, he's signing up for a pack of lies. You, the writer, are the liar and your reader is the sucker who is going to buy all these lies, hook, line, and sinker, as the old saying goes. It's part of the contract that you and the reader are agreeing to. Your opening promises that you are going to tell the sort of lies that the reader specifically wants to hear. This logic is fairly simple because each genre has a built-in audience and your opening winks a come-on at that audience like a saloon girl in the Old West.

If a reader plunks down $24.95 for a fantasy or science fiction novel, he expects fantastical elements and interesting explorations of themes that perhaps cannot be explored in a story that's based strictly on realistic elements. Of course some sci-fi stories are set in today's world because lots of chilling truths can be told about this world, especially about ecological nightmares or technology unleashed. So your opening can start in a galaxy far away or just down the street, but it promises that imaginative ideas will be explored.

Likewise, suspense novels are always about a crime and a criminal who needs to be caught. Besides the classic detective story, there are subgenres such as espionage, psychological suspense, romantic suspense, police procedural, courtroom procedural, whodunit, and cozies. Each type has varying degrees of violence and grit, but all are a thrill ride. And the opening must present a world in which all hell is about to break loose.

If you're writing a romance, in the opening pages love will be in the air, as the lovers collide, usually appearing at an inconvenient time. In a romance, readers expect to delve deeply into the hero's and heroine's psyches, want to watch the blossoming romance falter and fizzle before it finally blooms, and want all other aspects of the plot—even if it is set on another planet in the distant future—to rank secondary to the romance. But all this is promised in an opening that unfolds with just the right note.

An emotional opening prepares the reader for a heart-rattling journey, just as a philosophical opening promises a thoughtful exploration of themes, an action-packed opening promises a bronco-breaking ride, and a quiet beginning usually promises an intense exploration of characters' lives.

So start with a specific promise about the story that follows and then, drumroll, please, keep the promise.

Beginnings Matter

Let's get back to editors for a moment because, after all, they're in the business because they want to read something they've never read before and love nothing better than discovering a good story. It's your job to intrigue and deliver these enchanting moments of discovery.

But here's the rub—in the frantic, fast-paced world of book publishing, most editors and agents are notoriously pressed for time. Their desks are stacked high with solicited and unsolicited manuscripts and they spend a lot of time in meetings and answering e-mails and phone calls. This means that their first glimpse of your manuscript must immediately stir their interest.

In fact, beginnings, more than any other part of your work, are disproportionately important. And all beginnings must hook your readers to pursue your next pages. *Hook* is the term that means your opening is a grabber, a page-turner. Now, a beginning can be brief and enigmatic, lush and descriptive, or land the reader smack in the midst of intense action, bada bing; but your story lives or dies on the strength of your opening paragraphs. For a book-length novel to sell, the hook must happen in the first page, or, better yet, in the first paragraph. This is especially true if you're writing for the young adult or middle-grade reader.

Hook, Line, and Reader

Let's think about how to seduce a reader. The best beginnings are like forces gathering, about to be unleashed on the reader. With the first words, the writer establishes his credibility, introduces viewpoint and voice, and makes the reader care about people and the story unfolding. Obviously this is a tall order for a few sentences or paragraphs to accomplish. Also, since fiction and memoir are based on adversity, typically an opening introduces a character or person under stress and the story world starting to tilt off balance.

Effective openings set a story in motion and create momentum, tension, and suspense. They involve readers in the story and thus have immediacy. This means you need to plan your first moves for maximum impact.

- Openings also create involvement and sympathy for a character or memoirist depicted in the opening moments. If you're writing fiction or memoir, start with a threatening change in a character's or memoirist's situation. This *inciting incident* starts the action, often opens a can of worms, and creates imbalance.
- Introduce the protagonist or memoirist or important characters, and give the reader his first glimpse of their core personality traits. These traits remain *consistent* throughout the story, are *intricately linked to the plot*, and are *tested by the events, especially the troubles* in the story. In fact, a plot (or memoir) always *showcases* a protagonist's primary traits.
- Introduce or hint at upcoming conflict.
- Use specific sensory details to immerse readers in the story world and situation.
- Establish setting and milieu of story, including the era.
- Use polished prose, figurative language, and other artful flourishes.

Deal Breakers

I've talked with many editors and agents over the years and learned that there are specific types of writers we most enjoy working with; we each have particular tastes in literature as well as pet peeves in writing that make us throw up our hands in despair. I've singled out the deal breakers—the mistakes that lead to rejection—that I've spotted most often, and you'll find this section featured in every chapter about craft.

Here's what I want you to do: imagine an acquisition editor's desk on the day before Thanksgiving. It's piled high with manuscripts, mail, notes, and, in this case, a box of tissues, Vicks DayQuil, and three kinds of cough drops. I want you to imagine the editor is coming down with a bad cold, has forty-six e-mails to answer and paperwork to finish, and her in-laws are arriving later that evening for a ten-day visit. Then I want you to imagine her glancing through the opening pages of a pile of manuscripts during her lunch break and encountering some of the deal breakers I've spotted in opening pages over the years.

Country Roads

This type of opening takes the reader on a scenic tour without intrigue, tension, or conflict. Often these openings describe cloud formations, bees buzzing, and soft breezes. For example, one opening I read contained two and a half pages of a character driving along before the story opened with her arrival at her childhood home, and that scene *still* didn't include an inciting incident. It went something like this:

> Rowena zipped down the window so she could get some fresh air into the old Mustang and escape the smells of exhaust that filled the car. The summer air smelled of cow dung mixed with moist earth and apple blossoms. She had always loved this earthy, country smell. It reminded her of being a girl and walking home from school with her best friend Meg Seibert along the old

> Apple Tree Road. Sometimes they'd stop and pick clover or flowers to bring home to their mothers. Sometimes they'd talk about what they'd do when they grew up. There was such nostalgia in her memories, just as there was goodness in the sun on her face as she drove down the old country road.

Crash Course

This is an opening that tries way too hard to give too much information about a character, including his past, what he looks like, what he is wearing down to his socks, along with the present moment and the story world. Trouble is, too much too soon gives even smart readers a headache. Readers are not dim, and they certainly know when too much is tossed at them too soon. After all, you've got the rest of the book to explain things. Sometimes these openings include police-blotter descriptions of characters so as soon as a character walks into a scene, the scene is paused for a detailed description. Here's an example of a crash course opening:

> Mary Ellen walked into the room wearing a low-cut dress guaranteed to turn every man's head and make other women wish they'd worn their Wonder Bra. She looked good in the garnet-colored gown; it set off her flashing blue eyes and contrasted nicely with her pale blond hair piled high in an elegant chignon. She looked around the room and saw a scene of opulence as waiters tiptoed around offering champagne and sumptuous-looking canapés dotted with caviar, while meanwhile a four-piece combo played smooth jazz amid the hum of the partygoers. Mary Ellen had wanted to attend this annual event

at the Evergreen Country Club ever since she was a young girl living near the sawmill. Ever since she wore her sister's hand-me-downs and ate beans and corn bread for dinner, night after night. Mary Ellen had finally arrived.

The Dud Prologue

I'm a rare editor who has no problem with a good prologue. Trouble is, not many writers understand why a prologue is used to begin a story and that it needs to shine a light of significance on all the events that follow it. A prologue must be justified because it means your story has a double opening. It also must somehow stand apart from the rest of your story, and it needs a hook and to raise a question. Typically it shows the future or past life of the protagonist, or reveals events that will have a profound effect on the story. It can also be told from a different point of view, and most prologues are fairly short, though embedded with tension.

One prologue in a client's manuscript that was especially duddy began the day before the inciting incident and showed the protagonist packing to move to a new city, sighing over the contents of the boxes she was packing, worrying about her new life in a new city. In chapter 1, the following day, she was living in the new city with all the boxes and furniture magically transported three thousand miles in mere hours.

Another dud prologue I encountered featured a nameless, faceless villain wandering around muttering in an undefined cavern of horrors. Or at least I think it was supposed to be a cavern of horrors because it lacked details and menace. If you want to begin with a prologue, study the level of details used by published authors to make it zing. Remember, it must create a question that demands to be answered and must make us wonder about the people we're about to meet in the story.

Mirror, Mirror

Along with dreams, my least favorite openings involve a character looking in the mirror. Especially if she's heading off on a date or to the office. They always shriek, "In case you didn't realize it, you're reading a story!" Of course, these mirror-gazing scenes can make me want to take a match to the manuscript no matter where they occur in the story.

They look like this:

> Mary Ellen adjusted the collar of her navy blue blazer, then slipped on her favorite pearl earrings. Her startlingly blue eyes regarded her solemnly in the mirror. *He's the one*, she thought, as she inspected her teeth to make sure there was no spinach showing from dinner.
>
> The teeth were perfect, her coral pink lipstick on her rosebud lips just the right shade, and her ivory skin offset by the pale blue of her stylish blouse and long blond hair.
>
> "I'll do," she said out loud and picked up her purse from the hall table. "It's now or never—look out, world, here I come."

Not Much Going On

In these sorts of openings the protagonist sits in a diner killing time with a cup of coffee, or wanders through a grocery store picking out the perfect head of lettuce, or rakes leaves, or chills out by looking through her photo albums, or any number of ordinary tasks that simply don't contain tension. Just label this one deadly. While a status quo—the world of the story before it begins—can be shown in an opening, there is always unease simmering beneath, something about to unravel or crack. Openings mean something threatening is about to happen to someone who'd rather avoid the threat, avoid the heat, avoid the challenge about to be unleashed.

Paint-by-Number

This type of beginning is clichéd, as in the "it was a dark and stormy night" oldie but not so goody. Now, the truth is that a dark and stormy night creates a terrific milieu for a story—after all, we're all at a disadvantage when it's dark and nature is rampaging. But the trick is to make things fresh and not to overdo the foreshadowing.

So if your story begins with this sort of paint-by-number, you're likely doomed:

> It was a Saturday night in Sweetville and the storm that was looming looked like it was going to be fierce. It had already blacked out the moon and set the old elm trees around the town square swaying in the wind. You could just tell by the way the wind swept through the town that it was bringing something bad along with it.

Sensationalized

This means the opening is so explosive and disturbing that the rest of the story cannot live up to these events. Now, you can start off strong with a murder, kids discovering a body while playing in a crummy neighborhood, an accident, or a fight, but the story that follows must justify the beginning and proceed briskly so that the explosive opening gambit isn't an aberration. An over-the-top, sensational, grab-you-by-the-crotch opening requires an action-packed, fast-paced story that delivers the gusto. With possibly a bloodbath or two stirred in. Beware of writing openings such as this:

> The body was covered with maggots. Lots of maggots. Maggots munching on the eyeballs, maggots crawling out of the ears, and one slipping from a caved-in nostril. Where there weren't maggots it looked like something had been chewing on the corpse, with sharp, rabid teeth. Something ravenous and soulless.

Speedway

This opening also starts too fast and the reader never has a chance to get his bearings or understand the context for the actions that are taking place. In most cases the speedway opening means the protagonist is being chased by some unknown and unseen assailant and typically the details are vaguely drawn. When I read these sorts of openings, I feel like I've arrived late to a cocktail party and everybody is already drunk and arguing and breaking the glassware.

An example looks something like this:

> Jaden and I start running for our lives. Raldorm and the rest of the crew already have the holoprints, so now it's just a question

> of holding off the Death squad until they can slip back to the *Tempest* and off of Jupiter 3. We can make it happen.
>
> The soldiers take the bait and give chase, not realizing that we're merely bait. The strategy is working. Our armor, the latest in bulletproof Kevlar III, isn't quite as sophisticated as theirs, but at least we had enough time to deploy laser death rays around the station before they breached the hold. Their zip-bullets are flying everywhere, but somehow we're dodging them.
>
> "Don't look back," I shout to Jaden, as I dive for the atom-destabilizer device.

Tear-stained

In this opening, a sister to the Sensationalized type, the writer cranks out melodrama because a character is weeping or displaying other extreme emotions on the page even though readers don't know who the heck is crying and why. It's hard to develop empathy on the first page when we're still strangers. This is especially problematic when a character is hysterical, because if a story starts at such a shrill pitch, the reader worries how intense drama in the closing will play out.

> As Genevieve gazed longingly toward the shoreline, a single tear slid down her ivory cheek and she stifled a sigh. But try as she might to suppress her sorrow, more tears followed, and she collapsed against the railing, sobs racking her body, grief encircling her like a shroud.

Options for Openings

While an opening has a lot of heavy lifting to accomplish, happily there are many ways to begin. While I've read terrific beginnings in my clients' stories, I'm protecting their privacy in this book, so I use openings from published stories or novels. I'm sure you'll agree they all grab our attention and pull us into the story:

Dialogue

Beginning with dialogue makes for immediacy and makes readers wonder who is talking and why. Here is an example from a short story, *Your Better Half,* by K. W. Oxnard.

"I've misplaced my soul," you tell me.

"Men are always losing things." I laugh. "Look under your bed, or behind the pickles in the refrigerator. Do you remember what you were wearing when you had it last?"

Notice how you're drawn in with this poignant exchange? These characters sound witty and fascinating and the story feels alive from the first words.

Anecdote

Savvy writers insert these small stories within a larger story throughout a novel or memoir. If you begin with an anecdote, make certain that it relates to the themes or main actions in the story, as does the anecdote in John Irving's *The World According to Garp*.

> Garp's mother Jenny was arrested in Boston in 1942 for wounding a man in a movie theater. This was shortly after the Japanese had bombed Pearl Harbor and people were being tolerant of soldiers, because everyone *was* a soldier, but Jenny Fields was quite firm in her intolerance of the behavior of men in general and soldiers in particular. In the movie theater she had to move three times, but each time the soldier moved closer to her until she was sitting against the musty wall, her view of the newsreel almost blocked by some silly colonnade, and she resolved she would not get up and move again. The soldier moved once more and sat beside her.

The characters in *Garp* are quirky, to say the least. This anecdote tells us Jenny is a spitfire and we immediately wonder *why* she's so intolerant of men's sexuality.

Story Question

Donna Tartt's novel *The Little Friend* is about the aftermath and repercussions of the murder of a child. The prologue, which occurs twelve years before the story, immediately introduces this story question: Who killed a nine-year-old boy and why? The opening outlines the circumstances surrounding the murder.

> For the rest of her life, Charlotte Cleve would blame herself for her son's death because she had decided to have the Mother's Day dinner at six in the evening instead of noon, after church,

> which is when the Cleves usually had it. Dissatisfaction had been expressed by the elder Cleves at the new arrangement; and while this mainly had to do with the suspicion of innovation, on principle, Charlotte felt that she should have paid attention to the undercurrent of grumbling, that it had been a slight but ominous warning of what was to come; a warning which, though obscure even in hindsight, was perhaps as good as any we can ever hope to receive in this life.

After the prologue the story reveals how the family never recovers from this terrible event. And because the murder is never solved, it gives Harriet, the murdered boy's sister, a motive to search out his murderer. Which is when the situation spins into treacherous waters because we all know a child is no match for a murderer. Or is she?

Suspense

Suspense is created in fiction by rousing the reader's curiosity, by inserting unanswered questions and delaying answers and resolutions. Here are two prime examples of beginning with suspense.

The Dogs of Babel opening by Carolyn Pinkhurst presents a mystery that needs a solution:

> Here is what we know, those of us who can speak to tell a story: On the afternoon of October 24, my wife, Lexy Ransome, climbed to the top of the apple tree in our backyard and fell to her death. There were no witnesses, save our dog, Lorelei, it was

> a weekday afternoon, and none of our neighbors were at home, sitting in their kitchens with their windows open, to hear whether, in that brief midair moment, my wife cried out or gasped or made no sound at all.

In Jon Clinch's powerful novel *Finn*, the first sentence is a grisly image that asks the question: Who died and why?

> Under a low sun, pursued by fish and mounted by crows and veiled in a loud languid swarm of bluebottle flies, the body comes down the river like a deadfall stripped clean.

Both of these openings present startling facts—a woman falling out of a tree to her death and a body floating downriver. When death is announced so soon in the story, readers naturally want to discover how and why the person died and the fallout from the death.

THEME

A book's theme is the meaning that whispers beneath the events. Theme is not the message, it is more like the soul of your story and lends the story emotional depth. Themes help the reader understand the ramifications of the story events. An example of opening with theme is Cormac McCarthy's Pulitzer Prize–winning novel *The Road,* about a father and son's journey in a bleak, postapocalyptic world. The main themes are survival and hope. The survival theme is introduced in the opening page when readers land in a harsh and lonely world.

> When he woke in the woods in the dark and the cold of the night he'd reach out to touch the child sleeping beside him. Nights dark beyond darkness and the days more gray each one than what had gone before. Like the onset of some cold glaucoma dimming away the world. His hand rose and fell softly with each precious breath. He pushed away the plastic tarpaulin and raised himself in the stinking robes and blankets and looked toward the east for any light but there was none. In the dream from which he'd wakened he had wandered in a cave where the child led him by the hand. Their light playing over the wet flowstone walls. Like pilgrims in a fable swallowed up and lost among the inward parts of some granitic beast. Deep stone flues where the water dripped and sang. Tolling in the silence the minutes of the earth and the hours and the days of it and the years without cease. Until they stood in a great stone room where lay a black and ancient lake. And on the far shore a creature that raised its dripping mouth from the rimstone pool and stared into the light with eyes dead white and sightless as the eggs of spiders. It swung its head low over the water as if to take the scent of what it could not see.

The opening sets up the dark and dangerous conditions for the story and immediately announces the characters' vulnerability and connection—a father watching over his sleeping child and thus making us care.

Setting

If the setting is especially crucial to the story, as in a historical novel, using setting details in the opening can propel readers into another time and place and set the tone or mood for what follows. If you choose to use setting in your opening, it needs to be specific yet suggestive. An example is found in Thomas Keneally's *Schindler's Ark,* which was made into the film *Schindler's List.* It begins:

> In Poland's deepest autumn, a tall young man in an expensive overcoat, double-breasted dinner jacket beneath it and—in the lapel of the dinner jacket—a large ornamental gold-on-black-enamel *Hakenkreuz* (swastika) emerged from a fashionable apartment block in Straszewskiego Street on the edge of the ancient center of Cracow, and saw his chauffeur waiting with fuming breath by the open door of an enormous and, even in this blackened world, lustrous Adler limousine.

The details in this opening set against the onset of World War II are intriguing and lead to questions: How did the tall man become wealthy and how will he be involved in the war? Why is he a member of the Nazi Party?

Punchy First Sentence

Sometimes the best openings feature a first sentence that lands like a boxer's punch, immediately hooking the reader. Here are some examples:

> It is cold at 6:40 in the morning of a March day in Paris, and seems even colder when a man is about to be executed by firing squad. —Frederick Forsyth, *The Day of the Jackal*

The first time my husband hit me I was nineteen years old.
—ANNA QUINDLEN, *Black and Blue*

When the lights went off the accompanist kissed her.
—ANN PATCHETT, *Bel Canto*

It wasn't a very likely place for disappearances, at least at first glance. —DIANA GABALDON, *Outlander*

The day I killed my brother's girlfriend started with me hand-picking leaves off our front lawn. —E. R. FRANK, *Wrecked*

Derek Strange got down in a three-point stance.
—GEORGE PELECANOS, *Hard Revolution*

We slept in what had once been the gymnasium.
—MARGARET ATWOOD, *The Handmaid's Tale*

Notice how there is not a wasted word in any of these opening lines? To accomplish this sort of knockout punch, collect first lines and practice your own, over and over.

CHARACTER DESCRIPTION OR INTRODUCTION

If you begin with character details, these bits must have significance in the story. A terrific example is found in *Emperor of the Air*, a short story by Ethan Canin.

> Let me tell you who I am. I'm sixty-nine years old, live in the same house I was raised in, and have been the high school biology and astronomy teacher in this town so long that I have taught the grandson of one of my former students. I wear my

> father's wristwatch, which tells me it is past four-thirty in the morning, and though I have thought otherwise, I now think that hope is the essence of all good men.

When we hear a narrator describe himself in an opening, or at any place in the story, we naturally wonder if this assessment is accurate and the narrator is reliable. And when a character describes himself as being so connected with the past, readers want to know how his life and connections to the past will be threatened.

A Moment of Change

By design, most stories begin with a moment of change or just before a moment of change. Few of these changes are quite as memorable as when the protagonist in *Girl with a Pearl Earring,* by Tracy Chevalier, is first introduced to the artist Vermeer and his wife.

> My mother did not tell me they were coming. Afterwards she said she did not want me to appear nervous. I was surprised, for I thought she knew me well. Strangers would think I was calm. I did not cry as a baby. Only my mother would note the tightness along my jaw, the widening of my already wide eyes.
>
> I was chopping vegetables in the kitchen when I heard voices outside our front door—a woman's, bright as polished brass, and a man's, low and dark like the wood of the table I was working on. They were the kind of voices we heard rarely in our house. I could hear rich carpets in their voices, books and pearls and fur.

Well, once I learned that the protagonist's mother hadn't warned her about the visitor, that the protagonist is upset, and the visitors are wealthy, I'm naturally curious about what is about to unfold. Aren't you?

FORESHADOWING

Tobias Wolff's memoir *This Boy's Life* covers Wolff's harrowing adolescent years in a family that defines dysfunction. As Wolff and his mother are driving west to live with his new stepfather, an incident sets the tone for the wreckage the marriage is about to cause in their lives.

> Our car boiled over again just after my mother and I crossed the Continental Divide. While we were waiting for it to cool we heard, from somewhere above us, the bawling of an airhorn. The sound got louder and then a big truck came around the corner and shot past us into the next curve, its trailer shimmying wildly. We stared after it. "Oh, Toby," my mother said, "he's lost his brakes."
>
> The sound of the horn grew distant, then faded in the wind that sighed in the trees all around us.
>
> By the time we got there, quite a few people were standing along the cliff where the truck went over. It had smashed through the guardrails and fallen hundreds of feet through empty space to the river below, where it lay on its back among the boulders. It looked pitifully small. A stream of thick black smoke rose from the cab, feathering out in the wind. My mother asked whether anyone had gone to report the accident. Someone had. We stood with the others at the cliff's edge. Nobody spoke. My mother put her arm around my shoulder.

Wolff's life, like the truck, is about to topple off a cliff. The opening not only hints at upcoming danger, but reveals through his interaction with his mother that the memoirist doesn't always play fair.

Try This

Just for practice write five sentence openings to short stories, novels, or memoirs that you don't intend to write. In fact, try to write openings for genres that you typically don't dabble in. If you write historical fiction, instead create the opening to a contemporary suspense. If you write mainstream, try your hand at horror. The point of this exercise is to perfect vivid and compelling openings, and also to experiment. Especially try to write openings that are vastly different from your normal approach.

Quick and Dirty Tips for Writing an Opening That Captivates

As you've seen, there are plenty of options for starting a story. However, most of us have a deeply ingrained tendency toward reporting or expository writing. You must resist this impulse because it will likely lead to a wimpy beginning. Instead keep these suggestions in mind:

- Polish your opening lines until they gleam—every word a jewel.
- Try a new approach—sometimes the best openings come from using a technique outside of your comfort zone.

- Use specific sensory details so that readers land smack-dab in another place beyond their ordinary lives.
- Don't meander into the story—the first reader at a publishing company or literary agency doesn't have time to wade through pages looking for your hook.
- Don't open with a character alone simply thinking, or portray a nameless character wandering alone on a beach or in some vaguely defined space. Instead, give the reader a clearly drawn person to focus on and care about.
- A beginning must intrigue, but that doesn't mean it must shock, titillate, or manipulate the reader. Thrillers and suspense stories often have more intense beginnings because readers are expecting mayhem and excitement in the story that follows. But quieter stories might call for a quieter beginning. Don't mistake drama for melodrama and feel the urge to toss a body in front of a speeding car. Conflict can also be subtle. Instead, imagine your first words *seducing* the reader.
- Beware of unnecessary details and descriptions, dumping in backstory, and introducing too many characters in the opening. Get the story started, but don't bog it down with excess or the past.
- Make certain that your opening creates questions that can be resolved only by further reading.
- Make certain that your opening is crucially linked to the chapters that follow.

Resources

http://modena.intergate.ca/personal/gslj/firstparas.html

Max Perkins Editor of Genius, A. Scott Berg

First Paragraphs: Inspired Openings for Readers and Writers, Donald Newlove

Great First Lines, edited by Celina Spiegel and Peter Kupfer

The Sound on the Page, Ben Yagoda

Beginnings, Middles and Ends (Elements of Fiction Writing), Nancy Kress

Two

Underpinnings: Structuring Stories for Maximum Dramatic Effect

> Prose is architecture, not interior decoration, and the Baroque is over.
>
> —Ernest Hemingway, *Death in the Afternoon*

One bit of accepted wisdom that drives me crazy is when famous writers claim that writing is like driving in the fog without the headlights on and that you can make the whole trip that way.

Who are they kidding? Driving without headlights in the fog is maddening and a hazard to other drivers. And what's the point of stumbling along clueless and blind as your shoulders tense at each approaching curve? I'm all for writing being a process of discovery. And I'm all for writing being fun and a way to express our deepest passions. But I believe in headlights and want to suggest you need a more working-class version of the writing life. You need to see yourself as a skilled laborer, not an artiste who awakes each morning wondering how best to flirt with your muse.

This means you write with a fully loaded toolbox of craft and habits and understanding. And in the top shelf of your toolbox, please pack a blueprint for what you're writing. While building without a blueprint is okay if you're using scrap wood to knock together a tree house in the backyard, for most other structures you need a plan, a design, a way forward.

Imagine the underpinnings that are the basis for every structure in our world: bridges, skyscrapers, castles, and churches. Plans also are used to construct appliances and ships, airplanes, trucks, and cars. Now, when I cross a suspension bridge I want an engineer to have created an ingenious design that includes trusses, concrete pilings, and whatever else is required so it doesn't crumble into a pile of debris underneath me. And I want a team of engineers to have designed my car so that it can zip across the bridge.

Likewise, you need a blueprint to give shape to your stories, to keep them from crumbling into piles of meaningless words. In the manuscripts I've read over the years, it seems to me that what often spells doom for writers is if they don't understand the underpinnings of drama. Their stories meander or dead-end at odd intervals, and typically the ending isn't the logical progression of what went before.

I realize that not everyone can outline or plan their fiction before they write. Some people simply need to write in order to discover their stories and especially to find the truth of their characters. That's perfectly okay. But if you don't know *why* you're writing in scenes or creating plot points, you'll muddle along and end up with a lot of words, but those words won't add up to a story.

Three-Act Structure

Major blunders can be avoided by first understanding the underpinnings of fiction and learning what is supposed to happen to whom and why it's happening. To write a novel or memoir, you need to understand the three-act structure. Why? Because the three-act structure takes your ideas and characters and transforms them into a story.

Most manuscripts average about three to four hundred pages, and you can divide those pages into three parts or acts. The three-act structure has been around since ancient Greece and was first described by Aristotle in *The Poetics*. It's really fairly simple: a story needs a beginning, a middle, and an end. The three acts are the setup, complications, and resolution. While there are no set number of pages that define each act, about fifty pages or one-quarter of the story is act one, act two requires about half the pages, and act three about one-quarter of the pages.

Act 1: The Beginning

The first act has lots to accomplish: it introduces the world of your story, it must hook readers, and it begins the external conflict. This is done by introducing a *disturbance* or *threatening change* in the story world. This change is called the *inciting incident.* It needs to tilt the protagonist or another character off balance, revealing a character under stress. Here's your blueprint for Act 1:

- Amid the ordinary world of the story, an *inciting incident* occurs, shakes up the protagonist's world, and sets the story in motion.
- Protagonist and other major characters are introduced.
- Story problem, challenge, or conflict is introduced.
- The reader learns what is at stake—what the protagonist can win or lose.
- Setting details create the story world.
- Viewpoint or viewpoint pattern is introduced.
- Subplots are introduced once the main story is established.
- Flashbacks and backstory are introduced on a strictly need-to-know basis.
- It establishes the *cauldron*, meaning that there is a place or situation that glues the characters together as the conflict boils over.
- It ends with a crisis—typically the protagonist decides to accept the challenge.

Act 2: The Middle, or Body, of the Story

The middle of a novel is not a transition between the opening and the ending; it is the heart of the story where the most complications take place and it creates anticipation for the climax. Act 2 deepens the reader's understanding of the story world, heightens the conflict, makes things harder for your protagonist, and proves that a resolution is needed. It is the bulk of the novel. I once heard the middle described as a long and precarious bridge connecting the middle and the end, and some characters make it across and some don't.

In Act 2 subplots are developed and a major reversal occurs at about the midpoint in the story. One of my favorite illustrations of this midpoint reversal is in the film version of *The Wizard of Oz*. After Dorothy and her pals reach Oz, they believe that they are home free. But then comes the reversal, when the Wizard demands that they bring back the Wicked Witch's broom, the supreme test.

The second act ends with a crisis that plunges the protagonist into the Dark Night of the Soul. The Dark Night is the scene in which your character's worst fate looms, or he faces his greatest fear. Typically this situation thrusts your character into despair, fear of failure, or inner struggle, then finally he decides (consciously or unconsciously) to rise to the challenge. During the ordeal, the protagonist usually meets head-to-head with the antagonist, a dark force, and his own doubts. Often he is isolated. In literary novels the demon often lies within, but in most novels the inner struggle must be overcome so the protagonist can face down the outer struggle. In *The Wizard of Oz*, Dorothy's Dark Night happens when she is jailed deep in the witch's castle and her plight seems hopeless.

Your blueprint for Act 2 includes:

- Deepening conflicts and complications and the protagonist is tested by facing them.
- If appropriate, introduce time running out or a deadline approaching.
- Backstory, which provides important information and deepens characters.

- Characters becoming more emotional and committed to a goal.
- Stakes rising along with the protagonist's motivation.
- Ever-increasing obstacles, trials, and dilemmas.
- The protagonist's actions demonstrating that he or she is capable of change.
- Contrast between the protagonist and other characters in the story is illustrated.
- Demonstrates, as the middle ends, that the situation cannot continue much longer.
- An ending with the protagonist in a dire situation from which there is no turning back.

Act 3: The End

After your protagonist has survived the Dark Night of the Soul, he must face the biggest obstacle: he must win the race, chase down the criminal, or confront the villain. This is where your protagonist ventures into the deepest, darkest, most dangerous place where he would rather not go, as when Dorothy faces down the witch before she can return home. The ending of a novel is where the protagonist faces a physical or psychological death. Now this can be a showdown or a capitulation, as in a romance where the characters come to realize they're meant for each other. But it's always the place in the story where the trials the characters have experienced lead to a logical and inevitable conclusion. It can also slip in a twist that the reader didn't see coming.

Your blueprint for Act 3:

- Whatever the protagonist has learned in the Dark Night of the Soul can be put to use in the final tests and struggles.
- As the climax nears, the pace quickens, chapters are shorter, action starts boiling.
- The ending is often a smackdown, or somehow delivers the most emotion.
- The ending stems from the protagonist's nature, exposing his deepest self.
- The ending delivers maximum drama without extra words, and doesn't linger once it's over so the drama can be savored.
- The ending answers story problems or questions and ties up most of the subplots if they haven't been resolved previously, along with any loose ends.
- The protagonist in many story types undergoes internal and external transformations (there are exceptions in series fiction and action stories).

Blueprints

Now that you've got an understanding of the three acts, let's talk about a few structures you might use. Whether you're building a castle or a bungalow, it helps to plan your structure instead of taking a scattershot approach. Let's talk about a few of the most popular structures you might use to tell your story.

Chronological or Linear

This is a simple approach where the story moves forward in strict chronological order. One event follows another, resulting in a chain of cause and effect as it chugs toward the climax. In this format lengthy or complicated flashbacks are typically not included, although backstory can be briefly introduced through recollections, brief interjections, or dialogue. Generally genre fiction is more likely to be told in chronological order. An example is Harley Jane Kozak's *Dating Dead Men*.

Nonlinear

The story does not unfold in chronological order but slips in and out of time. An example in film that illustrates this structure is Quentin Tarantino's *Pulp Fiction*. Toni Morrison's novel *Beloved* also has a nonlinear structure.

Dual Story Line

This type of novel features two stories that often share equal importance. Sometimes the second story is told back in time, but sometimes both stories are told in the present. *Cold Mountain,* by Charles Frazier, has a dual story line, following the lives of two characters as they struggle to survive during the Civil War. Ron McLarty's *The Memory of Running* also has a dual story line, alternating chapters in the past and present that merge in the climax. *Snow Falling on Cedars,* by David Guterson, also has two story lines, one in the past that influences events in the present.

The point of a dual story line is that the stories intersect, and moving back and forth between them creates suspense because each story is constantly being interrupted.

Frame Story

There are several types of frame stories. In the first type are stories told within the framework of a story set in the present. Amy Tan's *The Joy Luck Club* is an example of this type, as are more classic models such as *The Canterbury Tales*. The frame provides a sort of umbrella under which to gather the stories.

Another frame story structure has a dual story line, with a story within a story, or sometimes two stories within a story. Typically it begins with the ending, then tracks back in time to explain how things came to be, then concludes in the present. The story in the past, or the embedded narrative, is the most important part of the whole, as in *Rebecca,* by Daphne du Maurier, *Frankenstein,* by Mary Shelley, and *Sophie's Choice,* by William Styron. Authors use a frame structure when they want to explore the why, or the psychological reasons for how things unfold. It's crucial that a convergence of past and present occurs, but the story from the past has the most weight or shines a light that explains all.

Multiple Viewpoints

In a multiple viewpoint story the reader is allowed into the lives and thoughts of several characters. The story can move forward in chronological order or move around in time, but it always follows more than one important character and typically the viewpoint characters' lives somehow intertwine. Barbara Kingsolver's *The Poisonwood Bible* and George R. R. Martin's Song of Ice and Fire series use multiple viewpoints. Multiple viewpoints work for stories of great scope and complexity and when characters are sharply contrasting.

Deal Breakers

Most writers are myopic. By the time we finish a manuscript we cannot see the errors on the page and especially cannot analyze the larger questions and structure. Published authors have agents and editors to help them see their mistakes; unpublished writers are at a disadvantage without these resources.

With that in mind, let's talk about the deal breakers related to the underpinnings, especially the big mistakes of structure that send a manuscript into the rejection pile.

All Hat, No Cattle

This is typically a manuscript in which somehow the main story question (Who killed Bernard? Which side will win the election or war? What really happened during Rebecca's childhood?) is buried. This problem sometimes starts in the first scene when the story doesn't have a firm launch, but sort of sputters to life and then meanders through a series of events. On the other hand, I've seen manuscripts that zipped off to a great start and then fizzled into a pile of dreck, as if the writer couldn't make up his mind about how to piece together a coherent tale.

Often the story question is buried under all sorts of excess, such as too much description and exposition. In one manuscript about 90 percent of the story was dialogue—looonnnng, endless chatter because characters gathered to chitchat, congratulate each other on their cleverness and cool, and to joke and rehash what had already happened in the story. But mostly it consisted of cute riffs and endless yak fests that seemed to be based on the writer's life rather than hurdles and snags to push the story along.

I've read manuscripts that juggled about ten subplots so that the main story was drowned out, and some that literally contained a cast of hundreds. I've noticed that writers of thrillers tend to create layers of villains and antagonists, so most of these stories contain four bad guys and endless henchmen. As I read I am forced to devise a scorecard to track the cast and all the divergences. Unless you're writing an epic such as the next *Winds of War* or a family saga, a cast this big and a myriad of subplots is too much for the writer and readers to keep tabs on. Populate your stories with as few people as possible and focus on the most important moments.

If too many characters are sinking your story, one solution is to ask yourself which ones will undergo significant changes and focus events around them. The secondary cast members work best if they cause things to happen in the story but don't necessarily undergo significant changes. If your secondary characters all have a character arc—meaning they grow and change—they steal attention from the main characters and conflict.

Excess also stems from writers borrowing from their lives rather than concocting a story based on make-believe. In one manuscript the protagonist constantly baked cakes because the writer was an amateur baker, and in another readers were forced to attend boring meetings about corporate strategies, including all the jargon that makes your hair follicles hurt, because the writer worked in the same industry as the story setting. To avoid all hat and no cattle, weigh each scene and event you include and ask yourself if it's pushing the protagonist toward his goal or opposing his goal. If not, get rid of it.

Bogged Down Under Backstory

While we've established that stories have three acts, they also have two main parts: backstory and front story. Backstory means all the events, influences, and histories of the main characters and setting before the story begins; front story refers to the events that occur after the inciting incident and lead to the climax. Knowing when to include backstory and when to leave it out is one of the biggest challenges of structuring fiction. Most writers err on the side of introducing it too early, introducing it in large info dumps, or burying the front story under too much backstory.

One manuscript I worked on had an intricate plot, and the backstory—secret societies from the 1800s, buried treasure, and political intrigue—was equally intricate. The story got off to a rip-roaring start with a man wearing a creepy costume appearing in the middle of the night and threatening the protagonist at knifepoint and demanding a key to buried treasure. However, once this happened, there was little aftermath of the attack and most of the next forty pages was backstory. Delivered, oh woe is me, by a historian in dialogue as he cheerily cooked up a huge pot of spaghetti.

There is no surer way to kill suspense than to answer every question before the reader wonders about it. Don't explain everything or answer every question up front or set things up too thoroughly because this destroys suspense. Instead, let your story unfold dramatically and trust that clarity will emerge eventually. The trick is to delay telling backstory until the last possible moment or include only tidbits that *matter and stir unease or questions in the reader*. Here's a tip I want you to remember: if you've spent a lot of time getting to know your characters and story, not all you know will end up in the story. In fact, you'll discover that much of what happened in the past isn't needed.

There is no neat formula about how much backstory you need since every story is different. In the first act, introduce backstory on a need-to-know basis; in the second act add more backstory to reveal motivations and keep the pot boiling; in the third act reveal as little backstory as possible because you want to keep the heat on and push toward the climax.

Episodic

I also read stories that are mostly episodic—meaning that one thing happens after another but there is little linkage between episodes. Characters ricochet through the story but their actions aren't tied to their motivations and they come through even the most desperate moments without a scratch or wince. This is especially a problem I find in suspense stories in which a detective is tracking down clues, but each witness interviewed or clue unearthed doesn't link together to create a coherent pattern. When you write fiction or memoir, keep cause and effect in mind as you plan your structure. Each scene needs to impact the following scenes down the line, and each action should cause emotions in the characters that further complicate future events. Fiction must punish characters, and readers need to witness how punishment accumulates and has ramifications that cause reactions, bad choices, and dilemmas.

Offstage

I read a manuscript in which the climax—hand-to-hand combat in an airplane that was flying at forty thousand feet—took place offstage, meaning the writer didn't describe the actual scene, but summarized the event after it happened. (And I hate to nitpick, but the protagonist jumped from the airplane—a passenger jet. I'm no astrophysicist, but if the door was opened, wouldn't everyone get sucked out?) If you'd been in the room with me as I reached these final pages, you would have heard a loud shriek of despair.

But that wasn't the only time I've encountered vital scenes inexplicably happening offstage, then discussed or summarized afterward. It's especially important not to summarize scenes that contain conflict. After you finish your main draft, it might be helpful to rank the most crucial events in the story. Make certain that the top-ranking scenes are dramatized, not reported about after the fact. Summary works best for transitions and less important information.

Obscure

I've read manuscripts in which the story was so thin it could have passed for a message in a bottle, or some in which vast parts of the story were obscured. Some manuscripts never connect the dots in the plot or leave too many subplots dangling or questions unanswered. I once worked on a manuscript in which a criminal organization the villain was involved with was never explained. It wasn't clear if the criminals were affiliated with Eastern crime families or the Russian mob or a separate entity. It was also unclear if they were smuggling drugs or illegals in from Mexico, or if they operated a legitimate front. Besides not knowing the criminal nature of the villains, it wasn't clear why they were making life hell for the protagonist, an amateur sleuth.

I've read a fair number of manuscripts that didn't fit into any discernible genre, but were not mainstream or literary fiction. I've read manuscripts featuring characters with broody good looks who wander around muttering about how life is cold and meaningless, but the scenes in the story never reveal why life is supposed to be cold and meaningless. And there was the story about the modern-day hobbit who hated being a hobbit and felt out of place in our techno modern world. Trouble was, we never learned how he came to exist in modern America.

Call me a cynic, but if I were a betting woman, I'd wager these manuscripts ended up with *rejection* stamped on them.

Sagging Middle

There's a good reason why the middle is the most difficult part of the story to write. Often the zest or excitement of crafting the beginning has worn off and the writer's energy is flagging while he's faced with a pile of choices and threads to be developed. And if you don't know what's going to happen next or how the whole shebang is going to conclude, writing the middle can be excruciating.

Perhaps the chief mistake that beginning writers make is that the middle of the story doesn't send the plot skittering off in a new direction with one serious, unpleasant setback. They also don't include enough surprises, twists, and difficulties that catch the reader off-guard and have the power to revive the story, increase interest, and push it forward with renewed momentum. Instead, the middle chapter is often choked with backstory and characters gathering to party or chat. Because the "job" of the middle chapters is to heighten the reader's curiosity and involvement and hold him until the ending, the middle scenes require a lot of deftness. In the middle chapters of most plots, the reader witnesses the protagonist's motivations becoming more intense and personal, and obstacles and setbacks increase and become more horrific.

Another danger is stories that veer off in too many directions because writers tack on subplots or introduce new characters. This danger can be averted by making certain that additions are clearly linked to the ending and by tying up some of the subplots before the climax. Beginning writers often try to resolve everything in the ending, but some of the subplots can be resolved in the middle.

In most fiction, with few exceptions, a character's fortunes, how he thinks and acts, and how he perceives the world will have changed by the end of the story. In short, his inner and outer worlds will never be the same by the end of the story. The middle of the story is a prolonged setup for this necessary transformation to take place.

Ask yourself questions about your middle as you plot. What is the antagonist up to and how is he standing in the way of the protagonist's goal? Is time running out? Are inner conflict and complications from subplots making life more difficult for the protagonist? The central scenes usually prove your protagonist is capable of change and is up to the task for the dramatic events that must occur in the ending.

Master Plots

Let's add to our understanding of plotting fiction. Some experts claim there are twenty master plots, some say there are thirty or more. No matter—sometimes if you can place your plot within a storytelling pattern, you can then use this pattern to make the most of the story. Here are examples of plot patterns that your story might fall into.

Adventure

Adventure stories are action-packed and typically not about personal growth or moral issues but are about how a character's *situation* changes. There is often danger, excitement, and ventures into the unknown. Some contemporary thrillers fall into the adventure category, such as Diana Gabaldon's *Outlander* series. *Tom Jones,* by Henry Fielding, and *Treasure Island,* by Robert Louis Stevenson, are also examples.

Chase

A chase story is often but not always an action story. The chase story is based on a high-stakes game of hide-and-seek and typically features lots of tension and twists. *Jaws,* by Peter Benchley, is a good example of a chase, as are *Jackie Brown* and *Get Shorty,* by Elmore Leonard, both made into films.

Contest

A contest might be found in a thriller, a courtroom drama, a gang war, a turf battle, a power struggle, as in William Golding's *Lord of the Flies*, or an emotional tug-of-war, as with the custody battle in the film *Kramer vs. Kramer*. Sometimes the contest is between good and evil, as in the Harry Potter series. We live in a world of contests showcased in our political system and sporting events. Readers respond easily when characters are pitted against one another, especially when they have the same goal and similar strengths.

Coming-of-Age

In a coming-of-age story the protagonist is usually young and the story focuses on his spiritual, moral, or psychological growth. Often the story begins when the protagonist is challenged to act like an adult or take on adult-like responsibilities. It is always about a character being tested by outer events and maturing because of them. Examples are *To Kill a Mockingbird,* by Harper Lee, *The Secret Life of Bees,* by Sue Monk Kidd, *The Body,* by Stephen King, and *The Little Friend,* by Donna Tartt.

Love Story

Another classic tale, in which two people meet, electricity sparks, then circumstances and their own natures drive them apart until the resolution. The resolution can be a happy ending, as in most novels written for the romance market, or a tragic ending, such as in *Romeo and Juliet*. Examples, of course, can be found in the romance and chick-lit genres, Jane Austen's novels, as well as mainstream fiction such as *Anna Karenina.*

Puzzle, Mystery

Most puzzles or mysteries evolve around a crime, typically a murder and the reasons for the murder or crime. A writer has many choices about using an amateur detective, such as Agatha Christie's Miss Marple, or a professional might be involved, such as a police detective, forensics expert, or lawyer. The mystery has many shades and can be inky black, as in Thomas Harris's *Silence of the Lambs*, or a puzzle can be a thriller that is more like a maze, such as Robert Ludlum's *The Bourne Identity*.

Quest

A quest is an enduring story type seen in novels such as *The Grapes of Wrath,* by Steinbeck, *The Road,* by Cormac McCarthy, and *Ireland,* by Frank Delaney. Characters are often on a life-defining journey that presents the protagonist or cast with a number of obstacles, and shows the importance of what they're searching for.

Revenge

A revenge plot doesn't need a bloodbath to succeed, but readers need to understand how the protagonist has been injured, why he must retaliate, and why the law cannot help him. Most readers, especially young readers, have a firsthand acquaintance with injustice and long for fairness. Examples are the films *Kill Bill* and *The Fugitive,* and *A Time to Kill,* by John Grisham.

While there are more classic plots and more structures that you can incorporate into your stories, these are basic ones that you can use again and again. But first determine your story's underpinnings, and then you can create the literary equivalent of a mansion, a skyscraper, or a castle.

Try This: Create a Blueprint

Fiction illuminates the significance of events. But first comes knowing your story because the more you know, the easier it is to write. One such tool is a blueprint for crafting your story or novel. Here are the elements of your blueprint:

Situation:
Story Question:
Protagonist's Name and Identity:
Protagonist's Goal or Desire:
Protagonist's Emotional Need:
Obstacle/Antagonist:
Internal Conflict:
Subplots:
1. ____________________
2. ____________________
3. ____________________

Complications:
1. ______________________________
2. ______________________________
3. ______________________________
Time Span:
Setting:
Resolution:

Quick and Dirty Tips for Plotting

- Start on the brink of change.
- Remember that in most stories, plots are designed to threaten your protagonist's safety and identity and push him or her to act in ways he or she doesn't want to act.
- Fine-tune your first fifty pages because you'll be showing them to editors and agents, and your story lives and dies on their strengths and weaknesses.
- Plot begins when something happens to send a character in a new, unexpected direction where he enters new emotional territory.
- Events are showcased within scenes, and we write in scenes most of the time because they happen in the now, causing the reader to worry. So stage adversity where readers can watch it unfold.
- Your protagonist needs a good reason for pursuing a goal, and this goal matters greatly in his or her life.

- Whenever possible, use the pressure of time running out.
- Middles often feature a major surprise or twist. Sometimes the protagonist is betrayed, sometimes he recognizes truths about another character's identity, flaws, or importance. In some stories a crucial clue emerges, but in all stories the danger—whether physical or psychological—increases in the middle.

Resources

The Marshall Plan for Novel Writing and *The Marshall Plan Workbook*, Evan Marshall

The Writer's Journey: Mythic Structure for Writers, Christopher Vogler

Plot & Structure (Techniques and Exercises for Crafting a Plot That Grips Readers from Start to Finish), James Scott Bell

How to Write Killer Fiction, Carolyn Wheat

20 Master Plots (And How to Build Them), Ronald B. Tobias

Three

Plot Is a Verb: Using Change, Adversity, and Action to Shape a Story

When forced to work within a strict framework, the imagination is taxed to its utmost—and will produce its richest ideas. Given total freedom the work is likely to sprawl. —T. S. Eliot

One of my most dreaded jobs is writing a memo to a client describing what is working and not working in his or her novel, memoir, or story. What really sucks about this part of my job is that often the parts of the story that are *not* working outweigh the parts that *are* working. That's when the pitiless, dragon-breath aspect of my personality must seize control, push away compassion, and explain truths the writer needs to face.

When I write these memos I first focus on what is working in the story, followed by the buzz kill as I break down the problems that are sinking the manuscript. I often spot big plot holes and often the story needs to be rebalanced, meaning it needs more or less dialogue or summary, more or less backstory, more or less foreshadowing, more or fewer subplots. It almost always needs more suspense, setting details, and character development.

The biggest buzz kill is when I need to explain that the writer doesn't have a workable plot.

Plotting Explained

In the previous chapter we discussed the broader strokes of plot structure; now let's break down what happens *within* the three-act structure. A story's structure disappears behind the events on the page but still has a framework holding up all the unfolding action as it evolves.

There are many definitions of plot. It has been called an ordered structure of significant events designed to create interest and suspense. But I would like to add that plot is *movement and a record of change*. These changes—inflicted on the protagonist or a group of characters—alter their fortunes, choices, and beliefs.

A satisfying plot:

- exposes characters via decisions, mistakes, and actions;
- reveals and dramatizes the conflict;
- resolves the conflict;
- gives the novel complexity and breadth.

With adversity as the basis, the plot builds by adding on complications, surprises, and developments, which in turn add more tension and forward motion. Plots are not drawn as a straight line; instead there are zigzags, dead ends, sidetracks, and crooked paths. Each adds more obstacles, more decisions to be made, paths to be chosen. At each turn, chaos, disorder, arguments, struggles, bewilderment, and dilemmas should result.

A plot simmers, boils, and then finally explodes in the final scenes. You cannot write a story in which the plot merely simmers—there needs to be increasing tensions, terrible pressures building, and options disappearing as your character is thrust forward.

A plot satisfies. The final scenes, when tensions are red hot and the character has reached a point of no return, must deliver drama and emotion, along with a logical conclusion. This is not to suggest that every plot ends with a shoot-out or a physical confrontation, because some stories are quiet and thoughtful. Sometimes much of the conflict is internal, not external. Nevertheless, the ending delivers a payoff; the tension and conflict are resolved. Decisions are made, goals achieved, plans drawn for a new life, a victory secured. Something important has happened, and the ending is like pressure released from a boiling-over pot. The release is real, palpable, and pleasurable.

Because fiction is based on change, consider the big picture of the plot, as in the Before (beginning) and the After (climax) before you start plotting. Typically the story presents these important changes:

- From lost to found.
- From problem to solution.
- From mystery to meaning.
- From question to answer.
- From conflict to resolution.
- From danger to safety.
- From secret to revelation.
- From confusion to order.
- From dilemma to decision.

- From ignorance to understanding.
- From unresolved to closure.

Plot Points

What most often sinks a story is a writer who doesn't understand that storytelling is based on adversity, change, and rising and falling action delivered via a series of plot points. In a story there are a number of dramatic spikes, along with key twists and turns. These spikes change the course of the story. They're called plot points and create the bones or skeleton of your plot.

A plot point is an event or complication that moves the story forward through a one-way gate. Once the protagonist passes through this gate, there is no returning to the way things were before, and the character commits to a course of action. Plot points crank up tension and introduce new elements and dilemmas. They are typically crises that the character must respond to and are defining moments in the story. Most plot points revolve around the main conflict. They keep revealing what is at stake and showcase the protagonist's weaknesses and strengths. Ever-increasing conflict with plot points as the building blocks creates the *story arc.*

Before you start writing your novel, imagine the big events and twists that will occur in the story. These are the plot points. Some are bigger than others, but all must introduce change. If you're writing an eighty-thousand- or eighty-five-thousand-word manuscript, you need about six major plot points, although successful novels sometimes contain three or four.

Plot points:

- introduce a threatening change.
- always have consequences.
- shoot events/drama off in new directions.
- can be revelations that allow the reader to see things in a new light.
- result in things never being the same afterward.
- ratchet up tension and suspense.

Act 1 establishes the everyday world of your story and shows what your character has to lose. The film *Titanic*, which has a frame structure, moves back in time and introduces the protagonist, Rose, boarding the ship. We learn that Rose feels confined by her high-society life and dreads her upcoming marriage, which has been arranged to save her family's finances. In Margaret Mitchell's epic *Gone with the Wind,* we meet the flirtatious belle Scarlett O'Hara living at Tara in the world of the pre–Civil War South.

The *first major plot point* occurs in Act 1 and typically ends the act. A crime might occur or a couple meets in a romance novel. The character sets off on an adventure, meets up with an evil character, or chickens out when asked to defend the kingdom. But no matter the outcome, this major event creates a point of no return, exposes the protagonist, and deepens the conflict. It also sets the story in its true direction and gives the protagonist a new goal. In *Titanic,* Rose contemplates suicide leaning over the bow of the ship. In *Gone with the Wind,* Scarlett meets Rhett Butler after learning that Ashley is marrying another woman—this sets the love story in motion.

Act 2 is all about complicating the original problem. In Act

2, Rose meets the penniless but free-spirited Jack Dawson, the antagonist, and falls in love with him. In *Gone with the Wind,* war is declared and Scarlett marries Charles, a man she doesn't love. As the act continues, Scarlett becomes a widow and moves to Atlanta, the South is defeated, and Scarlett must flee Atlanta with Rhett's help. To stir up more trouble, the *midpoint plot point* is a profound change in circumstances, usually a reversal of fortune that leads to the climax. In *Titanic* this is when the ship hits the iceberg. Scarlett cannot afford the taxes on Tara and out of desperation marries another man she doesn't love.

At the end of Act 2 another *major plot point or twist* occurs that is usually a major setback, disaster, or threat. This nadir is often when the protagonist's plan has failed, he's been betrayed, he's backed into a corner, or he experiences a terrible loss. In *Titanic* Rose leaves the lifeboat, abandoning her confining future, and returns to the ship and Jack. In *Gone with the Wind* Scarlett's daughter dies, further eroding her relationship with Rhett.

In Act 3 the climax and conflict resolution is the *final plot point.* It is often a showdown and the high point of drama and emotion since the reader witnesses how the protagonist has changed. In *Titanic* Rose chooses life even though Jack has frozen to death in the icy Atlantic. A much-changed Scarlett realizes she loves Rhett, not Ashley. If you're having problems coming up with plot points, keep asking yourself what is the worst thing that can happen to your character at this point in the story.

Sometimes it's difficult to map out plot points before you begin because you might not be certain of your story arc. But the more you know about where your story is heading before you begin, especially your ending, the easier it is to write.

Stir in Doubt

Fiction is about interesting people in a mess of trouble. If your protagonist is not in a boatload of trouble, the story doesn't matter. The stakes in the story must be significant and understandable so the reader cares about the outcome. If the protagonist's problem is not difficult to overcome, the story is out of balance. Likewise, if it is solved too quickly, that is, before the climax, imbalance results. If the solution to the problem is not in doubt, the story will lack suspense, which also makes it unbalanced.

The single dramatic question lies at the heart of the story and provides glue for your plot and raises doubts in your readers. In *The Old Man and the Sea* the dramatic question is, Will Santiago catch the enormous fish and restore his pride and reputation? Remember the stakes were established in the opening, when readers learn that Santiago doesn't have enough to eat. In *To Kill a Mockingbird*, the dramatic question is, can Atticus Finch defend his client against the trumped-up charges and face down the racism of the community? In *The Grapes of Wrath* the Joad family is striving for a new life. The question is, will they make it?

The dramatic question is always linked to the protagonist and his or her mission. In *The Firm* Mitch McDeere wants to escape the Mafia. In *Jaws* Brody is desperate to stop the marauding shark. In *Silence of the Lambs* Clarice Starling needs to capture the serial killer Buffalo Bill. When the mission features life-or-death stakes, the reader will stay glued to the page. A story doesn't need death hanging over the protagonist to work, but the character's well-being, happiness, and success must hang in the balance.

Adversity 101

Stories stem from adversity and are about a character's, or in the case of a memoir, a real person's, vulnerability. While there have been memoirs published about triumphs and good times, most clever memoirists, like their fiction-writing comrades, know that a reader turns the pages when the person in the story is in the worst trouble. Vulnerability is the key to making conflict sizzle because invulnerable characters rob a story of suspense, while vulnerable characters make us worry. While events in your story might lead to a happy ending, the road to happiness is paved with misery, danger, and gut-wrenching choices.

Thus your first job as a fiction writer is to imagine yourself as a sadist, a torturer par excellence who dreams up ways to taunt, torment, test, and ruin your protagonist. As a memoirist you're often revealing the shadowland of your past that most people would never want to inhabit.

When possible base the story on your protagonist's *greatest fears* along with smaller fears. It can be fear of losing his family, job, health, or country. Next, make sure the main conflict is *inescapable*. Think about the snow piling up around the Overlook Hotel, preventing escape in Stephen King's *The Shining*. As the snow blocks off escape, Jack is going mad, the snowmobile they could escape on is inoperable, and über-creepy ghosts are haunting the joint so that even the bathtub isn't safe. Or, note how in Michael Crichton's *Jurassic Park* the island isolates the characters among the gigantic beasts. Then stir in a big dose of human greed, and add a fierce storm to complicate matters, which in turn sets the dinosaurs free, including the devious, slavering velociraptors.

Adversity also comes in the form of *moral dilemmas.* Whenever possible, give your protagonist difficult moral choices or decisions—one of the most famous of these is in William Styron's *Sophie's Choice*, when a mother must choose between her son and daughter for immediate death camp extinction. But moral dilemmas come in all shapes and sizes. In Alice Sebold's *The Lovely Bones*, the protagonist, Susie Salmon, is murdered early in the story and looks down on her family, friends, and her killer from heaven. But Susie's ghostly attachment to her former life isn't working and if she keeps hanging on, she won't ever transcend into an afterlife and her family and friends won't be able to recover from their grief. There's nothing like a damned-if-you-do, damned-if-you-don't dilemma to heat up a plot. Your characters will want to avoid making the choice, guilt and repercussions follow the choice, and factors that complicate the choice will keep piling up.

Physical adversity also naturally creates a link between readers and characters. After all, we all know what it's like to feel pain and to be frightened of monsters, death, and howling hurricanes. If a character is cold, hot, thirsty, hungry, fevered, ill, exhausted, or broken, the reader leans in, twisting with worry. The possibilities for physical adversity are endless, as demonstrated by Stephen King and Dean Koontz, who can turn a seemingly benign situation into a heap of horror.

Physical adversity is often linked to a character's *personal demons*—a person with agoraphobia will be forced to go out into the world, a non-swimmer like the antihero Quoyle in *The Shipping News* will get dunked into the north Atlantic. Or a person afraid of heights will end up in a mountaintop gondola, which will stall or break, dangling thousands of feet above the earth, and rescue will seem impossible.

Deal Breakers

It takes more than a big idea to create a story that is so riveting it will entertain readers for three or four hundred pages—it takes planning and analysis. Now, you can cry me a freakin' river about how plotting is too left-brained and you prefer to write intuitively, or you can buckle down and learn how to hold together a story. Most poorly written stories can be fixed with a deeper understanding of structure and plotting, and by creating a deeper adversarial situation. With that said, here are some of the major deal breakers that screw up your plot.

Heavy-handed Foreshadowing

I call foreshadowing the whisper campaign of fiction because it plants seeds for what is to come, thereby adding plausibility to plot events and characters' actions. Sometimes writers don't trust the reader to pick up on subtle clues and so blatantly hint at what will happen later. This is especially a problem in suspense novels, because more than any other genre of fiction, readers want to connect the dots and make discoveries on their own.

When too much foreshadowing exists there are unexplained thumps in the middle of the night, telephones ring but no one is on the line, doors to mysterious rooms are locked without explanation why characters never venture into them, and settings remind readers of the cheerless hellhole in *The Fall of the House of Usher.* Ham-fisted foreshadowing also includes lines such as, "As soon as he stepped into the darkened house he knew something was wrong." Or "Denise wished she wasn't feeling that sick feeling in her gut that told her something bad was going to happen soon."

Limp Adversity

I've read manuscripts in which every time a detective interviewed a witness, the witness acted as if he'd been injected with truth serum; stories in which the villain admitted his evil deeds like a *Jerry Springer Show* confession; and a story in which the antihero went on a murder spree with nary a hitch or breaking a sweat. But fiction screams "no" at characters—again and again. Make sure the main adversity is daunting and most people and events in the story say "no" to your protagonist. After all, if Romeo and Juliet had the blessings of their families, there would be no story.

Or think of *The Old Man and the Sea* and poor old Santiago. Not only was he dragged far out to sea in Act 1, but once he won the tough match with his prized marlin, it was devoured by snarling sharks, and he was practically wiped out from his ordeal. If he'd been giggling and singing sea shanties throughout his fishing trip while snacking on Cuban sandwiches and sipping beer, then hauled in the big fish as the wind whooshed him homeward, the story would never work. (Okay, it was true that he did gnaw on that raw tuna—talk about fresh sushi.) Fiction punishes characters, and most memoirs reveal pains and truths that are difficult to witness.

Lonely Hearts

I cannot say it enough: if too many scenes in your story feature a character alone, the story won't work. Especially if in most of the scenes a character is thinking, musing, recalling the past, or sighing. Especially sighing. It will be boxed in and lack conflict and fireworks. One memorable story featured a protagonist who spent most of the story alone weeping and despairing. In fact, when she wasn't breaking down she mostly whined throughout the story. I don't know about you, but I cannot handle histrionics and self-pity in real life, so I'm not going to pay $24.95 to read about it.

Instead, imagine the drama as a play acted out on a stage—if a character is alone on the stage, usually within moments another character arrives to mix things up. Now, I realize that one-man plays are performed all the time, but for most writers a character hanging out alone is static and dull as dishwater.

In *The Old Man and the Sea,* Santiago is mostly alone in the wide waters of the Gulf of Mexico throughout his ordeal. But the story isn't based solely on inner conflict—he's up against the villagers, who believe he's an unlucky has-been; the sea; the marlin; the brutal, hungry sharks; and the dwindling capabilities of his aging, ravaged body. This means readers feels the pain of his scarred hands and cramped muscles, and worry about his survival. This means that even though Santiago is mostly alone, the conflict is staged and we can watch him fighting for his last chance. The solution here is that conflict—your protagonist's worries and doubts and struggles—must be staged and the adversary visible whenever possible. Put anguish into action and readers will care.

Excess

When a plot is excessive the story meanders and becomes buried under too many words and gimmicks. In one story the writer was so fond of excess, his story was buried under about nine subplots. Each scene featured most of the bloated cast—which you needed a scorecard to track—who were always hanging around chitchatting, and it was filled with all sorts of cute riffs and recipes for a perfect Cosmopolitan. Such gadgetry bogs down a story. The bottom line here is that every word, paragraph, scene, and subplot needs to be justified. If an element cannot be justified, especially if it doesn't add to suspense, tension, and understanding of the character; fire it. Write for a reader, not to amuse yourself or so your friends can recognize themselves in your story. If your novel has dozens of characters or more than three or four subplots, you're likely in trouble. (Conversely, if your novel has no subplots, you're writing a short story.)

Lousy Ending

Nothing makes an editor crankier than when she's muddled through a manuscript and the ending sinks the whole kit and caboodle. Endings must provide emotional impact and closure. They must cast a backward glance that sheds significance on all that has happened. I've read way too many endings that are implausible, silly, or just plain wrong.

Hollywood endings especially bug me—when the hero and his gal gaze deeply into each other's eyes as the sun sets in lavender and peach hues. This happened in a manuscript after the hero had hacked to death three bad guys without breaking a sweat, and with bodies strewn about (although he is, of course, unbloodied); their embrace was both innocent and fervent. I'm not making this up.

On the other hand, an open-ended ending often can be unsatisfying, although of course famous authors sometimes get away with it. At times writers use an open ending because they're planning a sequel, but more often it's because they want the reader to guess if the climax depicts a win, lose, or draw. Don't do this, either.

Sometimes writers cannot get off the page—after the climax they tack on another twenty or thirty pages of clutter and tying up loose ends or introduce the opening scene of a sequel. Or sometimes the ending is so abrupt it slams the door in the reader's face. Ditto for endings that come out of nowhere, when the villain turns out to be the protagonist's long-lost father, or a giant freakin' monster robot (never mentioned in the story) appears to destroy the villain, or the whole labyrinth of a plot turns out to be a government cover-up. One of the least satisfying endings I've read was tacked onto an elaborate fantasy story that ended with "it was all a dream." Most readers will see this as a cop-out because "it was all a dream" endings have been used before and have lost their element of surprise. The larger problem, though, is that this sort of ending sounds as if the writer couldn't find a way to conclude the story so he took the easy way out.

Shadowy or Snidely Whiplash Villain

A gaping plot hole happens when the antagonist or villain is only a shadowy presence in the story or isn't introduced until Act 3. Keep in mind that the antagonist, especially when he is the villain, is the second most important character in the story. This doesn't mean he's entitled to the same number of words or appears in as many scenes as the protagonist, but a reader wants to experience his physicality and strengths, wants to come to know how he thinks and what motivates him.

Another deal breaker is when an antagonist or villain is depicted as one-sided and evil, or stereotyped as a man in black who snarls and sneers and twirls his greasy mustache, a la Snidely Whiplash of *Rocky and Bullwinkle* fame. Too many writers create bad guys whose character traits and backstory are too thinly drawn and simplistic. Bottom line, we need to know what makes villains tick. And take note that greed and world domination aren't the only motivations for a bad guy, even if you're writing a comic book.

So What?

Some manuscripts simply never grab my interest or sympathies. By the time I reach the end I don't care that the protagonist was kidnapped by despots, or the government agent in the post–Patriot Act story was surrounded by backstabbing zealots, or the protagonist fell in love with her best friend's husband, or the amateur sleuth stumbled over a corpse on page 1 in the midst of an island paradise, and then was blamed for the murder. There are lots of reasons why I don't care but often the central predicament seems overcooked, far-fetched, or simply clichéd.

In these plots instead of feeling as if I'm caught up in a drama, it feels more like things are sliding into chaos and silliness or that I'm treading on overfamiliar territory. Besides, the manuscripts flunked the basic test for good drama: *characters who enter into fresh emotional and physical territory; protagonists who fascinate; a ticking clock or some intense outside pressure to resolve a situation.* Too often plots that sputter feature a protagonist who is a victim or reacting to action rather than instigating it. Too often I'm acutely aware that I'm reading a manuscript as opposed to a story. So start with a character the reader has never met or a predicament that sizzles with suspense and breaks fresh ground. Too many plot ideas are hackneyed or rehashing of stories that have been done to death.

Suspense That Fizzles

Many beginning writers craft stories that are not based on a question that *must* be answered. A whodunit that I worked on featured a murder on page 20, but the whole question of why the victim was killed was diluted by a plot that was a labyrinth of digressions and gags, all of which short-circuited the suspense. For example, in an early scene where the screwball detective visits the crime scene, he kisses his love interest as they're standing in a pool of blood while about twenty characters arrive to toss off one-liners about the dead guy. A crime scene, especially with a corpse oozing blood, needs to loom over the story with a chilling, sad reality. It cannot be a gathering place for high jinks and stolen kisses. It needs to horrify readers and make them want the mystery of his death solved.

But of course there are many ways to kill suspense. Your job is to dangle solutions, answers, and rescues for as long as possible, tossing in complications like hand grenades. Many beginning writers don't want readers to feel uncertain, and so load the story with predictable events or feature elements in the story that are glaringly obvious to everyone *except* the characters in the story. Suspense comes from a curious reader worrying about characters under pressure as the writer delays outcomes.

Train Wreck on Page One

It's your job to begin your story as close as possible to a moment of change, then take readers on a journey through this change. Beginnings matter a lot and it's easy to start too slow, but it's also easy to begin by overwhelming the reader with too much conflict too soon. I've read manuscripts in which there was literally a train wreck on page 1 and in which a protagonist drowned in the first paragraph. In one story the protagonist received a head injury on page 3 that led to blindness; and in another story the protagonist, who was on foot, was being chased by villains in a Hummer with the intent to smash him like a bug. Another featured about sixteen pages of nonstop action with unknown characters dodging bullets on a vaguely drawn spaceship. These beginnings were especially problematic because after these whizbang scenes, the stories slowed to a crawl.

While it can work to start off your story with mega-exciting action, as does Robert Ludlum in *The Bourne Identity* by pumping bullets into his hero and then tossing him off a trawler into the Mediterranean, there are a few things to keep in mind. First, like Ludlum, if you begin a story with a character in physical danger, remember that the reader doesn't know the character yet, so the opening must be especially well crafted. In the opening of *The Bourne Identity*, the language and description are so intense and create such immediacy that the skin on your neck prickles. Readers need to wonder how the protagonist landed in such hot water and turn the pages to find the explanation. This means the reader feels what the character feels and that the setting anchors the reader in a place as tension and suspense boil away.

No matter how exciting your opening salvo, pare the opening scene down to the essentials and then in the following scene or chapter, slow down a bit so the reader can catch his breath and be brought up to speed on things. This doesn't mean dumping in a big chunk of backstory or exposition. Instead, while keeping the momentum chugging ahead, reveal more of the protagonist in the aftermath as he's forced to make a choice or a decision or take action because he was blindsided or thrown off-kilter.

You also want to make certain that the story question is in place by the second scene or chapter if your bold beginning doesn't explain it. In *The Bourne Identity,* the story question is, Who is Jason Bourne? After he's shot, readers learn that Jason Bourne has no memory and no name. His face reveals he's had plastic surgery, and a tiny microfilm implanted in his thigh bears a number that leads to a bank account in Zurich. This information all comes out as he's recovering after the explosive beginning scene. As the story moves along, we learn that during duress and danger, he exhibits fighting and survival instincts, for which he has no explanation. So following Ludlum's example, train wreck beginnings need to be followed by an action-filled plot that justifies this forceful opening salvo.

Writing is easy (well, at least for a small percentage of us); plotting is hard. If you decide to outline or write by the seat-of-your-pants method, as you shape your plot you need to make decisions about what is going to happen next in the story and why.

One method of beginning and staying on track is to create a

one-sentence summary of your story. (An old man goes out to sea determined to catch a fish to salvage his tarnished reputation.) Then create a one-paragraph summary and then a one-page summary of the plot. The one-page summary reflects the action in the three acts and depicts the ending. From there, create a list of the sequence of events, or just start writing. This isn't a fancy method of getting started or tracking your story, but it forces you to step back from the plot and analyze if the sequence of events makes sense and leads to the climax. Which, of course, is what editors are looking for.

Try This

Write a scene in which a reversal takes place in the story that drives your protagonist in a new direction and creates a significant complication. A reversal often means your character's fortune changes for better or worse. As mentioned earlier, the *Titanic* hitting the iceberg in the film is a famous example. The major reversal in *To Kill a Mockingbird* is when the jury returns a guilty verdict. However, as you create the scene, make sure you don't state the fear or reactions of the character; show it via action, including dialogue.

Quick and Dirty Tips for Plotting

- Don't explain, just begin.
- Don't start with a theme or archetype. Start with a character reacting to a problem that is propelling his life in the wrong direction.

- Create situations in which your character is out of sync or a fish out of water. Don't send your character into a series of situations in which he'll feel on top of things.
- Your plot forces your protagonist to change in the ways he or she most needs to change. The opposition or antagonist in your plot is the agent for change. A wallflower character becomes more confident, a loser regains his belief in himself, and a hard-hearted, hard-driving workaholic softens and finds balance.
- The more intense your protagonist's needs and goals, the more complicated and interesting the plot. A character with a goal of remodeling her house isn't particularly captivating, even if her contractor is a drunk and a screwup. Now, if your character Lola, a person so burned by love that she's sworn off men for good (her husband drank himself into an early grave), wants to create a home that is a sanctuary where she can heal and take in homeless kids, and then meets a charming and brilliant contractor (who seems to have a drinking problem) and falls for him, while meanwhile the remodeling isn't getting done, and a kid whose life is in danger is out on the streets, well, then the plot will work.
- Worry, stress, and torture your readers by endangering your characters.
- Force your characters to act in ways that most readers would be afraid to.
- Illustrate your character's changes and development through actions and decisions, not summary.

- Whenever events happen in your story, they must be followed by some reaction or response.

Resources

How to Write a Damn Good Novel, How to Write a Damn Good Novel II, James N. Frey

Story, Substance, Structure, Style, and the Principles of Screenwriting, Robert McKee

Save the Cat! The Last Book on Screenwriting You'll Ever Need, Blake Snyder

How to Grow a Novel, Sol Stein

The Elements of Mystery Fiction: Writing the Modern Whodunit, William G. Tapply

Plotting and Writing Suspense Fiction, Patricia Highsmith

The Plot Thickens: 8 Ways to Bring Fiction to Life, Noah Lukeman

Writing Fiction: A Guide to Narrative Craft, Janet Burroway and Susan Weinberg

Four

Striptease: Stirring in Suspense

Suspense is made up of a crucial question and the delay in answering that question.

—PHILIP GERARD, *Writing a Book That Makes a Difference*

I have a confession to make: I've never seen a striptease act. I've never seen men prancing on a stage a la Chippendales, have never set foot in a strip club. Oops—come to think of it, there was that long-ago bachelorette party and the guy who came out in the cop uniform and peeled down to a skimpy bikini. But I've known strippers, some of them my students, and I've learned that they all like to dance and they all possess a certain joie de vivre and sass.

The most important thing I learned about stripping is that it requires mystique and confidence. These traits inspire the audience to imagine the body beneath the costume, imagine the person away from the spotlight. Imagination is sparked by teasing, flirting, and delay. And at the heart of a striptease looms the big question: *What's going to happen next*?

Before you start thinking too much about naked people prancing around, let's get back to writing, because storytelling requires the same delay and subterfuge and readers wondering what's going to happen next. And many writers want their stories buck naked by chapter 2 rather than revealed slowly, layer by tantalizing layer. Let's discuss how the lessons of stripping can apply to writing (even if you never go near a go-go pole).

Suspended

Why is delay so important in storytelling? Because once you've teased readers with a tantalizing opening, you need to delay answers and solutions. Delay in turn creates unbearable suspense, and suspense manipulates readers' emotions. Once the inciting incident threatens the protagonist, the writer's job is to prolong this trepidation for as long as possible. So seduce the reader via the opening scenes like a stripper strutting onto the stage amid catcalls and whistles, and once he's involved in the protagonist's life, perturb him as he worries about outcomes. Suspense forces a reader to stay engaged and is part anxiety, part curiosity. Suspense unsettles the reader, plunges him into nail-biting angst.

Suspense is also caused by threat—someone is endangered and his life is about to plunge into a living nightmare and the reader is suspended, forced to wait until the end of the story to learn how it all turns out. Suspense is woven into every scene and makes the world of make-believe enthralling. This works for memoirs, too—if the reader isn't worried about the person telling the story and wondering how it all works out, he won't keep reading.

Suspense is then stirred by time running out, a sudden scream in the dark, an inner conflict that stirs in doubts, the surprise that leaps into the scene when least expected, the cliff-hanger at the end of the chapter. Suspense builds and satisfies when the reader desperately wants something to happen and it isn't happening.

When a reader is caught up in suspense, when he is tiptoeing in the dark along with the character, experiencing firsthand the smells, sights, sounds, and peril, then he transfers feelings about the protagonist into a generalized worry about the state of the world and his own personal safety. This means it's your job to be diabolical because suspense causes anxiety, and anxiety forces readers to keep tiptoeing ahead, into your story.

Before we go further let me clarify something: suspense is used in all types of writing, not just action stories, thrillers, and mysteries. It starts with an intriguing story question and is not only created in moments of physical danger, it's generated by all sorts of techniques designed to keep readers wide-eyed until the wee hours. Perhaps your protagonist hates confrontations, while the antagonist believes nothing clears the air like a screaming match. The protagonist's avoidance tactics can create the suspense building up to the scene.

Tough decisions, moral dilemmas, and choices also stir suspense because characters and real-life people are most revealed in the choices they make. If you're writing mainstream fiction, perhaps a long-ago family trauma (the protagonist Kelly was abandoned by her father when she was two) now must be dealt with when Kelly discovers her father has a life-threatening illness. She has a chance to forgive or to remain bitter about her past. The reader needs to care and wonder how Kelly will choose.

Or maybe in your young-adult story, the protagonist, Alex, a sixteen-year-old dweeb, is forced to choose between going along with his peers or staying true to himself and his dweebish ways. If Alex, who has always been ignored by the hipsters at his school, goes to a party and turns into a hilarious stand-up comedian after an encounter with a beer bong, and attracts admirers who laugh at his quick wit and his spot-on mimicry of their teachers, then the reader is going to wonder how this newfound popularity is going to affect him. Will he start drinking to fit in? Will he quit the chess club? The reader's curiosity will be especially piqued when, after the party, Alex snubs his best friend, Jake, who is one of the biggest losers in the school.

Another trick to build suspense is via the story structure. If you tell the story through more than one viewpoint, every time you slip into another viewpoint to deal with other matters, it prolongs the reader's need for an answer from an earlier viewpoint. The same thing happens if you write a story set in two separate times and bounce back and forth between the time zones.

Here are more techniques that stir suspense: readers love a good fight and fights create suspense, but again, not all fights mean fisticuffs and blood splattering. Maybe the protagonist's mother wants her to marry the proverbial boy next door, an insurance adjuster, but she's got the hots for a starving artist. Create suspense by giving readers information that the protagonist doesn't know—you might achieve this by slipping into the villain's or antagonist's viewpoint from time to time. Make sure the stakes are big—the protagonist needs to find the serial killer before he kills again and because he's targeting victims close to the protagonist. Create a series of complications that make it difficult for the homicide detective to achieve his goals—the electricity goes out, his partner is killed, he's kicked off the case. Complications always intensify the conflict. Create a situation where the protagonist is in over his head—fictional characters need to be vulnerable, or ill-equipped, or in the dark, or outside their comfort zone, so that doubt is planted that he'll succeed.

Suspense is jacked up by the mood and setting of a scene. The more intense, complicated, or scary the scene, the more important it becomes to weave in atmospheric details. Perhaps the attack needs to happen in the dark, or the declaration of love by candlelight, or the harrowing escape during a blizzard.

Since you're trying to snag (sometimes jaded) agents and acquisition editors with a story they simply cannot put down, let's add one more trick to your writer's tool kit. To amp up suspense, orchestrate your scene and chapter endings so they don't wind down, but instead keep the reader hanging. When a reader reaches the end of a chapter he naturally wants to set the book down—your job is to not allow this to happen. This means endings are the perfect places to create cliff-hangers, revelations, and surprises. You've got a whole range of devices that could work: characters bursting onto the stage, narrow escapes, lovers sharing their first kiss, lovers breaking up, or posing questions that aren't answered.

So plan your structure so that a good portion of your endings feature a character in a precarious situation or inject an exciting new development. But use this technique with care—too many cliff-hangers and the reader feels manipulated. Also make sure that the endings that don't include a cliff-hanger or a surprise are still embedded with intrigue and tension.

Tense

Fiction isn't written to delight readers. Its purpose is to rattle their nerves, elevate their blood pressure, and mess with their sleep. A contented reader isn't one who keeps turning the pages until dawn.

Along with suspense, the urge to keep reading is caused by tension. Tension is a penetrating force in fiction and memoir and is created in each scene and on a word-by-word basis. Tension is stirred by unease and dread woven into every aspect of the story. Tension, along with suspense, jabs at the reader's senses and nerves. Tension invades the setting, such as when the characters are picking their way through the forest as night falls with whispers, hoots, and rustling, descriptions that prickle the reader's nerves. This is similar to when a movie viewer is on the edge of his seat, glued to the unfolding action, and cellos are playing an eerie accompaniment, heightening the tension. So you need these undercurrents to seethe in every scene, although from time to time you'll pull back so that the reader can set down the book.

A terrific way to induce tension is to make things uncomfortable for your protagonist in *every* scene. This means he's not lollygagging through the story, he's hungry, tired, thirsty, worried. He's up against hostile witnesses, subzero temperatures, as meanwhile the main conflict is exploding, his bank account is tanking, and his girlfriend cannot understand why he's working so many long hours.

As you plot, plan for small obstacles, tribulations, and tensions on a scene-by-scene basis. Thus if your character Al is waiting for a bus (after his car was stolen in the previous scene), the bus runs late, it starts raining and he has forgotten his umbrella, and a fellow passenger wearing a kilt and orange high-top sneakers arrives at the bus stop. The guy in the kilt seems a few sandwiches short of a picnic and, to prove it, begins an increasingly animated and hostile conversation with an invisible Great Dane.

Remember, too, to say no to your character's comfort and ease in scenes whenever possible because this increases tension. If it's a scorcher in mid-August, make sure your protagonist's air-conditioning breaks down or he's forced outdoors under a blistering sun. Make him exhausted, craving a cigarette or a drink. But don't offer relief until the last possible moment. Get him tangled in an argument when he's trying to fall asleep after an exhausting day, break the key off in the lock when he's desperate to get inside, and send him out on a moonless night so finding his way in the dark is treacherous and dangerous. If your detective is trying to wrest information from a witness, make certain the witness is suspicious, hostile, or uncooperative. In other words, use every element of fiction to say no to your protagonist.

Tension is also depicted in dialogue, especially what is left unsaid or suggested via subtext. A tense dialogue exchange can be as exciting as a professional tennis match with volleys ripping across the net, including accusations, denials, demands, and power plays.

If your character is alone in a scene (which is generally to be avoided), then he's roiling with inner conflict, frustrated because he cannot solve a puzzle, worn out by the story events, is served bad food in his favorite restaurant, or steps in a puddle and ruins his new shoes. Or if he's in a car traveling to a scene, perhaps the familiar route will stir uneasy memories that might lead to a flashback, which will of course create more tension. Or, if he's unable to sleep, perhaps he switches on the bedside lamp and sees the photo of his dead wife. The point is that you're always striving to create unease and discomfort in doses large and small because they create tension.

Tension is also generated by using words for their emotional connotations and fright factor. This means you're paying attention to the *sounds* of the words we use. *Shriek* or *screech* contain more of a fright factor than *yell* or *holler*. Someone can *break out* in nervous laughter or *squeal* with nervous laughter.

Deal Breakers

Over the years I've suggested to about 90 percent of the writers I've worked with that their stories need more tension and suspense. Sometimes when I'm working on a manuscript or leading a critique group, a writer's mistakes are obvious, but then at times I read along and know something is wrong with the story, but I cannot quite put my finger on the underlying problem. So I go for a walk, deliberately imagining the story unfolding as a kind of movie in my head. Often these walks unlock some answer. I list questions that the story raises and note if they are answered. I list scenes that seem flat, noting if each one introduces new conflict or complications. I also list the characters and ask if I know what each one wants, and I always puzzle out the theme and examine the whole so that it is showcased. You might try these tricks to analyze your story's strengths and weaknesses.

Here are deal breakers that prompt my suggestion that the writer should twist the knife deeper. Chapter 9, "Never Write About Wimps," focuses on characters, but I also need to mention a few character types that sink suspense.

Cookie-Cutter Villains

Beginning writers tend to create cookie-cutter villains who exist simply as a source of evil, or as a sadistic, rampaging killing machine. In most thriller manuscripts I read, villains are motivated by greed or power and most have facial scars and greasy hair and smell bad. Typically the reader never understands why these badasses need or want or like to commit dastardly acts. If readers don't understand a badass, they will not be significantly threatened by him, and this kills suspense.

Consider, also, that a handsome or erudite villain is creepier than an unwashed clod, and a complicated villain makes for a complicated story. Take this to the bank: all the characters in your story need to be complex and understandable. Now, this doesn't mean you want your sister to date the villain, but your reader must understand why he's bad and how he got to be that way. So if appropriate to your story, give the bad guy a childhood trauma or history or a dilemma or agenda that explains his actions in the story.

Invisible or Overexposed Villains

A villain threatens the protagonist and others he cares about, which creates tension and fear in readers. However, readers hate it when they can immediately spot a villain when he appears in the story because it spoils the fun of reading fiction. In one manuscript I read, the villain was introduced in the opening chapter when he was hauled into the ER after being involved in a car wreck. The admitting nurse, the protagonist, called the police because of his high blood alcohol level, which set in motion a revenge plot—he was going to get back at the nurse.

The opening chapters, however, were from the villain's viewpoint and included his previous crimes, and his intention to murder his mother was also revealed. Talk about naked. In most stories the villain needs to exist as a *threat* that builds over time—the reader needs to imagine what he is capable of, not know all about him and his motivation from the get-go.

Another problem exists when the villain is offstage too much in the story. Now, there are no hard-and-fast rules about when a villain should appear in a story and when a character should stir the reader's suspicions. Fiction writing often requires misdirection, and that isn't easy. Sometimes you need to cleverly conceal a villain in the opening chapters. However, too often beginning writers feature a villain insinuating himself in a murder investigation or hanging around the edges of the story, as was the case with a janitor who popped in and out of scenes carrying potentially lethal tools, and, in another story, the villain who seduced the protagonist in chapter 3. While the villain doesn't need to be center stage, since that space belongs to the protagonist, readers needs a chance to get to know him (or her) over time and thus to fear him.

But I Digress

Digressions often sneak into a story because the writer has researched a topic and wants to slip in this knowledge or has an opinion about a subject. Digressions take readers away from the action and onto dry ground. Repeat after me: my job is to entertain.

I've read manuscripts that detailed six generations of family history that had little to do with the plot, and manuscripts that explained how a ship was built although the ship wasn't central to the story, and another that described how the canals in Amsterdam came into being although only two scenes occurred in Amsterdam. So save your research for a magazine article and explain only what needs explaining.

How many words you spend on a topic telegraphs its importance in a story. Some writers mistakenly want to pause to describe every piece of machinery, every sunrise, every turret, hallway, butler's pantry, or floor plan. Trouble is, not all story parts are created equal. A reader of a historical or sci-fi novel will patiently allow you to build the world of the story because it's a place he's not familiar with, but for most stories, consider yourself more like an Impressionist painter than a still-life artist.

COINKIDINK!

Coincidences and contrivances sink suspense whenever they appear in a story. I recall one tale in which a character was kidnapped and driven out to the desert. Problem was that the kidnappers, blood-thirsty badasses, allowed the character to bring along an oversized tote bag filled with handy gadgets that she used to survive her ordeal.

In the same scene the kidnap victim read a map as she was sitting in the backseat of a van. Trouble was, the map was in the front seat, and she read it by using the rearview mirror. Try this; it is an impossible feat.

In another manuscript the protagonist eavesdropped on crucial conversations and spied on action in half a dozen scenes.

Problem was, the character needed to be *in* the scenes, not spying on them. This sort of secondhand witness to events was used in novels written in past centuries but comes off as amateurish in contemporary novels.

Then there was the suspense manuscript in which a murder took place at a private school. A few hours later the teacher sent her second-grade charges outdoors to search for clues about the murder. I ask you, would you want this bimbo teaching your kiddies? And guess what? The kids found clues to the murder because the victim conveniently stashed a notebook in plain sight, which the kiddies discovered. And the notebook was filled with cryptic notes in the victim's handwriting, all clues to the identity of her killer.

This category also encompasses acts of God or deus ex machina, a term from ancient Greek dramas for when a story conflict is solved by some improbable means. Examples of these duds include lightning striking the villain, a gigantic wave sweeping the murderer overboard into the Atlantic just as he's about to take deadly aim at the protagonist, or the protagonist receiving an unexpected inheritance that solves all his problems.

Early or Unnecessary Flashbacks and Backstory

In real life you and I imagine the future and remember the past daily. In writing stories, including memoirs, we can also meander in and out of time. A flashback is a scene from before the story time frame that adds richness to the story and chronology and shines a light on the events. However, you need to be especially careful of adding flashbacks early in the story, because backstory is revealed only as needed. The first chapters exist to arouse readers' curiosity, introduce the status quo and the protagonist's dominant personality traits, and establish conflict. Readers don't need a lot of explicit information about what happened to your protagonist in previous years—you need to get the story rolling. You also need to make certain each flashback is sufficiently dramatic and tightly written and filled with vivid language and zippy verbs.

Unnecessary flashbacks simply prove that the character once lived or had adventures or traumas before the story began. But writer, beware. Too many flashbacks confuse the story's chronology. Like all parts of your story, flashbacks need to be justified because they stop the story (which stalls suspense) and they lack immediacy because the events are already over.

Flashbacks need a purpose in the story and are best used to *reveal a character's motivations, to explain crucial influences, and to set up crucial events*. Flashbacks should explain something vital to the protagonist's character arc or to the climax—they are not mere excursions into another time zone. So don't venture into the past without a reason—use flashbacks to make the protagonist's choices and the ending plausible, or to foreshadow. Any other use of flashbacks is like a stripper standing around pulling items out of her purse to show to the audience. Ho-hum.

Easy-Peasy

Storytelling boils down to conflict and opposition, and both stem from a single word: no. And although it sounds simplistic, your job when plotting is to say no to just about everything your protagonist (and often your antagonist) wants or attempts. True, you'll throw in a yes now and then, but not too many, and not until the last possible moment. In the best stories, more than one person, situation, or force says no to your protagonist, and from every quarter. In fact, the no's, the tortures, and the refusals thwarting your characters' large and small desires and goals should be adamant, constant, and tortuous.

I often encounter characters that have uncanny luck and ease, especially when it comes to murder and subterfuge. A middle-aged female character on a killing spree offs her victims with a drug overdose without a hitch. The victims don't catch on when she shows up with her paraphernalia, don't struggle when she lunges at them with a needle, but instead cash in their chips with remarkable cooperation.

In stories that involve a stalker or identity theft, the stalker or thief always has complete access to the victim's home and identity from the opening pages. A killer escapes from prison and immediately flags down a ride, kills the driver with his bare hands, then heads off to easily find the detective who was responsible for his imprisonment. In a damsel-in-distress story, family members, neighbors, and coworkers all pitch in to help the protagonist find the culprit. In fiction, the opposite happens, and fellow cast members don't always cooperate and often thwart the protagonist's goals. Whenever possible, isolate and endanger the protagonist; do not make things easy for her.

Elephant in the Room

An elephant in the corner means that there is an obvious danger, truth, or story element that characters do not notice or that is ignored for the writer's convenience. Although the elephant has left a twelve-foot trail through the jungle and trampled the village and squashed villagers, no one believes in its existence. You'll catch me yawning at these ploys. In one manuscript teens were disappearing from a small town and instead of the townspeople freaking out, sending out an Amber Alert, and forming search parties, they let days pass and rationalized that the kids were off on an adventure. Of course, by the time they realized that the kids weren't simply AWOL, their corpses had grown cold and maggoty. In fiction every action or plot point should create a reaction, not avoidance. In another story, despite a growing body count, horny teens kept driving to a remote make-out spot and getting it on even though a murderer was snuffing out young lovers with the ease of King Kong stepping on cars. Don't do this, either.

Hollywood Ending

Endings matter a lot, but Hollywood endings try too hard, with outcomes that are happy and uncomplicated and thus unrealistic. Or they're over-the-top, sweetened-with-saccharin goodness and try too hard to tug at readers' emotions. When the feel-good ending is cotton-candy pink, all the suspense that came before it is dissipated. Good endings make readers think and ponder the significance of the story and the human condition.

Hollywood endings can also be predictable and can be spotted in the first act. I've read endings with shoot-outs that would require the skills of a professional sniper; a poor kid from the ghetto becoming a superstar billionaire; a child awakening from a coma; and, oh horrors, an "it was all a dream" ending. Most of all, endings need to be realistic or possibly bittersweet—the protagonist wins in the end but the price paid or losses accumulated steal sweetness from the victory.

Introspective

When a reader spends too much time in a character's thoughts, it can be wearying; and when a writer relies on introspection to reveal a main character, it waters down suspense. In most stories most of the time characters need to be interacting with other characters—preferably those who have differing agendas. Interior talk helps build the story and develop character. It doesn't exist to prove your character has a pulse and firing synapses.

Insights into characters are best staged, not a process of watching them mull over events that already happened or calculating their risks. Readers want action; they don't want to hear a character's every thought. Remember that strippers dance—they don't perch on a chair and look out at the audience.

Also, beginning writers often create amateurish-sounding introspection that looks something like this: Delia thought longingly back to the night when she first met Jason. The sky had been the most amazing shade of purple as the sun set when she turned the corner and spotted him putting change into a parking meter. She wanted to meet him immediately and thought that he was cute and interesting-looking. That was the beginning of a magical summer.

Police Protection

I'm also surprised at how easily some characters are given police protection in the stories I've read. As in round-the-clock cops patrolling the protagonist's neighborhood, trying to prevent a crime and keep the protagonist safe from the villain. These days, cops are too overburdened and understaffed to offer police protection unless the person is a senator or a billionaire, in which case a private security firm would be hired. But of course the bigger issue here is that police protection kills suspense—stories require that the protagonist be vulnerable and on a collision course with the villain, not existing in a safety zone.

To-ing and Fro-ing

As a story unfolds, let readers know when you're moving around in time and space. Which is when many writers resort to excess and have their characters to-ing and fro-ing in every scene. At times it's important to show readers how a character arrived at a scene or is moving around, but sometimes it's not and you can simply employ a *scene cut* or move the story directly from one scene (an empty office building at midnight) to a new scene (the protagonist's apartment, where she's pouring herself a glass of Cabernet). You don't need to depict the protagonist slipping into her coat, walking across the office, switching off the lights, stepping into the elevator, trudging through the parking lot, and driving across town. In a well-written story the reader can leap with you into the new setting.

Now, if as the protagonist unlocks her car door the villain hurls himself at her and holds a knife to her throat, that's a place to carry the reader along with her. Or if a rapist is waiting in her apartment wearing her lingerie, you might want to foreshadow this by inserting shadows in the parking lot or some other creepy detail like a burned-out light in the hallway. The point is that you can skip over ordinary movements, especially those found in stories set in contemporary times.

PIMPING

In fiction and often in memoirs, bad things happen to characters and people we come to care about. Such is storytelling. But pimping means that the writer has used gore, sex, or over-the-top violence for shock value, even though it's not an integral part of the plot. Too many of these sensationalized tactics and you anesthetize the reader. Way too many and an editor might wonder if you're a closet sociopath. Which is never a good thing.

Now, it's always tricky for a writer to know when to draw the line in a story, especially since humans are sexual and violent beings. When is something too graphic, too nutty? My clients' stories have featured a hit man splattering the brains of a toddler, a creepy pedophile getting it on with ten-year-olds, a sociopath who collected pubic hair from his victims, and detailed accounts of rape, torture, and incest.

So before you add the X rating and start painting blood-smeared canvases, consider the purpose of your tactic. How many maimed corpses do you need to tell a riveting story? A story often works best when the protagonist is touched personally by a single, needless death. Is the violence used to create empathy for the characters? Does it change things, up the stakes, reveal truths? Are you commenting on good and evil? If you add a sex scene, does it show the emotional connections between characters or some other facets of their personalities? Or better yet, are these scenes used to create or resolve conflict?

Pimping also means you're telegraphing to readers that your

characters' lives and hearts don't have value. So keep in mind that sometimes the more graphic or violent the moment in a story, the more it needs to be understated.

Premonitions

It's also surprising how often characters in beginning writers' stories have premonitions and forebodings of imminent disaster early in the story. In almost all these stories the characters' neck hairs prickle or a disaster is prophesized in a nightmare.

In the revenge plot mentioned earlier, the nurse immediately had a premonition that the villain was gunning for her. In another story a mother sensed something was wrong and rushed to her daughter's school just before terrorists arrived to strap bombs to the doors and herd all the kiddies into the gym. In fiction you want your protagonist in the dark some of the time, not quite trusting her feminine intuition or gut instincts. Or, instead, the reader, not the protagonist, should guess that danger is afoot. To create suspense, the protagonist should always be wrong about something and quite often underestimate the antagonist or villain.

Pulling the Plug

Sometimes writers pull the plug on a scene instead of allowing it to explode into high drama. It looks something like this: The story begins when Beth, a children's librarian, starts receiving phone calls at the library from a stranger who describes moments in her life that no one should know about because she lives alone. The number of calls escalates, and then he begins calling her at home, then phoning in the middle of the night. Beth changes her phone number and starts screening her calls.

Then a single white rose is left on the seat of her car, even though there is no evidence the car was broken into. Then she receives e-mails demanding to know why she has broken his heart.

She walks home alone one night about two-thirds of the way into the story. Of course, if any of us were being stalked we wouldn't walk alone in the dark, but this is fiction. As she walks along she has a spooky feeling someone is following her. Instead of finally allowing the reader a close-up of the stalker (who has still not made an appearance), she runs into old friends from college emerging from a liquor store and is whisked away to a party, amid high fives and "what have you been doing all these years?" questions. Instead of making the scene scary, the writer pulled the plug.

Now, sometimes for the sake of delay you need to pull the plug. But in general don't eliminate possible dangers to your character. Make things worse and worse with close calls and increasing dangers, especially in the second and third acts.

Special Powers

Unless you're writing for the comic book industry, it's important that your characters don't possess an excess of special powers. I often see this problem in stories that feature amateur sleuths—characters who possess such an unlikely blend of traits and skills that it makes your head spin. These characters can run for miles without tiring, although they're overweight, out of shape, and middle-aged; they can solve unsolvable crimes, although they have no background in detection; they're impervious to pain; they never eat or sleep; they tap-dance through the story as if on a cloud. The beauty of amateur sleuths, and indeed of casting protagonists or antiheroes who are ordinary blokes or gals is that *readers identify with their weaknesses*, along with the way they solve the story problem. So before you make your character a superstud or give him psychic abilities, ask yourself if these traits are believable and necessary to solve the story problem.

One of my client's protagonists was a MacGyver type who, armed with string, duct tape, and a Swiss Army knife, saved the world. He was so tough and amazing that nothing fazed him—he had a black belt in karate, spoke eight languages including Cantonese, could defuse a bomb with a paper clip and scale a fifty-foot wall (because bad writers create fifty-foot walls), was able to follow a criminal's trail in the jungle like a human bloodhound, and made love in marathon sessions with only a pause for another sip of champagne.

In one manuscript I read, a character with no athletic prowess and wearing a dress and pumps leaped from a speeding train and then scrambled to her feet without a bruise. Later, this character, who had no background on a cattle ranch or as a rodeo performer, and was in fact a rather ordinary Southern woman, lassoed the bad guys with a neat rope trick. (Don't get me started about the conveniently available rope.) Yet another character in another manuscript took out his opponent, his lover's husband, with ninja-like deadliness, although the guy didn't have martial arts training. Remember, your job as a writer is to torture not only your characters, but also your readers—make them sweat, fret, and worry. Concocting superpowers or uncanny resourcefulness in your characters doesn't allow readers to worry about their plight.

Trivial Intervening Actions

Some writers cannot help themselves—they simply need to describe or explain every aspect of the story. This habit can be especially distracting and suspense-busting when it comes in the midst of an argument, confrontation, crisis, or fight. It looks like this: Margo stomps into the kitchen, her heels clicking against the cold granite tiles. She walks across the room, ignoring Jason, and pours herself a cup of Swiss Mocha from her state-of-the-art Italian coffeemaker into her English bone china cup. She adds a dab of cream and an exact teaspoon of sugar, then slams the refrigerator door with a resounding clatter. Still holding her coffee cup, she straightens her spine and tosses her shoulder-length raven hair, then walks up to Jason until they are only inches apart, her eyes mere slits of rage. She demands of him, "Just who do you think you are calling me a slut?"

To Be Continued

By now I hope you understand that when we write stories we want to inflict physical effects on the reader, just as a stripper has an, um, physical effect on the audience.

But to keep a reader leaning forward, you need to keep him hanging, and even in the midst of good times in the story, he needs to anticipate that trouble is ahead for your characters. In your first draft, keep employing a "to be continued" approach; you can even type the words into your first draft to remind yourself *not* to solve problems and *not* to provide answers.

There are so many difficult decisions to be made when crafting a story, but ones that seem to trip up writers are the decisions about when to include information in the story and when to hold back. If you're concerned that your scenes are lagging, remind yourself that your job is to take the reader where he *doesn't* want to go. He wants the characters to get it on, solve the case, find the missing kid, or resolve the family drama. Your job is to thwart that desire. Remember, too, that fiction evolves around letting readers inside the hidden lives of people and places. And readers expect and want to live inside the characters—inside their souls, their secrets, and their flaws and desires. Trouble is, this intimacy with characters is happening when their lives are a tormented mess, some of their problems subtle, some overt, all complex.

Try This

No matter what genre you're writing, craft a murder scene. Experiment with an imaginative yet realistic means of murder—I once imagined a story set in a Mexican restaurant in which the victim is killed by having habanero peppers stuffed into his mouth, and then being swathed in industrial-strength plastic wrap and lashed to the prep table. Take readers step-by-step through the victim's final breaths, but remember, understatement often works best, and delay the outcome so readers are forced to keep reading.

Quick and Dirty Tips for Keeping Readers Worried and Uneasy

- Delay. Delay. Delay.
- Whenever you write a scene, ask yourself, What is the worst thing that can happen next?
- Unpredictable plots are based on unpredictable characters whose reactions to events aren't always what readers expect.
- Give someone in the story a secret that casts suspicion, and reveal the secret at the last possible moment.
- Never create characters who are invulnerable to danger. Create characters who make mistakes with fatal consequences. Orchestrate a character's missteps so they're based on his flaws. Mistakes, large and small, shape believable characters, and by witnessing these missteps, the reader worries if the character will ever get his act together.
- Make certain that your protagonist is somehow thrown off balance and weakened by the story events.
- The more a character desires something, the more suspense you create.
- Use red herrings and false alarms to throw off the reader.
- If there is a villain or some evil force in the story, introduce him/her/it early or at least hint at his/her/its presence.
- If possible, use time running out to increase the suspense.

- Create realistic hindrances to your protagonist escaping or being rescued.
- Use the setting to capitalize on the suspense—a deserted mansion, a lonely coastal highway, a snowstorm that strands people in a mountain cabin.
- To milk the suspense and tension, orchestrate your protagonist reaching safety, but then make the safety an illusion.
- Tense endings force a protagonist to act in ways that the reader would be afraid to—confronting the antagonist, running into the burning building, or escaping the murderer's clutches. The ending supplies the most vicarious thrills and action in certain genres.
- While fiction is imbued with tension and suspense, if every moment is fraught with horror and nonstop action, the results are melodrama and a story that exhausts the reader. The solution is to intersperse *breathers* throughout the story where you turn down the tension a notch.
- As a novel progresses, keep raising and personalizing the stakes.
- Look for opportunities to make your character out of sync with his surroundings. Send a rookie cop to a grisly crime scene. Force an introvert to attend a gala. Place an impoverished character in an environment of wealth.
- Do not open scenes with characters waking up or end them with characters going to sleep—this kills suspense.

Resources

Study pacing and techniques in suspense movies *noting* how directors make the story taut and when information is withheld. *Sleeping with the Enemy*, *The 39 Steps*, *Rebecca,* and *Gaslight* are good choices.

Read *The Road,* by Cormac McCarthy, to note how tension and suspense invade and push every scene.

Conflict, Action & Suspense, William Noble

www.heretocreate.com

Writing and Selling Your Mystery Novel, Hallie Ephron

The Art of Deception, Ridley Pearson

The Elements of Mystery Fiction: Writing the Modern Whodunit, William G. Tapley

Five

Blood, Roses, and Mosquitoes: Writing from the Senses

My object is to show what I have found, not what I am looking for.

—Pablo Picasso, from an interview with Marius de Zayas

I'm afraid it's time to get all Judge Judy on your ass because this is one technique that you really need to get right. Editors look for writers with an uncanny knack for reflecting life experiences with accuracy and originality. You see, from the opening paragraph, when an editor reads a manuscript, he or she wants to tumble headlong into the world of that story. He wants to feel as if he's in the hands of a spinner of yarns and travel like a delighted tourist through the story, discovering again and again unexpected pleasures. No matter if you've written a romance, mystery, or memoir, an editor wants to gobble it up like potato chips. An editor wants to believe.

In my work, what happens too often is that instead of sensing that I'm entering a story world, I feel like I'm plowing through a pile of words that don't add up to something magical called *story*. Now, I could spout off about wavering tone or narrative slackness, or try to explain why a manuscript too often feels like a murky fog bank in which the characters bounce around for no fathomable reasons, or I could complain about saccharine tales with clunky morals. But the first reason I won't believe in your story is if it's not alive. Readers want an experience when they open a book, and most are yearning for escape. So let's talk about how you can make this happen.

Begin with the Tangible

There are many places to begin a story—with a character, a dialogue exchange, or a crisis like a deep plunge into the icy lake of storytelling. But no matter if you start a story with two elderly women stumbling onto a corpse while walking along the shore or the long-ago memory of the night your stepfather moved into your house, here's a foundation from which you can always begin: all stories must start with the artifacts of everyday life. A reader wants to enter the story world you're describing in the same way he enters his house at the end of the workday.

I often recommend to my students that they write for an imaginary reader. In fact, I prefer an imaginary reader whose life is a swampland of bad luck and misery. Let's call our hapless reader Lauren. She works at a crappy cubicle job where she feels trapped. And as with many crappy cubicle jobs, she has a brainless bully for a boss, and on this particular day she's had a run-in with her boss. Lauren would like to utter the "take this job and shove it" line, but her savings are meager and her prospects even thinner. So after staying late at work because of her boss's demands, hungry and tired, she heads for home.

Because Lauren lives in Seattle, she's driving in the gloom

amid a downpour. Which is when she gets a flat tire. And discovers that her cell phone battery has run down. At the side of the road, she narrowly misses getting run over, but with the help of a stranger, manages to limp to a gas station on one of those tiny doughnut tires. Luckily, the gas station is able to fix her tire—the only bright spot in her day.

She finally arrives home, exhausted and soaked. In her bedroom she's peeling off her sopping clothes when she realizes that her beloved but elderly cat, Otis, is unusually still on her bed. You guessed it, Otis has moved on to the Great Litter Box in the sky. Weeping, she manages to bury Otis in the backyard in a muddy flower bed and straggles back inside to again change her wet clothes. By now ravenous, she trudges down to the kitchen and realizes that between working late and the flat tire, she forgot to stop at the grocery store. She scrounges around and finds a packet of microwave popcorn and slips it in. While pouring herself a hefty glass of bourbon she smells the popcorn burning—somehow she set the timer wrong and it has been zapped far too long. Dumping the blackened kernels into a bowl, she retreats to an armchair, determined to somehow push this lousy day out of her mind. That's when she opens *your* book. That's when Lauren's surroundings and miserable day need to disappear and the world of your story takes their place.

The sensory details of the real world have a potent and reassuring reality. Similarly, when we open a book or enter a story we want to be welcomed there with the reassuring artifacts of reality. The reader will find himself wandering around in the story noticing the new snow frosting the fir trees, or the peculiar, musty smell of your grandmother's attic, or the chilly, labyrinth passages of a thirteenth-century castle.

So for now, let's ignore the many adages about writing and simply concede that art is in the details. And the biggest job of details is to stir emotions in the reader. The more senses you use in your story, the more you'll affect your reader. Sensory details pierce the reader's heart and mind, creep into his imagination, and set off mini-explosions of understanding.

Sensory description contributes to every part of storytelling and stirs the reader's memory and helps him make connections and experience the story emotionally and physically. Thus life is breathed into fiction and memoir by translating the senses onto the page, producing stories rooted in the physical world. Action and dialogue arrest the reader's attention, but sensory details assure the reader that they're actually occurring. That means blood, roses, and mosquitoes or whatever proofs your story demands.

The Sensory World

Reading is an intimate experience and requires that the reader enter an intimate world. Since the real world is made up of things—cumulus clouds, paperback books, and overstuffed chairs, California Zinfandel, your favorite pen, the belching city bus, the gloomy winter sky—your story needs to mimic reality. The trick is to choose details that are so vital and convincing that the story would suffer without them. Details should affect the outcome of the piece and help us understand theme and meaning. Details also unify the plot, especially when they change over time, as when a family hits the skids and starts moving to increasingly seedy apartments.

But herein lies the writer's dilemma. Which details do we

choose? Sometimes it seems like there is a blizzard of choices. Which ones are important? How many do you add to flesh out a scene? What is overkill? When are details boring, self-indulgent, distracting?

Let's look first at the *why* of using details. Sensory descriptions paint a vivid picture with words. Use description to anchor setting in fiction, to create a mood, to make things happen in a story, to foreshadow events, and to reveal characters. Without description, ghostly characters move about in vague buildings or fuzzy landscapes.

Details also reveal *distinctiveness* and *significance*—the places in the story where the reader should slow down and pay attention. Not every scene plays out with the same speed, intensity, or importance. Some scenes are transitions, some introduce set pieces—the most dramatic events in the story—and some scenes happen in settings the reader has visited earlier. In these scenes, you don't need as many details—you can zip through, revealing the essentials. But for major events, lavish more words on details and your readers will linger there because the level of drama demands it.

Because sensory details engage readers, weave them into the beginning of books, scenes, and chapters. Many writers scatter sensory details in dribs and drabs across the landscape of the story when instead they're needed throughout to maintain the illusion of reality. A lack of sensory details leaves your reader lost and baffled. Your story line is the map of events that takes readers from beginning to end. The sensory information fills in the map so readers can follow the story's trajectory and forge ahead when they reach a new fork in the road.

Bring details to readers through all the senses, through everyday elements like the smell of coffee brewing, the chill and clank of ice cubes, the distinct scent and flavor of oranges. Details can telegraph meaning, as in the beige walls and mix of stale air, disinfectant, and been-in-bed-too-long funk of patients in a hospital. Or they can be precise, like the musky smells that linger on the sheets after lovemaking or describing a baby's skin as soft as rose petals.

When someone wants to create intimacy, *touch* works best—a caress, a kiss, a hug, stroking your hair, or holding your hand. In the same way, have your characters touch and be touched by other characters. Drape velvet or silk on a character's skin, or punish a character with a cruel, rough rope binding his wrists, biting into the skin. Or make us feel the leathery skin of the old farmer's hand. Make weather assault the characters—the cloying heat of a Louisiana bayou, the burn of frostbite, the scalding heat of a midday sun. When elements touch your characters, readers feel it, too.

In the real world, we're bombarded with *sounds*. They annoy or jangle our nerves, such as the blare of heavy traffic or a scream in the night. They soothe and lull like the song of the ocean or birds singing or a lullaby. Sounds tug the reader into the *present*, as when we hear a car backfire or a gunshot ring out. Sounds focus the reader's attention, which is why dialogue is so convincing in scenes.

Taste is also intimate and can serve several purposes in your story. If your character eats bacon cheeseburgers and fries regularly, we'll make assumptions about his health habits. We'll also make assumptions if your character's refrigerator is stocked with tofu, hemp milk, sprouts, and apples. But you can also weave in tastes as proofs of reality, to slow pacing when your character whips together a meal, and to make readers believe in the story world.

Scents are also important to fiction because our olfactory senses are wired directly to the limbic, primitive part of the brain. Among other functions, this so-called "lizard" brain stores our memories and emotions. Often there is nothing as savory as garlic roasting in olive oil, as heady as the perfume on your lover's neck, as homey as cookies baking, as lovely as the fresh smell after a spring rain. Especially use smells for unpleasant or scary associations in your stories—funeral flowers, cheap cologne, dirty hair, a decomposing body, a restaurant Dumpster on a hot day.

Sight is most commonly employed in fiction writing since we use it the most as we go about our days. The world is full of colors, light, landscapes, and the tiniest of visual details. They anchor readers in a place, a moment, and allow them to experience action. When visual details are embedded in stories, the reader implies meaning, imagines what the child's avoidance of her uncle's hug means and why a character turns her face to avoid a kiss.

Now let's look closer at the reasons we use senses in our writing, because there are three main purposes that sensory details serve in writing.

Blood: To Stir Emotions

As discussed, one of the big jobs of description is to evoke emotions. Unless you're a surgeon, few of us encounter blood regularly in our daily lives. Blood is natural, blood is also freaky when it comes from a beating or an accident, blood is symbolic, and blood is vivid.

Blood is usually used by writers to pull out the stops to evoke fear or horror. But obviously you cannot go for the gusto in every scene, so when you write scenes, ask yourself each time, What do I want my readers to feel in this moment? As you ponder this question, seed the scenes with sensory details that bring about emotions.

In life, there are good reasons for our skin to crawl or our hearts to race—the loud bang or phone call in the middle of the night. The friend who phones weeping. A child's illness. A co-worker's unjust accusation. In stories try to install those same effects in the reader. So add the shrieks, the sinister suggestion, the betrayal.

And details push these emotional reactions into the reader's nervous system. After all, there's a good reason why spooky stories or scenes take place during a dark and stormy night. When the heavens are shrieking with thunder, lightning is slashing the inky sky, and we're huddled in our homes, the elements can bring on feelings of vulnerability and unease. Anything can happen when nature is rampaging in real life and in fiction, and details are the key to bringing about emotions.

Roses: To Bring the Familiar to Life

Because most readers are bombarded with a nonstop media onslaught in daily life, it's especially important that your details be selective and persuasive. And often a few small details, carefully chosen, can convey reality. It's also necessary that the familiar be convincing in a story. If the scene that takes place in a living room in your story includes an overflowing ashtray and a lumpy couch and unframed posters on the wall, and other artifacts that we recognize, then we'll believe in whatever else happens in the scene. So that if a couple argues or one person threatens divorce in that room, we're more likely to believe in their actions because we can smell the ashtray and the despair that permeates the place.

Mosquitoes: To Convince, Especially When the Story Has an Exotic Setting, and to Show Consequences

Most of us have encountered the tiny kamikazes of the insect world. If you're hiking, barbecuing in the backyard, camping, or merely trying to sleep at night, when one or two have infiltrated your space, you know what capable torturers mosquitoes are. You know what it feels like to be prey.

When they buzz around your tent, you believe. Details are the mosquitoes of writing. The more exotic your setting—a planet in a far galaxy, a fairy kingdom, Ireland in the seventeenth century—the more details are necessary to anchor the reader to this outlandish story place.

Details, like mosquitoes, also prove the consequences of events. After a mosquito bites, you're left with the annoying, itchy swelling (which is from the mosquito's saliva). Similarly in stories, icy weather should bring shivers and layers of wool; heat waves make people cranky; darkness makes characters more uncertain and vulnerable; smoke stings the eyes; cheeseburgers are usually greasy and filling; cell phones have individual ring tones; and perfumes can intoxicate or choke. If the protagonist drinks too many beers, he becomes stupid, clumsy, and logy, and he should wake up the next morning feeling like hell. Make your readers itch.

Deal Breakers

Now that we've explored the reasons that we use sensory details, let's clarify how details, like so many parts of writing, can go wrong.

Empty Soundstage

I wish I had a dollar for every scene I've read that takes place on an empty soundstage. Indoors there is no lighting, no sound, no floor, furniture, or colors of any sort. Outdoors there is no sky, sun, moon or stars, plants, planets, trees, grass, roads, animals, insects, birds, flowers, or weather.

Years ago one of my most talented students wrote a story about a young man who traveled to the States from Scotland in the 1800s and ended up being conscripted into the army and fighting in the Civil War. It was a fabulous story, but it so lacked in details that the drama never came to life. The writer especially lost an opportunity to show the new world through his protagonist's eyes. And because he was from a remote Scottish village, the world he was encountering was exotic.

Here's a tip that might be helpful: when you watch films, pay attention to the decisions made by production and set designers. Every time a sensory object appears in a scene, especially if it's repeated, ask yourself why the director and design team chose to include it.

Faulkneresque, or Someone Left a Cake Out in the Rain

Sometimes when I receive a certain type of manuscript I wonder if the writer has been influenced by Faulkner, Toni Morrison, James Joyce, Haruki Murakami, or other writers who are experimental and difficult to read. It seems some writers believe that if their readers are constantly scratching their heads over their stories and their tales are bloated with details, symbolism, and motifs that it all somehow translates to *lit-trah-shure*. Grab a clue: stories need to be accessible in order to work. And a story that is a tortuous labyrinth of description is often a sign of a bloated ego.

In these stories, in which there is often some cheesy adaptation of stream of consciousness and far too much introspection, made-up, airy-fairy descriptions and phrases populate the pages as writers describe things like the Sanskrit of beingness; the wounded trees of childhood's crippled dreams; longly risqué revelries of nothingness; the masturbatory elegance of gloved toes; frisky, enchanted Cleopatra butterflies flitting in the meadow; and semitransparent envelopes of joy.

When I read this sort of blather I'm reminded of the worst song lyrics of all time, "MacArthur Park," that includes a lament about a cake left out in the rain. It goes: "I don't think that I can take it 'cause it took so long to bake it and I'll never have that recipe again." A cake turning into a puddle is supposed to have some deep significance or symbolism. I don't think that I can take it, either. The advice here is easy to swallow: sound like yourself, not a cake in the rain.

JELL-O

When I was a kid I loved Jell-O—especially with bananas and whipped cream. I didn't care that the colors were improbable and that it was wiggly and strange. Well, I'm not a Jell-O fan anymore, and I especially dislike finding descriptions in writing that are as flat and bland as a Jello-O recipe. Jell-O descriptions never take readers deeply into a moment so that we can understand characters. Typically the details are so mundane they don't paint a picture in the reader's imagination and instead mostly feature character descriptions based on appearance, not inner traits. It looks something like this: My sister is petite, a teenager with blond hair and blue eyes. She always wears skirts and sweaters and sometimes she wears glasses when she reads. She is usually carrying her pink backpack and cell phone.

Problem is, we cannot know characters strictly by their appearance, and if this character was in the midst of a group of three hundred other girls, we likely would not be able to pick her out. In the most vivid characters their appearance is an expression of personality and their personality traits are showcased in the plot. If a hot-tempered, blustery sort of character is caught in circumstances that call for cool and sensitivity, then we want to know how he's going to react. Jello-O descriptions of characters are not the key to their being—desires, fears, and dominant personality traits are.

In Your Face

Excess and purple prose buries the meaning in your sentences and wearies the reader. In-your-face descriptions are subsets of purple prose and are especially annoying when they describe characters or people. It looks like this: Allison Sorrow walked in the door looking like a movie star. She brushed her blond hair the color of the sun from her face and took off her sunglasses, revealing eyes as blue as the Pacific. But her head was only the crowning glory of a body that demanded to be kissed from head to toe. How was I going to make it through this meeting without touching her? I asked myself.

It's not easy to describe characters (or anything) that the viewpoint character finds attractive or repulsive. But avoid gushing, hyperbole, and sounding like Geraldo Rivera on speed. Instead, combine description with action and dialogue, scattered throughout in palatable bits.

Ordinary Details

This is similar to Jell-O descriptions and probably the most common problem I see with description: ordinary details that don't slip into a reader's bloodstream. Effective details are like adrenaline or drugs or wine. Ordinary descriptions mean characters wear blue sweaters, ceilings are high, dogs are furry, snow is white, carpet is thick, books are interesting, storms are wet, and kittens are small and frisky. And let's not forget green grass and blue sky. Yawn.

Using ordinary details, a room is described like this: I stepped into the large living room. Along one wall was a giant window overlooking the backyard. Against another wall was a brown couch and yet another wall held a fireplace. Margo was sitting in an armchair near the fireplace.

Another yawn.

Instead, find the perfect, quirky, or extraordinary detail that serves as shorthand to paint a bigger picture. One of my favorite examples is from Amy Bloom's short story *Silver Water.* In the story, Rose, at fifteen, is experiencing a psychotic break, and then the story chronicles the progress of her illness. When it first happens, as her father tries to talk to her, "she sat there licking the hairs on her forearm. First one way, then the other." I've never forgotten this perfect expression of losing it.

Police Blotter

With this problem in writing, the writer pauses at every moment to provide a police-blotter description of each character that walks into the scene. Problem is that this stops the story and seems contrived. Sometimes the writing is matter-of-fact, sometimes it, too, can be in-your-face. Here is an example: Richard was easy to spot, tall, maybe about six-three, with sandy-blond curly hair, and he was extremely well built, not to mention handsome. His aquiline features were graceful. His facial features resembled the gods of Roman mythology that Alicia had seen pictures of in her art history studies. Richard had a long nose, blue eyes that sparkled. Somehow Alicia sensed that Richard would be reserved or shy.

Somehow I sensed that the writer needed a subtler method of introducing characters, and I hope you agree.

Text Message

Confession: I am not fond of texting. The keys on my cell phone are too small, and since I spend so much time at a computer, I'm looking to escape from technology and gadgets as often as possible, and I don't care if my BFF, a BAC, or LOML loves 2 text, I don't. And texting doesn't make me LOL, it drives me batty. For the life of me I cannot imagine why people need to be in constant contact with their pals and why they want to reduce language to acronyms and smiley faces.

In a story it looks like this: Anna was angry as she pulled out of her parents' driveway. Past the Martins' house. Past the park. Through town and away. Away from childhood. Away. And all the bad memories. Toward a new beginning.

BWDIK?

Weather Report

Please don't begin every scene or chapter with a weather report. Please don't tell readers every time the sun shines. Just don't. Weather is a great addition to a story but it needs to create a mood and characters need to interact with it, as when they splash through puddles, or turn on the windshield wipers, or huddle against the cold. Unless your story is about a monsoon wiping out the continent, weather should not be reported on constantly as a backdrop because it will look like you cannot figure out how to write descriptions that deepen the story.

Zombie Parade

Writers tend to feature characters who either emote and weep and gnash their teeth all over the place or who resemble a zombie parade. Not that I've ever seen one, but in these stories characters never wince, laugh, grimace, sigh, raise their voices, groan in ecstasy, wink, stumble, blink, grin, or blush. Not only must your characters have human emotions and reactions, but you need to find fresh and interesting ways to express them. Most of our communication in life is nonverbal—difficult as this is to achieve, some of this must end up in your stories.

More "Jobs" for Sensory Details

Now that we've covered the main reasons why we use details and the most common mistakes, let's add a few more "jobs" that details can accomplish. What beginning writers often overlook is that description can create mood and atmosphere. At times we want the impact of a scene to make readers feel a certain way—pensive, edgy, or sad. Carefully chosen sensory information can work like a film score, since music plays on our emotions and unconscious.

While music stirs the filmgoer's emotions and shades the impact of the scene, it must be appropriate in each moment. It cannot draw too much attention to itself and away from the action on the screen. And it must be *felt,* as when the eerie strains of a cello foreshadow that the protagonist is venturing into dangerous territory; or violins shriek when the killer bursts into the room, with his demonic eyes gleaming; or low, lush notes serve as the backdrop to a love scene. Music cues audiences to pay attention and helps filmgoers remember crucial scenes; details in writing serve the same purpose. A film score also creates continuity and unity in the film, as do details sprinkled throughout a story.

Similarly, writers create atmosphere and mood—lighthearted, hilarious, musing, dark, or suspenseful—depending on the needs of the scene. Details can always be used to heighten dread or suspense, as in a horror story, an extremely sensual genre. The description of the story's setting—a graveyard or a haunted house or a coastal town—can enhance the horror and terror and isolate the characters.

To illustrate how senses are employed in a scene, imagine this scenario: your character Stella Horne, a private investigator who has been hired to solve an insurance fraud case, is heading to an appointment with Marianne Mathers, a key witness and young mother. Stella drives her Honda Civic to a less-than-fashionable section of town for the interview. Pulling onto Mathers's block, she parks in front of her house, avoiding a cloudburst of broken glass on the pavement.

Climbing out of her car, she notices that the house, a rundown rental property in need of a coat of paint, and the overgrown yard have a neglected, bleak air and the front door is slightly ajar. And this is not the kind of neighborhood where people leave their doors open. She looks around the block and notices that it's eerily quiet and most of the drapes in the neighboring homes are closed as tight as coffin lids. She notes, too, that many of the homes have bars on the windows and doors.

Stella isn't carrying her gun because this case is fairly routine; so the reader is starting to squirm, wondering if Stella should approach the house, if things are safe. Stella rings the doorbell. No answer. She opens the door a few more inches, peeking in and calling for Marianne. Still no answer.

She pushes the door, with its peeling paint and greasy doorknob, and steps inside, leaving the door ajar. The first thing she notices is that the heat is blasting and the place feels like a hothouse. She looks around at the clutter of toddler toys and piles of laundry waiting to be folded covering a seen-better-days plaid couch from Goodwill, sniffs the stale aroma of old ashtrays and wet dog, a diaper pail that needs emptying and other unpleasant smells she cannot identify. In the corner of the living room, the pump from the murky-looking aquarium emits a low hum; otherwise, all is quiet.

Along with Stella, the reader is growing uncomfortable, fearful of what the other rooms might reveal. The writer, via the senses, is activating these fears by depicting proofs of reality. The writer has invaded the reader's senses because that's his job.

Tangible, sensory details also *establish credibility for future events.* If your reader has been wandering around in a farmhouse and sees the worn plank floor and cast-iron stove, notices the empty whiskey bottle and sour smell of dirty dishes, when the grieving widower stumbles into the room, the reader will believe in his aching emptiness because he's seen the whiskey bottle and the flies hovering over the sink piled high.

Specific details *slow the pace,* force the reader to savor the words and imagine the things or events that you are describing. Sentences filled with the commonplace, the vague, the indistinct, and with clichés are sentences that readers gloss over. These sentences don't enter the consciousness of the reader because they don't connect. Specificity connects.

Specific details are concrete and *make abstract concepts understandable,* emotions real, fuzzy ideas clear. I often mention the old example to my students—don't lecture me about the horrors of war, instead show me a child's discarded shoe by the side of a road, then I'll understand the horror. Abstractions don't involve us, and although issues such as racism, intolerance, despair, and poverty are obviously important, we cannot grasp them without details to latch onto.

Sense of Place

While setting is the time and place your story occurs, and includes geography, climate, or architecture, it can also include richer attributes such as the historical moment the story plays out or its social or political context. Sometimes the context will be overt, sometimes it's more of the subtext of the story. The context could be an intellectually stifling suburb or the Bohemian spirit of Greenwich Village in the 1950s. Because particular places and times have their own personality and emotional significance, choose a setting that fits your story's premise. Maybe a coming-of-age story about a naïve person needs the bustle and sophistication of New York City. A story about power struggles can be set anywhere, but if you want to comment broadly on good and evil, some Tolkien landscape like Middle Earth works best. If you need to isolate your character as he faces physical challenges, then the misty Yorkshire moors or a remote island might be the right context.

Setting details are multipurpose, multitasking tools, and have been described as a literary Leatherman. When a reader first opens a story, setting is the doorway through which he or she ventures into the story events. It includes the political, social, religious, cultural, and historical background of the particular time and place. It also includes the monetary system, superstitions, science, medicine, and technology of the times. If your story is set in ancient Rome, slavery would exist, powerful emperors and senators would rule, the classes would be strictly stratified, and a pantheon of deities would be worshipped. Senate debates would occur, the wealthy would live in villas and ride in horse-drawn chariots, gladiators would battle in public contests, and a vast army would exist.

There are many other purposes that setting can serve, such as antagonism when your character needs to climb a mountain to escape, and symbolism when dawn breaks on a new day and optimism reigns.

Setting details can also create convincing characters since a person's home or workplace is extremely revealing. The things a reader spots, or perhaps smells, in a setting can whisper volumes about his mental health, habits, and efficiency. Consider your detective's office—does it reveal he's prone to eating Krispy Kremes or Chicago-style pizza at his desk? Perhaps there is a bottle of whiskey or porn stashed in a lower desk drawer. Or maybe it's a place of sterile, orderly perfection—pens aligned in spooky precision, not a paper out of place, not a speck of dust; excessive neatness is always a curious, if not unfortunate, trait in any person.

Try This

If you believe that your scenes and descriptions lack sensory information, use a highlighter pen to highlight each sense with a separate color—yellow for sight, pink for smells, green for sounds, etc. Try this in a few chapters where you suspect that the level of detail is skimpy. What you should see on your pages is a rainbow of colors. If only one or two senses are represented, go back and start filling them in. You might also want to highlight the senses in a short story or a single chapter from one of your favorite authors, then compare it to the level of detail in your work.

Quick and Dirty Tips for Writing Descriptively

- Sensory details are the doorway through which the reader enters your story.
- Description begins with the writer. You cannot insert perfect details into your stories or prose unless you go about your days with awareness and curiosity. Collect, gather, cultivate, and observe all the nuances of life, including nature, weather, and lighting, but especially people.
- Description is sparing yet revealing. Description does not equal inventory. It is often most effective at its briefest and cleanest. Spark the reader's imagination, don't provide a portrait.
- The best descriptions help illuminate themes and create tone and mood.
- While details signal importance, they should appear natural.
- Descriptions can serves as transitions to move readers in time and place, such as *Later, as dusk cast long fingers across the lawn . . .*

- Use figurative language and comparison to make your descriptions soar, reinforce meaning, and add music to your writing.
- Don't always state the obvious, especially when describing characters' reactions and emotions. Try being indirect.
- Effective description sometimes evolves over time and can grow or change as the character or story deepens.
- Keep description fresh. Strive to inspire readers with a detail that they have never read before.
- Introduce major characters with substance and a presence that readers can experience through the senses. Here are three guidelines that will never fail you: (1) Always link information about the character to the plot and conflict; (2) Use choice details, not exhaustive lists; (3) Instead of using a police-blotter approach, use finely crafted language, including metaphors and comparisons.
- Introduce characters with flair. Even if your character is not dashing, a reader's first glimpse of him must somehow impress. At the very least, the reader needs to know if a character is young or old, male or female, attractive, ugly, or in between.
- Whenever possible, assign characters, including minor and walk-on characters, at least one physical characteristic that will remain in the reader's memory.
- Use details to reflect an era: at the beginning of a novel or story, the reader needs to know if it is morning or evening, spring or fall, if the scene is happening indoors or outdoors. But he also wants to know if the story is

set in 1860, 1990, or in the future. The era should permeate every aspect, particularly influencing characters' values.

- As in the real world, the naming of things—bird species, street names, architectural styles, dog breeds, hairstyles, and fashion accessories—brings accuracy and proximity and reveals a writer hard at work. Don't mention categories of things—cats, underwear, or cars; instead bring us closer, make your stories vivid. Write about a Siamese with her distinctive baby whine, comical-looking calicos, plaid boxer shorts and lacy red Victoria's Secret garter belts, Volvos and Mustangs, baby blue Jaguars with white leather interiors.

Resources

Word Painting: A Guide to Writing More Descriptively, Rebecca McClanahan

Descriptionary: Third Edition, Marc McCutcheon

The Writing Life, Annie Dillard

One Writer's Beginnings, Eudora Welty

How Fiction Works, The Last Word on Writing Fiction—From the Basics to the Fine Points, Oakley Hall

Six

Bling-Bling: Reining in Style and Language

Words are sacred. They deserve respect. If you get the right ones, in the right order, you can nudge the world a little. —TOM STOPPARD, *The Real Thing*

While your approach to writing might be like Goldilocks's expression of "just right" as she plunders the Three Bears' house, over the years I've observed that most writers fall into two broad categories: those who overwrite and those who underwrite. Those who overwrite produce overwrought or wordy outpourings; those who underwrite create anemic briefings. If you fall into the second classification, your stories tend to be thin and unformed and the reader is left drifting through your pages like someone underdressed in a blizzard, lonely and shivering; squinting ahead at a formless horizon, bewildered about why he is wandering in the cold so unprepared.

But by far, many writers fall into the first category and their work is overwritten or filled with bling-bling—in fact, way too much bling. When a rapper struts onto a stage bedecked in massive gold chains and diamonds, with dental grills glinting, he makes an impression about his style and values. All that bling makes a statement.

When writers use too much bling, the statement they're making is: I don't trust my readers and I like to emote on the page. Typically too much bling means their work is drowning in purple prose, modifiers, excess details, and fancy-pants words.

You see, bling stems from inexperience and not trusting in the reader as your partner in this enterprise. Each reader brings his life experiences and understanding of human behavior and how the world works to your pages. If you leave out minor details and don't describe every giggle or frown, the reader can still imagine the scene in which the protagonist meets her future mother-in-law. This partnership does not mean that the reader is doing the heavy lifting for you, the writer. Instead, he is an active participant in your story in a game of the imagination.

Subtlety is a fine art but this does not mean a story is vague, nonvisual, or formless. Contemporary fiction and memoir must be sensory, especially visual. But keep this in mind: your reader, inundated by cell phones ringing, e-mails zipping through time and space, and reality TV shows blaring, does not need to be spoon-fed every fact and detail, or have everything explained. Readers come to your story with a vast storehouse of images, memories, and information. Your job is to *remind* them what is in their memory storehouse, not serve as a nonstop tour guide who points out every highlight.

Readers want an *experience* when they open a book, but giving them an experience doesn't mean piling on. It means choosing and choosing well. Leave some details to readers' imaginations; and resist spelling out every emotion, thought, and grimace.

Deal Breakers

This chapter is about how language can get in the way of the story. Here are deal breakers that you might recognize from your own stories.

Overkill

One manuscript I edited was a rewrite of a screenplay. Which was where the writer tripped up because instead of telling a larger story by creating backstory and subplots, he inserted modifiers and excess details and descriptions to pump up his word count. Like other writers guilty of bling, he was convinced he needed to pause for every cloud and bird twitter, every wink and trip from sofa to doorway.

Now, while the plot had lots of potential, he also had the odd habit of using black to describe nearly every object in the story. Thus his protagonist wrote in a black journal, wore black leather boots, along with a black belt and black shirts and pants. There was also black furniture in his bedroom and he slept under a black quilt and a dark sky. His character was a sort of ninja-warrior-poet-philosopher so the writer felt black was the perfect color to underscore his character's traits. Trouble was, every time he wrote in his journal (which he did much too often) we were reminded it was a *black* journal. Likewise every time he slipped into his midnight-hued duds.

In fact, I counted *black* six times in a single paragraph. We also were given constant weather reports and comments on every dish served at every meal, and the same settings were described a dozen times with few variations. The effect was numbing, and I was especially bothered by how redundant the whole was.

To be clear: it's not that you cannot use colors or the same setting in your writing. In fact, many writers choose a setting such as the sea, a forest, or a garden because they can change over time to indicate time passing, decay, or some other aspect of the story. Perhaps an elderly character is sinking into illness or dementia so her once-glorious garden becomes neglected and choked with weeds. Or if a particularly dramatic scene is about to unfold, a roaring sea, a storm, or a desolate, scarred landscape with tumbleweeds drifting past can underline the moment.

The trick is to match your word proportions to your purpose. Good description enhances every part of writing; excess distracts. If you spend three paragraphs describing an alley, then the reader expects a dead body or a similar dramatic outcome to be associated with that alley.

Purple Bling

Then there is the kind of bling that is overdone and purple and makes me suspect the writer has read one too many bodice rippers or Sidney Sheldon books. The writing is extravagant, euphemistic, and clichéd; the brunette heroine has *raven* or *ebony* hair or, better yet, *a tumble of silky raven hair framing her heart-shaped face*, along with *sparkling sapphire* or *emerald* eyes. Poor children are *waifs*, pools are *limpid* and the heroine leans over them so her *pensive* or *brooding* or *pitiless gaze* is revealed; and walks are *halting* because she's *shaken to the core* since *she's been in the belly of the beast*. The problem with purple prose is that it calls attention to itself instead of performing its job—telling a story—and it tries too hard to manipulate the reader's emotions.

The hallmarks of purple prose are that it is excessively emotional, lyrical, figurative, and abstract. So it's the opposite of concrete, spare, and simple language. Now, we cannot all write like Hemingway or Raymond Carver, nor do we want to sound like a newscaster. There is a time and place for lush descriptions and heightened prose. And sometimes heightened prose works, such as in many passages found in works by Charles Dickens and Herman Melville. But these writers wrote for an earlier era and consciously chose when to use heightened prose and when to back off, while amateur writers pile on words and clichés like a glutton mounding his plate with every entrée and side dish offered at a single-price buffet.

Purple prose is found most often in character descriptions and love scenes; there is a lot of *quivering* and *throbbing* going on, breasts are *mounds* or *globes*, men in lust display a *bulging ardor* or a *raging beast of desire* or a *dragon of desire,* and couples in lust are *locked in a primal mating ritual* or *dance*. But purple bling can infect any aspect of writing, including storms that feature *distant thunder* and *menacing clouds crouching on the horizon* stirring up *violent gusts of wind* that *rattle frightened shutters* and send *frothy snowflakes*. Purple writing often seems breathless or silly, as when describing a person's *core of being* or *every fiber of being*, or the *slow burn of anger* and *being touched to her innermost soul.*

Stuck

Another problem with purple prose is that the writer often repeats phrases, particularly physical descriptions, so the sparkling sapphire or emerald eyes keep blinking back tears in scene after scene. Now, one writer's purple prose is another's lush description—but if you irritate or distract even one reader, you've gone too far.

So control purple prose by considering the context of your descriptions. There are times to slow down in stories, to make the story world deep and shimmering. It might be a love scene, or two characters meeting for the first time, or a funeral. Or you might want to describe a slum neighborhood to set up the scene that comes next, when the witness stumbles across the corpse in a Dumpster. Or you might want to use description to suggest symbolism, atmosphere, or mood.

But in these moments, use a fresh turn of phrase or a newly minted metaphor. Brain research has shown that the pleasure centers in the forebrain like surprises of all types. This aspect of physiology works in writing, so insert a series of surprises and reversals in your story. Dump hackneyed expressions and resist using predictable idioms, images, and tired phrases. Instead, lasso surprising word combinations and push the envelope of language.

Also, in every scene you write, ask yourself what kind of emotions you want to evoke in the reader and judge how important the scene is. There are moments to drive past instead of stopping the tour bus to point to every architectural detail.

Show-off

Another kind of bling is the show-off kind. A good work of fiction or memoir meets the reader at his own level. When show-off bling is present, it often means the writer is writing *down* to the reader or writing to impress or display an elaborate vocabulary. (Imagine the rap star's dental grills gleaming under stage lights.) Just as readers don't want to be jarred from the fictional world or a riveting memoir by excess, they don't like to feel illiterate. Thus, if a reader is constantly consulting a dictionary when reading your prose, you're dragging him from the story. Words in manuscripts such as *capacious*, *accretion*, *plangent*, *occluded*, *viridian*, *arboreal*, *sylvan*, *verdant*, *obdurate*, *luculent*, *longueur*, *rubescent*, and *mendacious* always pull me from the story. Just say no to showing off.

Some writers have difficulty keeping their message clear and simple. Instead of using everyday words, they strew through their stories formal, unfamiliar, or highfalutin words that sound important but usually don't infuse a sentence with meaning. Why not? Because generally simple, short words are crisp, powerful, and easily understood by the largest audience.

Simple words are usually of Anglo-Saxon origin and are punchier than those of French or Latin origin. *Ask* is more direct than *question* (French) or *interrogate* (Latin). Now, if your detective is interrogating a suspect in a murder investigation, that's probably the best word for that sentence. But for most purposes, *ask* will do.

Simple words constitute our first vocabulary—mama, daddy, dog, cow, nose. Simple words are close to our hearts and easily understood. Consider this segment from Winston Churchill's speech: "We shall fight on the beaches, we shall fight on the landing grounds, we shall fight in the fields and in the streets, we shall fight in the hills, we shall never surrender." Powerful, right?

But writers fond of bling long to impress, so they abandon simple words and instead choose their longer, more formal cousins. It's a mistake. The truth is, simpler words are unpretentious yet contain power and grace.

Examine your fancy vocabulary and choose familiar words instead. Pompous words are alienating, boring, and outdated. Replace *numerous* with *many*, *additional* with *extra*, *facilitate* with *help*, *proliferate* with *spread*, *terminate* with *end*, *compensate* with *pay*, *transpire* with *happen*, *commence* with *start*, *converse* with *talk*, *concurrence* with *agreement*, and *sclerous* with *hardened*. Depending on the needs of your story, good writing mimics the way most of us talk when our conversation is lively and entertaining. Good writing sounds genuine, true, and conversational. Not like a scientific or college lecture, or a senator grandstanding on the Senate floor.

Now sometimes formal words are needed, but use them with awareness, with judiciousness, and when you need to sound solemn or learned. Not to prove you were an English major.

Little-Word Pileup

Beware, also, of using too many prepositions, once described as "the carbohydrates of writing," as these little words pile up on the page and dull your message. Prepositions put distance between important words and appear before nouns. But if your sentences contain strings or clumps of prepositions, you need to strip them down. For example, instead of writing *went up in flames*: burned. Instead of *at a later date,* write *later*. Instead of writing *in the vicinity of*, near. Instead of *on a regular basis*, regularly. Instead of *as a consequence of*, because. Instead of *drew to a close*, ended. Instead of *a large percentage of*, many. Instead of *in the not-too-distant future*, soon. Instead of *has the appearance of*, looks like.

Here's an easy tip for trimming prepositions: beware of using *basis*, *manner*, *fashion*, and *way*. For example, instead of writing *on an annual basis*, write *annually*. And instead of *Jonathan found Rick in an accidental manner*, write Jonathan found Rick. Or instead of writing *Jared spoke in a muffled fashion;* Jared mumbled. *Randal fell in a precipitous way*, Randal plummeted. *A skilled writer communicates his truth in an honest way and in a simple manner.* Oops, a skilled writer communicates honestly and simply.

Ye Olde Corny Language

Another smaller but still annoying form of bling is using archaic words like *upon* when you mean *on*, or *amidst* when you mean *amid*, and *betwixt* when you mean *between*. This language most often appears in fantasy or historical fiction stories and in sermons and ceremonies. However, I've spotted it in all sorts of manuscripts. The problem is, if you're deliberately choosing archaic language, it's hard to pull off with accuracy. If you're writing a story set in the past, it's important to avoid substituting an antique version for every modern word because the story will sound silly and stilted. This is especially problematic in dialogue, as in: "*Hail, fair maiden. Pray tell what bringeth thee to the castle on this so lustrous a morn? Be it the rumors of scoundrels and knaves roaming these glenden hillsides?*"

Other offenders are: thee, thou, thine, ye, ere, fore, hither, mayhap, nary, nigh, sooth, therewith, twain, verily, shall, sage advice, whereof, and yon. Methinks these writers were English majors and wrote papers on Chaucer and Shakespeare. Their characters have locks or tresses, not hair, and orbs, not eyes, and a countenance, not a face or expression. The trick to using archaic writing is that it needs to be sprinkled carefully into a story.

One more note on bling. Most of these bad habits evolve from our school years writing term papers and reports. We wrote long and formally to please teachers. Forget your teachers and those bad habits. While you're at it, erase the idea that "showy" suggests intelligence in the writer. Wordy, pompous writing is a turnoff and tires the reader. After years of reading manuscripts, I've developed megalogophobia: fear of writing big words. I'm hoping it's contagious.

Eliminate Bling, Word by Word

Good writing enchants but is not gaudy. Readers want clean prose, real words, normal language, yet at the same time vivid descriptions and scenes. So how do you achieve this tightrope walk?

Whoever first said less is more must have been describing modifiers, especially when it comes to adverbs because they weaken sentences. Modifiers are defined as words that change or limit other words. Writers often wrongly believe they need them for emphasis and insight. That writing without modifiers is naked, stark, without music.

The truth is that often inserting modifiers means we're shoring up imprecise nouns and verbs. Effective writing relies on nouns and verbs to deliver the punch in our sentences. Nouns are the workhorses and verbs are the engines of our sentences. You especially want to collect potent verbs that elicit responses in the reader. Modifiers have lesser value and impact. The overuse of modifiers is also a dated, Victorian style of writing, from a time when many sentences were laden with them.

The trick, too, is to remember that verbs *show* and modifiers *tell*. Think about it: you can write *I looked out at the falling rain* or *The rain splattered onto the bricks.* The second phrase has more potency because it causes a visceral response in the reader; we sense the verb *splatter*, we can almost hear the rain splash on the bricks, but we don't necessarily experience *falling* as a modifier.

Thus, be stingy with modifiers and pluck out excess, one by one, and focus on nouns and verbs. By the time you're working on your final draft, ask yourself if every word adds to the whole. An easy way to do this is to print out the chapter or the manuscript and highlight every modifier. I recommend using a glaring color like lime green. If your pages feature lots of green dabs, you're likely in trouble.

After you've highlighted the modifiers in your pages, test whether you can justify each one. Adjectives modify nouns, pronouns, and gerunds (verbs ending with -ing functioning as nouns, such as swimming in "He loved swimming"). Start streamlining by getting rid of clichéd and redundant modifiers: little kittens, yellow daffodils, really surprised, cheerful grins, and the like.

I discover *suddenly* in most manuscripts I read, and it's never necessary. Things that happen unexpectedly in stories don't need to be explained as being sudden; the reader will understand this phenomenon. *Suddenly a loud sound shattered the silence of the night.* Or "*Look!" Alan shouted suddenly. "There's the ship at last!*" If a ship were to appear on the horizon, readers can imagine how the sunburned, shipwrecked victims would perceive it and broadcast the news.

Instead, choose adjectives that are unusual and add precision and understanding. For instance, if the grass is described as withered, brown, or brittle, that conveys information about climate conditions. We *expect* green grass, but harsh or burned grass tells the reader that you're describing the end of summer or a drought.

Imagine that your perfect modifier causes a thrill or twinge in the reader. Consider this description from the third chapter of *The Great Gatsby,* where Fitzgerald describes Gatsby's summer parties in his blue gardens:

> At least once a fortnight a corps of caterers came down with several hundred feet of canvas and enough colored lights to make a Christmas tree of Gatsby's enormous garden. On buffet tables, garnished with glistening hors-d'oeuvre, spiced baked hams crowded against salads of harlequin design and pastry pigs and turkeys bewitched to a dark gold.

Did you feel the thrill when he paired *harlequin* with salads and *bewitched* with turkeys? The context for these sentences is that the reader is about to meet the mysterious Gatsby and needs details of the opulent parties to stir interest in him and his wealth. And the language, with every word perfect and weighted, convinces us of Gatsby's wealth and power.

As you justify each adjective, be sure to examine adjective clusters. Sentences with a string of adjectives clustered before the noun are difficult to read: The sickly sweet, redolent ________.

What? Perfume? Jam?

The terrifying, dark, dank, stifling ________. What? Basement? Jail cell?

The brooding, morose, uncommunicative ________. What? Murderer? When we string modifiers in front of nouns, readers are forced to imagine and separate each adjective, waiting until the noun arrives with its meaning and clarity. And by the time the noun arrives, its appearance is anticlimactic.

So avoid listing modifiers before a noun and instead at times use sentence modifiers instead of word modifiers. That means the modifier shows up to the right of the noun. So you might write a sentence like: *I stepped into the garden, a place dotted with Italian fountains and statues and roses nodding in the afternoon sun.*

Adverbs are dangerous. In her book *Sin and Syntax*, Constance Hale notes that "Adverbs are crashers in the syntax house party. More often than not, they should be deleted when they sneak in the back door." Adverbs should be the *last* words hauled out of your writing toolbox. Adverbs modify anything except nouns and pronouns, so they are slippery devils—they can slink into any sentence.

The worst adverbs shore up wimpy verbs, usually with an -ly suffix. Instead of *Madison walked slowly, Madison moved quickly, Madison ate hurriedly*, how about *Madison dawdled, Madison loped, Madison devoured the fries.* The best verbs paint a picture for the reader and don't need modifying help: lope, creep, stumble, whip, twiddle, bludgeon, ransack, babble, grunt, shimmy, snuff. Notice how these verbs communicate oomph and meaning?

Another adverb problem is found in attributions, the "he said," "she said" parts of writing that describe dialogue. Here is the problem: adverbs should not describe the dialogue—its meaning and intensity should be contained within the exchange, not *explained* in the attribution. Novice fiction writers add phrases like *she said menacingly* or *he whispered softly* or *she demanded harshly.*

These adverbs bog down dialogue exchanges, and increasingly attributions are becoming obsolete in today's fiction.

Two more adverbs need our attention: qualifiers and intensifiers because you need to put the kibosh on them. These words intensify or qualify nouns and verbs, and are plunked into sentences to lend emphasis or focus. However, they're unnecessary and usually signal an unsophisticated writer. Notice how these adverbs aren't needed for meaning: The fire *completely* demolished the office building. The accident *totally* severed the dog's tail. Samantha was *absolutely* flabbergasted when Jim appeared with roses.

Here are the most often-used intensifiers: absolutely, definitely, particularly, actually, basically, decidedly, quite, very, really, totally, madly, dearly, utterly, absolutely, completely, mainly, usually, too.

COLORLESS VERBS

The first thing I notice about a writer is his or her verbs. Pallid verbs always signal a weak writer or at least one who is not sufficiently aware of language. Colorless verbs that are especially annoying are: get, got, do, did, put, walked, went, gone, run, ran, see, saw, crossed, turned.

Also avoid using am, is, are, was, were, being, be, been combined with an adjective. This looks like *Lola was sad as she walked around the apartment noticing all the reminders of Ben.*

One big problem when using these types of adverbs is that you sound like the actors on *Hannah Montana*. As in, Jenny is *totally* fabulous in that outfit and is so *completely* hot I'm *utterly* jealous. But the language is sophomoric: really big, very slow, extremely typical, quite lovely, and actually pleasant. Instead use more precise language, such as gigantic, plodding, typical, stunning, and charming.

Qualifiers qualify or allow you to hedge your bets in writing. They include: basically, generally, somewhat, a little bit, very, quite, kind of, sort of, probably, rather, mostly, mainly, as a rule, fairly. This might sound like a small point, but readers want precise observations. Please don't write that your character is sort of pretty or kind of nice or rather intelligent. Either a person is nice or pretty or smart or she isn't—take a stand.

Here's a little anecdote: when I was studying journalism and English in college, I had a professor who was a Pulitzer prize–winning journalist. If we used *very* or *quite* in a story, we received an F. It was one of the best lessons I've ever learned about writing.

Try This

Here's a simple writing exercise I learned from the late Gary Provost that will wean you off modifiers. Remember, adjectives *tell* and verbs *show*. For example, instead of *shiny necklace*, trade the adjective *shiny* for a verb: *the necklace glinted* or *the necklace sparkled, gleamed, flashed, glimmered, shimmered, twinkled*.

Create sentences based on these word pairs, but trade adjectives that tell for verbs that show.

1. happy baby
2. frisky puppy
3. frightening monster
4. fast car
5. tired miner
6. impoverished teacher
7. silly singer
8. crazed criminal
9. skimpy dress
10. paltry meal

Quick and Dirty Tips for Killing Bling and Blah, Blah, Blah

- Use specific nouns. Thus, use *Victorian* instead of a stately, large home with ornate trim built in the late 1800s, *Cheerios* instead of crunchy cereal, and *.44 Magnum* or *Glock* instead of a lethal hand-held pistol.
- Save lush passages for choice moments in the story, especially decisions, revelations, and reversals. If you use heightened prose every time your character feels an emotion, the whole will become contrived.
- Control your sentence length. Bling tends to make sentences longer. You want a mix of long, short, and medium-length sentences throughout.
- Search out and destroy adverbs. Replace with vivid verbs or actions.

- Sniff out sentences that use a form of "to be" (was, is, are, were, being, be, been, am) followed by an adjective. An example is *Tom was nervous as he tiptoed into the dark alley.*
- Omit redundancies like grotesquely ugly, grim reminders, complete surprise, and happy coincidence.
- Make certain every sentence adds something new.
- Show, don't tell. Especially avoid classifying emotions. *Bob slammed into the room, roaring, "I hate that bitch!"* is showing. *Bob came into the room sounding very angry* is telling.
- Avoid clumping descriptions in paragraph after paragraph because it stops the scene. In general try to weave description into action.
- Use figurative language sparingly to season your writing, but don't overuse it. We use figurative language to impart layers of meaning and to compare two unlike things.
- Generally avoid heightened prose in endings—often the best endings are concrete or understated.
- Respect word territory. If you use an unusual word in a sentence (effervescent, rococo, unremunerated, infelicity), don't repeat it in a nearby paragraph or, better yet, use it only once.
- Read poetry, noticing metaphors and what poets choose to emphasize and how they create emotions in the reader with the fewest possible words.
- Analyze book titles and headlines of all types, noticing how often writers tweak clichés and familiar phrases.

- Read screenplays if you're writing fiction. Not only are screenplays written in the classic three-act structure, but a screenwriter describes only what is seen and heard on the screen. Anything the character thinks or feels is implied through action—a trick many fiction writers can emulate at times.

Resources

The Vocabula Review at www.vocabula.com

The Dimwit's Dictionary: More Than 5,000 Overused Words and Phrases and Alternatives to Them; *Thesaurus of Alternatives to Worn-out Words and Phrases*; and *The Disagreeable Dictionary*, Robert Hartwell Fiske

The Dictionary of Concise Writing: 10,000 Alternatives to Wordy Phrases, Robert Hartwell Fiske and Richard Lederer

The Miracle of Language, Richard Lederer

For screenplays available online, go to: www.scriptshack.com or www.scriptpimp.com or www.simplyscripts.com.

Seven

Conflict: Can't Live with It, Can't Write without It

Plot is characters under stress.

—Henry James, "The Art of Fiction"

Here is an easy message every writer can swallow like chocolate: happy characters are boring, and if there is no conflict, there is no story. The best parts of fiction happen when the main character is caught in an assload of trouble. This is the stark, withering truth of storytelling. If your characters are complacent, relaxed, living the good life, the reader quickly loses interest. The more woes and worries, the more compelling the story because conflict gives it a reason for being and conflict defines characters. Thus, fiction is the opposite of real life, because in real life most of us avoid trouble. When we read fiction, however, we're watching people suffer, and when we write fiction, we propel our characters into a personal hell. Let's also clarify that while events in your story might lead to a happy ending, the road to happiness is paved with misery and risk.

There is nothing as unsatisfying and lacking in suspense as a story line where problems are easily solved, clues appear as if by magic or intuition, love is instantaneous and seldom rocky, people always agree and are agreeable, and everyday conditions never interfere with the protagonist's comfort. A story provides a reason for people to fight instead of turning tail. When your story features conflict, your protagonist's chief flaws and strengths will be exposed, and as he's threatened and worn down, this creates suspense.

As your protagonist becomes more and more entangled in obstacles, make certain that what he fears most is on the stage. These fears will be specific to your character: he'll never fill his father's shoes in the family business, or he'll never make the rank of detective. Then, as these fears are exposed, toss a wrench into his plan. Your thirty-four-year-old female protagonist finally achieves the promotion at a high-tech company, but then becomes pregnant. A character is poised to marry the gal of his dreams when his younger and more charming brother, who has been out of the country, appears on the scene, vying for the girl. The cop is about to be promoted to detective when a rival for the job plants drugs in his locker.

Since publishable writing is built on successfully executed conflict, a shorthand for fiction (and this works for memoir, also) is to slam your character into a cauldron of hot water, make the cauldron inescapable, turn up the heat to boiling, and keep the heat on so that the pot, or plot, boils over.

Types of Conflict

The inciting incident, the first threat, sets the story in motion and tilts the protagonist off balance. Balance in the story world and the protagonist's inner world is not restored until the climax, and along the way the protagonist is rarely happy, relaxed, or in sync with his surroundings. Although moments of normalcy are used to control the pacing and make the whole believable, the best parts of the story are where adversity is staged and boiling away. The harder a protagonist falls, the more emotionally charged the story and the deeper the reader's connection to the character.

For our purposes, think about the external conflict as the *dragon* in the story because this reminds us that it can be seen, heard, and felt, while internal conflict—your character's emotional and psychological struggles, or inner conflict—can be called the *demon*. Remember, too, that adversity always shines a light on the human condition, teaching us what it means to be human, especially during our lowest moments.

Shorthand for Effective Conflict

- External conflict involves two or more characters or some form of opposition. Internal conflict requires that the situation have serious ramifications.
- Give characters opposing goals, agendas, and strong motivations.
- Make sure the stakes for each character are high.
- Stage confrontations as if they're happening/unfolding in real time.
- Embed dialogue with tension, subtext, and power exchanges.
- Know your protagonist's deepest fears.

Here are the types of conflict you can use in your story:

Man Against Man

A character is pitted against another character or group. Think *Fight Club,* by Chuck Palahniuk, *The Great Gatsby,* by F. Scott Fitzgerald, and *The Grapes of Wrath,* by John Steinbeck.

Man Against Nature

These are stories about survival that pit characters against storms or weather, creatures, floods, fire, environmental or biological calamities, and other natural elements. The idea is that some danger is rampaging and out of control and the clash, which catches humans in the crosshairs, is always nail-biting and brutal. *The Old Man and the Sea* is an example of this conflict type, as is *Stormy Weather,* by Carl Hiaasen, and Michael Crichton's *Jurassic Park.*

Man Against the Supernatural

This conflict exploits our childlike fears of the unknown and unknowable, and the conflict is always heightened because the adversary often has supernatural powers. Ghosts, haunted houses, unexplained phenomena, all provide a good scare and unsettle the reader with dangers and menace that don't let up until the climax. Stephen King's *The Shining* and *Carrie*, and Shirley Jackson's *The Haunting of Hill House* are good examples.

Man Against Himself

While many stories are shaped by a protagonist plagued by antagonists, or physical danger, or nature unleashing its horrors, internal conflict (or the protagonist's inner anguish) can be equally compelling. Sometimes the inner conflict is the basis for the story; sometimes it exists alongside the outer conflict. The inner conflict or demon means the protagonist is typically faced with tough choices, dilemmas, and decisions. *Death of a Salesman,* by Arthur Miller, and the film *American Beauty* showcase inner conflict.

Man Against Fate

If fate is the conflict, then the protagonist has little or no control over his circumstances or cannot escape his destiny. Or, the story question asks if people can ever escape their fate or if there really is free will. This might mean the protagonist is an innocent bystander thrust into a dangerous situation—one of Alfred Hitchcock's favorite devices—or it might be that the character is born into extreme poverty or a lowly caste. Kurt Vonnegut's *Slaughterhouse-Five* is an example, as are many stories and novels in The Foundation series by Isaac Asimov.

Man Against Society

This type of story sets a character against the beliefs, values, or laws of a society. The protagonist is always out of sync and is sometimes an antihero, and thus exists to showcase society's flaws. *Handmaiden's Tale,* by Margaret Atwood, *Fahrenheit 451,* by Ray Bradbury, and *Minority Report,* by Philip K. Dick, are examples of protagonists in conflict with a repressive or out-of-whack society.

Man Against Machine

When machines turn on humans, or we're living a dehumanized, geeked-out existence, the results are scary and often creepily prophetic. This conflict is most often found in science fiction, as in Aldous Huxley's *Brave New World*, or the film *The Terminator,* about an evil cyborg, or *The Matrix,* which is about freeing humankind from the bondage of a race of machines.

Man Against God

These stories question the existence or benevolence of God, or God is messing around in the universe and lives of humankind. Often the theme is that when God is a player in human affairs, we all best watch out. *Childhood's End,* by Arthur C. Clarke, *Frankenstein,* by Mary Shelley, and *A Canticle for Leibowitz,* by Walter Miller, all illustrate this central conflict.

Stir in Internal Conflict

In many genres the main conflict is an outer conflict, meaning your character is faced with daunting, visible opposition. Inner conflict often means a character is thrust into a new situation or relationship where his old attitudes, beliefs, habits, and values are warring with the need to change and grow. Inner conflict forces the character to face his emotional truths, weaknesses, and vulnerabilities. When your characters wrestle with internal conflict they doubt, worry, make difficult choices, or take risks. It always propels a character to change, transform, or fundamentally shift his thinking. These necessary changes always come at a high cost. When not handled carefully, inner conflict can be static (as when characters spend too much time fretting instead of acting) or can depict a character who seems self-involved. Also, external conflict tends to make for a faster-paced story, while internal conflict slows it down.

The solution is that characters need to strain, gasp, and cling to their strength and sanity through most of the story. Characters can also grapple with jealousy, lack of confidence, overconfidence, or secret desires. Inner conflict can be the character's Achilles' heel, can stem from a subplot such as a dilemma with an elderly parent or teenager, or the emotional toll of a divorce. Readers can relate to these troubles.

The most compelling internal conflicts arise from emotional scars. Most characters have emotional scars or perceive themselves as somehow lacking. They can stem from childhood or an earlier phase in life, and abandonment, abuse, trauma, or loss, or other scars and insecurities are part of the inner conflict and play a role in the story events. And because fiction strives to dramatize character growth, a story often depicts a protagonist realizing something important about himself. And in these struggles, your character is deeply revealed, while a reader develops empathy and worries about the outcome.

What Conflict Is Not

Conflict is orchestrated, believable, and enthralling. When conflict fails, or simply isn't conflict, it is most often for these reasons:

- Behavior or actions that are not caused by characters' motivations or strong desires.
- Bickering, squabbling, and disagreements between characters, unless they escalate into a clash and emotions change during the confrontation or a threat or ultimatum is issued.
- A protagonist who doesn't act and react to conflict, doesn't have goals, or doesn't care (desperately) about an outcome. Again, the formula is simple to understand: no adversity, no story.
- A protagonist with no choices, problems, or dilemmas.
- A situation in which there is little at stake and the protagonist is not at risk.
- A situation in which complications don't arise from the main story question.
- A situation where the outcome is not in doubt. Typically when a story features the forces of good and evil or two sides of opposition, the sides are fairly equal, or the protagonist appears to be outgunned, or the protagonist has some chance of success but isn't aware or certain of this in the first half of the story.

Deal Breakers

With these criteria in mind, I need to mention something that both puzzles and fascinates me as an editor. Over the years I've read stories that were half-baked or too bizarre to follow, stories that were about as fascinating as watching elderly shuffleboard players on a cruise ship, and stories that weren't stories—more like a collection of unrelated words. But most writers have terrific story ideas and wade into the shark-infested waters of storytelling where their characters have dark intentions and twisted fates.

As I'm hoping to elucidate, stories most often fail because of a lack of attention to detail, proportions that are unbalanced, characters that aren't developed or aren't believable, and the like. Often these problems are correctable. But when the central conflict fails in a story, it's often doomed, so it's best to invent your central conflict before you commit your story to paper.

Bloodbath

Creating conflict isn't as simple as adding violence to a story. I read a manuscript that was a splatterpunk bloodbath with a zombie munching his way through entire neighborhoods—well, mostly it was the human brains found in the neighborhoods, but you get the idea. Then there was the story in which the villain was a master swordsman who stormed around in a homicidal rage hacking off heads as if stepping on ants. In yet another manuscript the villain kept snipping off the toes of his eight-year-old victim and mailing them to the child's parents.

A little blood (or toes) goes a long way, folks, and sometimes it works to underplay it. (A shot rang out. And then Ron was down and I was alone in the dark.) Too much violence and the reader becomes numb. But the bigger problem was that these stories failed to prove that violence or abuse in any form damages the victim, steals a part of his soul, and that the damage lasts. Uzis spraying a wide swath and ricocheting and splattering glass and body parts don't necessarily accomplish this.

Cast of Thousands

I've read manuscripts in which every scene included at least a dozen characters—they popped in and out like jumping beans, ad-libbing, jabbering, and cluttering each scene until I was dizzy. In a manuscript I read recently there were three people in a key scene and two looking in on the action. The scene kept moving from the action to the onlookers' views of the action and the result was messy.

Every time you add characters into a scene it strains the reader's ability to track each person's position, to grasp who is saying what and what each character wants. Now, conflict can be based on warfare or a large group set against one another, a la *Winds of War*, or it can follow multiple viewpoints through a story. The trick, however, is to make readers care and worry about the fates of the main characters. When you feature a large cast, make certain that every character is necessary to drive the story and that scenes contain the least number of characters needed to accomplish the scene goal.

Jumping

If jumping conflict occurs, characters jump from one emotional level to another much more intense emotion (boredom to hysteria) or characters develop without the necessary transitional steps. Often this takes the shape of inexplicable violence, as when two people argue, then without warning one pulls a knife and stabs the person he disagrees with. I've read stories in which a timid housewife became a brazen slut overnight, a staid family man turned into a meth addict without any previous indication that he was the addictive type, and a husband murdered his wife because she mocked his manhood.

If your character is going to undergo a dramatic character arc or transformation—from cad to caring lover, from addiction to sobriety, from coldhearted to warmhearted—the reader must witness the various steps of growth along the way. Conflict is the crucible that forces characters to change, but both conflict and characters must build over time and *then* explode.

No Big Deal

You need to thwart your protagonist's happiness and plans, not simply inconvenience him or her. The goals and desires in fiction always matter, and the refusals are always difficult to swallow and create wrist-slashing angst. Here's an illustration: if your character Melinda, who is in a funk because her boyfriend just dumped her, heads to the hardware store to buy cherry blossom paint to redecorate her bedroom (the ex-boyfriend hated all things pink) and she's given the wrong shade of paint (it looks dismally like Pepto-Bismol), that setback doesn't cause much tension. Sure, coming home with the wrong color is annoying, but it's not the sort of scene that torments the character or elicits much sympathy in the reader.

Now, if instead Melinda meets a hunky employee at the hardware store who refuses to respond to her flirting, and, as she's paying for her paint, feeling rebuffed, a wild-eyed meth addict bursts into the store brandishing a gun and orders everyone on the floor and robs the place, including Melinda's purse, now that's conflict that causes sizzle and empathy. And it's the sort of twist that pumps life into a scene and story line. How will the clerk respond to Melinda now? Will the robbery make her forget about her ex-boyfriend?

No Subplots or Drowning in Subplots

Subplots are miniature stories woven into the main story, like threads woven into a tapestry, complete and intriguing in their own right, and serving to contrast, reinforce, or divert attention from the main plot. Typically a shorter novel (sixty to eighty thousand words) contains at minimum a main story line, a second story line or a subplot starring the protagonist, and a second subplot featuring a secondary character. A longer novel (one hundred thousand–plus words) adds additional secondary characters or viewpoint characters in lesser story lines. If you don't have subplots in your novel, it's not a novel, it's a short story.

Subplots have fewer words and scenes than the main story line. In one thriller I worked on the subplot (the protagonist's troubled marriage) was of equal length to the main story. Thrillers typically aren't based on the protagonist's inner life or relationship problems because they're based on danger.

Another manuscript was simply drowning in subplots. The story needed to be about eighty thousand words, but it topped one hundred thousand because there were at least nine subplots cluttering the story line. As a reader, I soon lost track of the main story and had an extremely hard time keeping track of the many threads.

And here are deal breakers for specific genres or story types:

Horror That Doesn't Horrify

Horror fiction is built around the notion that characters will not be safe wherever they go, and there is no place to hide as long as the monster roams free. Now, horror can exist in a Gothic tale, thrillers and techno-thrillers, science fiction, fantasy, and other subgenres. There is typically some form of a monster, vampire, or ghost creeping into the protagonist's days and nights, and that force seems unstoppable, although sometimes horror is about the beast within. It's hard to create original ideas for horror—most I see are knockoffs of classics or Stephen King plots, but it's also difficult to scare readers. It requires complexity, an original and bedeviling adversary, characters readers can identify with, impeccable research into all aspects of the story, and an ending readers don't expect. It also requires clever surprises and dangers scattered throughout and setting that adds to the fright factor, but not too much description so the story bogs down. To make horror conflict work best, make sure it scares the writer.

Lackadaisical Thrillers

The audience for your novel will determine its level of conflict and what the protagonist stands to lose. Thrillers are a high-stakes game in which bodily harm or death hangs over the protagonist throughout the story and never lets up. There is also a driving need to stop the villain. Thus a thriller needs sociopaths, terrorists, corrupt governments, rogue operatives, or other skilled types who can exact maximum physical punishment. Since there are many subgenres of thrillers, they can also be written about some kind of a disaster—nature, weather, toxic microbes, or nuclear disaster. Spy and techno thrillers are written about some form of political intrigue, and you need to make certain the reader understands exactly who the players are and what is at stake.

Often in lackadaisical thriller manuscripts the main intrigue is vague or muddled and I never quite understand who the villains are or why they're in the game. Or, I've read manuscripts in which the protagonist is at risk, but the ramifications for the world of the story aren't large enough, and the risk is aimed mostly at the protagonist, when it should threaten a wider group. I've read thrillers in which there are a number of spectacular action scenes, but the whole story line is thin. Or the bad guys are so evil and deadly that the protagonist is mostly prey through the story, running for his life like a scared bunny.

Mainstream Ho-Hum

A mainstream or literary story does not fall under a genre or category such as romance or science fiction. It is often based on deep inner conflict or a character overcoming serious flaws, and his journey of understanding always comes at a heavy price. Mainstream novels can feature a coming-of-age story or a character struggling to find fulfillment or answers to life's big questions. It can also be about redemption, forgiveness, or understanding, and there is always attention paid to language and voice. The biggest problem I see in mainstream is when the plot is flat or pointless—the situation doesn't seem to matter enough and the story wanders around, following a character without a compelling conclusion. Mainstream fiction should inspire the reader to think about the story and the character's choices, and provide insights into the human condition. As in the advice for writing horror that scares you, write a mainstream story that lies close to your heart.

Misaligned Mysteries

Mystery plots are built on a protagonist struggling to uncover a murderer, but of course, that will not be easy because the criminal will do everything to elude capture, including increasing the body count. However, there are several tricks to writing a mystery. The first is the ingenuity of the crime—it needs to be a dastardly act that takes moxie, brains, and a cold heart. The second is to load the story with red herrings to throw off the reader and litter it with twists and surprises the reader doesn't see coming. By the story's end, order needs to be restored in the world so we can all sleep at night.

But what happens most often that sinks stories is that I never quite understand why the criminal committed the crime. The villains rarely have secrets or plausible motives, and they're shadowy or merely sadistic freak shows. Or their attempts to cover their ass aren't sufficiently sneaky.

Another problem that will sink a mystery is a detective who isn't somehow unique, quirky, or fascinating or the person best suited to take on the case. These detectives often seem like rehashed versions of Columbo, Miss Marple, Sherlock Holmes, Kinsey Milhone, Stephanie Plum, and the like. Typically the protagonist isn't sufficiently entangled in the case or doesn't have an emotional stake in solving the mystery, and the emotional stake is far-fetched, as when a neighbor the protagonist isn't particularly friendly with is murdered and the amateur sleuth sets out to find the murderer like a bloodhound after a rabbit.

Finally, mysteries don't quite fly when the story world isn't sufficiently intriguing. Now, a murder can happen in a school or in a suburban neighborhood, as in manuscripts I've encountered, but the world of the story must be vividly imagined, with weather and everyday details that make it believable. Then you need to prove that the criminal in this world has access to weapons and motive for murder.

Romantic Notions

Romance plots are built on thwarting the protagonists' relationship and devising all sorts of ways to force them apart. The key to writing romance is to prolong the conflict until the end and to plant misunderstandings and fundamental differences between the two well-defined lovers. He's a yuppie, she's a farm girl; he's a corporate lawyer, she's an animal-rights activist. When writing romance, devise plausible reasons for keeping the lovers apart. If the reason for their troubles is trivial, the story fails. Readers need to understand their flaws, weaknesses, agendas, and emotional needs because this creates the conflict. Romance stories that don't work typically don't delve into the backstories (because at least one of the characters needs to fear love) and personalities of the main players and are thin as playing cards. Romantic conflict must deliver the intimate tango that keeps the reader engaged.

Exerting Pressure

The main conflict always threatens the protagonist's identity, self-concept, and vulnerabilities. And all obstacles reveal his core traits and values and force him to change in the ways he needs to change. For example, if your character is the sort to fold or wimp out under pressure, the story's refusals and obstacles will force him or her to grow stronger.

For conflict to sizzle in a story, it's important to understand exactly how your protagonist reacts to pressure and threats. Some of us cave in when we meet opposition; some of us grit our teeth and pull from deep inner resources and face the music or the bully or the monster. If you've written a mystery with a subplot that complicates the detective's life, you need to know if the detective obsessed with his case will give in to his wife's pressure and take some time off. Or even though his marriage is endangered, will he keep working long hours trying to find the killer?

It's also not enough to know that your protagonist will start cracking under pressure; you must know *how* he'll crack. Let's say someone threatens a protagonist's family. How far will he go to protect them? Will he install a new security system or buy a gun?

Then, thinking of all the ways we're faced with opposition in the real world, understand how your protagonist reacts to authorities, tragedy, defeat, rudeness, bad weather, someone who refuses to return his affection, or a driver cutting him off in traffic. As you write scenes, implanting opposition along the way, make certain that his reactions are in sync with his core personality traits. Is he hot-tempered or patient? Is he analytical and thoughtful, or blundering along by the seat of his pants? Will his reactions make things worse instead of better? Does he keep his doubts and worries to himself, which further alienates him from other cast members? Or does he talk too much and this makes people not trust him? Be sure to turn some of his decisions into dead ends, wrong choices, and huge blunders, and reveal how he deals with his mistakes. Is he self-critical, clueless, easily shamed by his mistakes? Does he accept defeat gracefully or does every small failure nag at him?

But before you get too carried away with your mercenary plans to torment your protagonist, remember that he needs to win once in a while. No wins or no progress in the narrative can also mean no character arc. So every so often, throw your protagonist a bone. He finds the next clue, makes love, handles the press with aplomb. When the protagonist finally wins a small yes or achieves a goal in a scene or chapter and progress happens, it makes the successes in the ending believable. Also, because readers need to put down a book from time to time and because pacing cannot be as relentless as a runaway train, you need to bring down the temperature and tension in a story at intervals. A win for your character, as well as a slower or interlude scene, provides the pauses and quieter moments needed.

Try This

Write a scene in which a character who is normally peace-loving uses a weapon against an adversary. Stage the scene so the character's reaction is logical and believable and he or she is defending emotional or physical territory.

Quick and Dirty Tips for Powerful Conflict

- Write stories with meaningful conflict that exists on at least two levels, featuring characters with clearly defined goals.
- We write conflict into stories because readers can always relate to it—we all know what it's like to be refused, be rejected, have our hopes dashed, or have our plans for the future destroyed by an outside force.
- Force a character to make tough choices that he or she would rather ignore. Make certain these choices reveal and define the character.
- Typically at least one character needs to change or make a sacrifice in order to resolve the conflict.
- Depict a character protecting real or emotional boundaries.
- Give a character dilemmas that clash with his beliefs and values.
- All types of conflict in a story must be some sort of test.
- Create a series of turning points that send the story in new directions; these events should create more complications that, in turn, demand solutions. Conflict is always the mother of more conflict.
- Conflict is not merely a misunderstanding or a character having a bad day; the demon or dragon stirs up serious trouble and always pushes the character to take action.
- Avoid creating a plot based on a single conflict; instead layer in several conflicts of varying importance.

- The best conflict stems from your protagonist's worst fear presented at the worst possible moment.
- Genre determines type of conflict: a romance involves conflict that is staged within a relationship; mysteries are built on conflict involving a crime; thrillers involve conflict that stems from extreme and physical danger for the protagonist with potentially huge ramifications.
- When possible, give characters feelings of helplessness or hopelessness, but at the same time make certain they are generally proactive and fighting against these feelings.
- Insert rising complications as the story goes along.
- Place characters in situations where the odds seem stacked against them, and in scenes that make them uncomfortable.
- Reveal what characters gain or lose through their choices and struggles.
- Link choices and problems to a character's emotional core.
- Give a character dilemmas that clash with his beliefs and values.
- If possible, link the inner conflict to a long-buried emotion or memory.

Resources

Action & Suspense, William Noble

Writing the Second Act: Building Conflict and Tension in Your Film Script, Mark Halperin

www.scriptsecrets.net

Characters Make Your Story, Maren Elwood

Stein on Writing: How to Grow a Story, Sol Stein

Creating Short Fiction, Damon Knight

Secrets of Screenplay Structure: How to Recognize and Emulate the Structural Frameworks of Great Films, Linda Cowgill

Eight

"She said winsomely": Avoiding Dialogue Disasters

> Many writers think—erroneously—that fiction should be a mirror of reality. Actually, it should act as a sifter to refine reality until only the essence is before the reader. This is nowhere more evident than in fictional dialogue. In real life, conversation is round-about, filled with general commentary and polite rituals. In fiction, the characters must always get right to the point when they talk.
>
> —Dean Koontz, *How to Write Best-Selling Fiction*

There are certain techniques that set writers apart—the maestros from the hacks, the geniuses from the dullards, the wizards from the wimps, to borrow a phrase. One technique that especially reveals your skill level is how you handle dialogue.

It seems that some writers just have a knack or natural ear for dialogue. Their characters sound real and individual and drop hilarious quips with such ease it leaves you laughing out loud. Their dialogue crackles with electricity and tension. Some contemporary novelists and screenwriters who write great dialogue come to mind—Carl Hiaasen, Quentin Tarantino, George Pelecanos,

Janet Evanovich, Charlie Huston, Cormac McCarthy, and Elmore Leonard. When their characters talk, we feel like we're in the room. And not only are we there, we're holding our breath and we're ready to duck or dash for safety if things heat up.

These writers have learned an essential truth: dialogue is never a copy of real-life speech—it's more like conversation's greatest hits. It's always crisper, punchier, and embedded with subtext—the sea of emotions that runs beneath a scene but is never spoken out loud. Good dialogue is spontaneous and natural, but it leaves out the boring parts of life and is often a power struggle or power exchange. We use dialogue because it shows instead of tells. Its other uses are to:

- create and advance action in the story.
- visually break up the page and attract the reader's eye.
- bring people or characters to life when they speak.
- reveal a character's background, social status, and education.
- quickly and painlessly deliver essential information.
- insert opinions other than the writer's.

In real-life conversations we hear the regional inflections in the speaker's syllables and spot their Boston, Brooklyn, or Brahmin origins. We hear emotions, stifled or overt, longing that is barely expressed, subtle flirting, or laughter bubbling inexplicably beneath a starchy exterior.

But translating what happens in live speech onto the written page takes finesse and (usually) a liberal editing of the common, the clichés, and the unnecessary ramblings.

Putting Dialogue to Work

In real life many people are colorless, many people blather on and on or have little of importance to say. In real life we've all stifled a yawn and wondered how soon we could edge our way out of the room away from the proud mother who is bragging about her son the dentist who has just met the perfect girl, especially when she begins describing the young woman's extended family and pedigree. But fiction isn't life, it's artifice, and dialogue never rambles or is dull, and it always multitasks in a story. In fiction, dialogue:

- increases the pace. It is one of the fastest delivery systems in fiction.
- creates a sense of immediacy and reality; readers feel like they're in the scene.
- pushes the story forward by heating up conflict, adding information, telling a lie, or revealing a secret or difficult truth.
- adds conflict and tension to the scene.
- quickly dispenses and condenses backstory.
- imparts humor.
- reveals a character's core traits, the way he or she sees the world.

So here's the trick to writing dialogue. If your dialogue doesn't accomplish one of these jobs, fire it. If your dialogue accomplishes only two of these jobs, pump it up. The best dialogue is like a juggler on a unicycle—sometimes breathless and teetering, always entertaining.

Deal Breakers

There are so many deal breakers when it comes to dialogue that it's difficult to list them all. Sometimes I read ultra-crappy dialogue that is generic, that is, it isn't filtered through each character's outlook or worldview, personality, and mood. Sometimes the dialogue is pointless or characters simply gather together to reminisce or pass the time. Good dialogue explodes the scenes and taps into characters' personalities, and consequently opens up your story. Without further ado, here are the most common dialogue disasters:

"As You Know, Bob"

This type of dialogue is implausible because the characters already know the information but are chatting for the sake of dispensing information. It goes something like this:

"As you know, Bob, ever since Mom and Dad died in that head-on crash, things have been tough around here."

"They sure have, Jim. Thank God you found that job in the button factory to support us all. And what would we have done without Mom's sister Alice moving into the attic to help out with the younger kids?"

"I know, Bob. She was a godsend. But then let's not forget

how the church ladies brought over all that fried chicken and potato salad—that was a big help, too."

"Yes, and it helped a lot when the button factory gave you that promotion so we could keep up on the mortgage."

"You're right, because things were really tight then since little Peggy was hospitalized with pneumonia right after Ben, our youngest brother, fell from the roof."

Enough said. You can spot the fakery here. Just say no to "As you know, Bob" dialogue.

Chitchat

Often writers include chitchat in their dialogue because they wrongly believe it lends an air of reality to the story. The truth is, chitchat is deadly in a story. It looks like this:

"Hi, Bob," said Genny after walking into the party and spotting her old high school chum.

"Oh, hi, Genny," answered Bob.

"It's great to see you again."

"You too," said Bob, grinning.

"How's the world treating you these days?"

"Can't complain."

"Me either. But I am surprised to see you here. I didn't know you knew the Nelsons."

"Andrew and I work together."

"Oh, I didn't know that."

"Yup. For the past five years. Say, can I get you a drink?"

As you can see, this is dull as dishwater. Don't do this. Dialogue is more like an exchange of live hand grenades than watching a chess game.

Clipped

Beware of characters who sound like an Englishman after dental surgery ("Precisely. I say. Exactly. Just so.") or like Sergeant Joe Friday, with his rapid-fire, staccato delivery in the 1950s television show *Dragnet* ("This is the city: Los Angeles, California. I work here. I'm a cop." Or "All we want are the facts, ma'am."). While dialogue is necessarily concise, if it is too clipped and understated, it will not contain the breath of life. Rather, snappy dialogue *suggests* the pauses, sloppiness, and silliness of real life.

Drama Queen

Sometimes characters are drama queens and every time they open their mouths what comes out is excessive or hysterical or crazed or outraged. When a drama queen or two is talking, it looks something like this:

"Jason, you cannot possibly mean that! Tell me it's not true!"

"Bambi, I'm afraid it's true. I've never loved you, although I've tried all these long years."

"But what about our darling children and our splendid secret times? What of our soaring passions and shared intellect and our gourmet meals together? I cannot imagine an existence without these delights."

"I wish I shared your joy in our marriage. Alas, my heart

doesn't soar when I see you as I return from my toils at the bank each evening."

"No, no, my darling! I refuse to hear this. I refuse to believe these harsh denials."

"I'm afraid that truth is often cruel. And I must be true to my heart."

"My heart is now in shards and I can scarcely breathe for the pain you have caused me."

Etc. In life drama queens are exhausting, and in fiction they are doubly so.

Expert Witness

Some genre writers, such as mystery writers, have special problems because they need to introduce a series of witnesses or experts to explain important facts or happenings in the story. The trick is to keep these exchanges crisp and entertaining and keep jargon to a minimum. So you might want to use a character who is quirky or a character who is giving information under duress to create tension in the scene. Break up long dialogue with action and reaction along with mannerisms, gestures, or small bits of setting woven in to keep the scene from bogging down. A badly done expert witness might sound like this as he testifies in a murder trial:

"Detective, could you please describe your actions on the night of October sixth, 2007?"

"Certainly. My partner, Detective Lance Quiver, and I were called to the scene by the officers who first answered the nine-one-one call. We received their call at ten-eighteen P.M. and proceeded down Morrison Street at the normal speed limit, thirty miles per hour, and arrived at the scene, 1070 Laurelhurst Drive, at ten twenty-seven. When we arrived there were already a number of vehicles on the scene and the coroner, Dr. Sam Barbar, was pulling in also. We shook hands and remarked how unseasonably warm it was. The moon was just beginning to rise and it aided us as we picked our way through the woods around the old mansion. The mansion itself is set far off the road, but we didn't drive into the driveway in order not to contaminate the crime scene. So we carefully walked in, using our flashlights and the moon to guide us. As we drew closer a young officer, Matthew Collins, was placing crime-scene tape around the garden. The garden is to the right side, or north, of the home at 1070 Laurelhurst Drive. It's a large plot, about half an acre by my reckoning. Another officer, Barbara Rowenski, was setting up several spotlights on the scene, while at the back of the house, several officers were questioning the gardener, Bill Jenkins, who had made the nine-one-one call. According to Jenkins, he'd forgotten to turn off the sprinkler system before leaving work that day so had returned at about ten oh-five to remedy this problem when he discovered the body. . . ."

As you can see, this sort of rambling discourse takes much too long to give readers what they most want: new and juicy information about the corpse as well as a hint or two about why the corpse is no longer breathing.

Info Dumps

Similar to the problem of the expert witness, be careful of using dialogue to dump exposition or backstory information on the reader. Fictional characters need to carry on conversations, not expound or exchange essays.

James: "Verily, I say, Roberto, the Romans have been dominating our people for decades. They are a scourge upon the land and our women."

Roberto: "Tis true. But many a stalwart lad has joined their legions and gone on to glory in the battlefield."

James: "But Rome is an oppressor. They've ravaged this continent to fill their coffers and enslaved thousands."

Ugh. Don't do this, either.

Memory Marvels

When I work on a memoir manuscript in which there are long segments of dialogue, I usually worry about the credibility of the writer. The reason is simple: most of us do not journey through life hauling around a tape recorder. So a memoirist typically relies on memory to supply conversations that happened years ago. This means that dialogue in memoir should be brief and accurate.

The only exception I've ever run into was a writer who wrote a memoir about putting her son up for adoption when she was sixteen. Thirty years later, mother and son were reunited, and when they met, the son's wife videotaped much of their first days together. This meant the manuscript was filled with long exchanges, in fact pages and pages of dialogue. Trouble is, most of what we say in life is repetitive, as was the dialogue in her memoir. You need to justify every word of dialogue in a memoir.

Name Dropping

Name dropping is one of my pet peeves in dialogue, and I always eradicate it with red ink when I spot it in a manuscript. This means simply that characters repeatedly refer to one another by name. We don't do this in real life. In fact, when most of us phone a friend or family member we don't announce, "Hi, this is Tom speaking." Most people on the other end of the line recognize our voice so we don't need to identify ourselves. A name dropper's dialogue looks like this:

"Hi, Mary, lovely to see you again," said Jill.

"Jill, it's nice to see you, too," said Mary.

"Mary, I'm wondering if I can ask you a big favor?"

"What sort of favor, Jill?"

"Well, Mary, can we go someplace more private, because, Mary, this is really difficult for me. I would only ask you, Mary, because you're such a caring person."

On the Nose

"On the nose" dialogue is a screenwriting term. It means the speaker says exactly what he means at all times, and explains exactly what he wants or needs. On the nose is especially egregious when characters stand around (or maybe lie around) and talk about how much they love each other. Trouble is, people (and characters) often speak in code, have a hidden agenda, cannot admit the truth, or search for words. Often the more painful the subject, the more people talk in circles to avoid the truth. And on the nose isn't memorable and lively and spiked with tension; instead it's clumsy and obvious. Here's what on the nose sounds like:

"We need to stop Alec before he kills again!"
"We're all in this together."
"We need to hurry. Time is running out."
"I'm angry at you for sleeping with Jim."
"I'm deeply hurt that you think I'm fat because I've gained weight since I had the triplets."
"I've been living a lie."
"I cannot bear the thought of living without you."
"If only I could wear ladies' panties, I would feel fulfilled."
"I've been terribly lonely ever since Al died of lung cancer in 1998. He and I first met when we were both twenty and life has been empty without him ever since."

The point is that good dialogue often *hints* at what the character means but doesn't state it explicitly. Effective dialogue zigzags around the truth and is as much about revealing as it is about concealing.

Another point is that often in our stories we want characters to *telegraph* emotions rather than state them explicitly. So when a character is angry he punches a wall or goes out drinking, or when a woman fears her boyfriend is cheating on her she eats a pint of Häagen-Dazs or goes on a shopping spree.

Preaching and Speech Making

The problem with preaching and speech making in fiction is that it is often the writer's thinly disguised opinion on weighty matters like the death penalty, immigration, child abuse, or race relations. Now, there's nothing wrong with writing about topics that matter to you—in fact, your best writing will often stem from your passions. But it is wrong to concoct characters who give speeches to espouse your views. This sort of dialogue dud sounds something like this:

"Bill, you know as well as I do that life is just not fair," Roger Bosworth, Bill's attorney, began. "And that justice is not always served."

"Yes, I know. But I thought you could help me beat this rap," Bill answered, twisting the thin cloth of his jail uniform. "You gotta get me out of here. This place is driving me crazy."

"I wish I could, but the odds are stacked against young men such as yourself. Don't you know that the incarceration rate for young Afro-Americans is ten times higher than for other prisoners? Don't you know that the law is blind to the plight of the poor and disadvantaged? Now, maybe a jury will care that you were raised by a single mother and abandoned by your junkie father, but it's more likely that they'll turn a blind eye to your sordid background and instead see you as a danger to society who deserves to be locked up and forgotten."

Sometimes preaching and speech making can be stiff-necked and long-winded or sound like a rant. And sometimes preaching is necessary—but make sure it's a man of the cloth or a politician expounding, and as with all parts of dialogue, hit the high notes, not every note.

Adverb Explosions, or Fifty-pound Speech Tags

Good dialogue doesn't rely on speech tags (she said wearily, he spoke warily, Bob ventured sullenly) to express emotions or describe what is being said. In general, keep the speech tags to a basic "he said," "she said" format because we want the tag to be invisible. In fact contemporary authors are dropping speech tags more and more from dialogue exchanges.

Use substitutions for "said" sparingly (she expounded, elaborated, queried). While the best attributions are simple, use verbs when it's necessary to describe the quality or volume of a voice, but not to describe the content of what's being said. Here are examples of adverb explosions:

"Why doesn't my mentally deranged mother accept me for who I am?" Brenda asked pityingly, wiping the flow of tears from her wide blue eyes.

"How could you?" Alan shouted accusingly.

"When will you love me as I love you?" Belinda whispered longingly, her words beseeching him to answer.

"Aha! I knew you were cheating on me, you strumpet!" Timothy shouted, his voice at once accusing and triumphant, his accusation both judge and jury.

Write Naturally

Dialogue comes naturally when you know and trust your characters. As your characters begin spinning a web in your imagination, something magical happens—they just might take over the story. They'll leap off the page and start talking, and if you're smart, you'll listen. Sometimes this feels a little spooky, as if we're taking dictation. But it's the character talking to us, whispering her lines, surprising us with a joke we'd never thought of on our own. Just listen.

Try This

Imagine a character who works in a skyscraper in downtown Chicago or New York. Now imagine that this person is having a lousy week—an argument with her spouse or teenager, bad news from her doctor, and a pile of overdue bills littering her desk. This morning she's off to a late start because, among other things, she lost her keys. Finally, she leaves home without them, not sure how she'll let herself back into her apartment at the end of the day. As she dashes into the office building with only seconds to spare, she lunges toward the elevator and squeezes through the door. Oh yeah, she's been late for work three times already this week and her boss is gunning for her. Then the elevator screeches and clangs to an ominous halt after it lets out a passenger on the seventeenth floor. Now write the conversation that occurs between her and the other three elevator riders as they're stalled between floors. Distinguish each character, but try to leave out the most obvious statements about their situation.

Quick and Dirty Tips for Writing Dialogue

- Eavesdrop on life, paying attention to how a variety of people talk.
- Listen for places where people don't say what they mean.
- Collect quick comebacks.
- Learn the rules for punctuating dialogue and avoid exclamation marks.
- Ask yourself what your characters are feeling as they talk.
- Read your dialogue scenes out loud to hear where they lag, become entangled, or are just plain dull.
- For realism, look for places in your story where your characters might interrupt one another, their sentences trail off unfinished, and their dialogue overlap.
- Don't think too hard or overanalyze what your characters need to say. Good dialogue comes from our instincts and intimacy with your characters.
- While it's fine to demonstrate what the speaker is doing or to insert gestures and mannerisms, don't make the character's actions overshadow what he says.

Resources

The First Five Pages, Noah Lukeman

Write Great Fiction: Dialogue, Gloria Kempton

Writing Dialogue for Scripts: Effective Dialogue for Film, TV, Radio and Stage, Rib Davis www.script-o-rama.com

Watch *Glengarry Glen Ross* or read the screenplay, noting the realism, pacing, and rhythms of the dialogue.

Watch *The Visitor,* a film written and directed by Tom McCarthy, because it exposes the United States' immigration policies via drama, not preaching by the characters.

Read Hemingway's "Hills like White Elephants," a story that is chiefly told in dialogue, noting especially how tension is embedded.

Read a variety of established and contemporary playwrights: David Mamet, Tennessee Williams, Neil Simon, Caryl Churchill, John Guare, Wendy Wasserstein, Tony Kushner, Wole Soyinka, Edward Albee, Suzan-Lori Parks, Arthur Miller, and Wallace Shawn to study the range of possibilities for character speech. Note especially what is left out of conversations, how characters of varying ages and social status are portrayed in an ensemble, and how dialogue drives the story.

Nine

Never Write About Wimps: Creating Potent and Memorable Characters

Fiction writers too often forget that interesting characters are almost always characters who are active—risk-takers—highly motivated toward a goal. Many a story has been wrecked at the outset because the writer chose to write about the wrong kind of person—a character of the type we sometimes call a wimp.

—JACK M. BICKHAM, *The 38 Most Common Fiction Writing Mistakes (And How to Avoid Them)*

Let's think about famous characters who linger in our imagination years after we've read the novel: Scarlett O'Hara, James Bond, Atticus Finch, Huckleberry Finn, Sherlock Holmes, Hester Prynne, Harry Potter, Frodo and Sam, Elizabeth Bennet, Randle McMurphy, Jo March, Dracula, Jane Eyre, Hannibal Lecter, Clarisse Starling, Voldemort, and Holden Caulfield. The list goes on and on.

One trait these characters share is that they're not wimps. No siree, they're people of action who speak their minds, kick ass and take names, and, most important, who act when in real life *we'd* be cowering, or wetting our pants, or scrambling for an exit.

Scrappy, shrewd, Scarlett struggles to save Tara and solve enormous problems as war rages and the world around her goes to hell; Huckleberry defies society by floating away with Jim, the runaway slave; Randle McMurphy in *One Flew Over the Cuckoo's Nest* tries to bring dignity to a group of lost men under the thumb of a dictator; and Frodo sets off for adventures into a world so big and scary and teeming with danger that his butt is always on the line.

Or, for example, imagine the sleuth who stars in a suspense story. When the sleuth stumbles over a dead body, he examines the crime scene for clues before the cops arrive and is then pulled into solving the murder. Now, if you or I chanced on a corpse, we'd likely vomit in the gutter or try, with shaking fingers, to dial 911. But we wouldn't hang out with a corpse. As for hunting down dastardly fiends or facing most kinds of danger in the manner of fictional heroes? Gotta take a pass.

Buzz Kill

Your characters can be neurotic or despicable, vain or shallow, but they must always be vivid, fascinating, and believable, and their actions, decisions, and motives must propel the story to an inevitable conclusion.

The biggest buzz kill a writer hears is when a reader pronounces that his protagonist is bland, boring, or predictable. Often these pallid creatures plod across familiar ground, mouthing banal lines and twisting into hackneyed mannerisms and gestures. Writers are shocked when their characters are called wimps since they've been hanging out together for the year or so that it's taken to pen the story. Especially when the protagonist seems like a pumped-up version of the writer.

But before we go further, let's define the protagonist in your story. He or she is the main character who will be most hurt and pays the price for the events in the story. In a memoir, the person narrating the story has a unique vantage on the events of the past and has uniquely paid the price for those events. In many but not all stories, the protagonist will also be most changed by what happens in the story. (In some genres or series fiction the focus is on action, not character arc.) For example, in *To Kill a Mockingbird* Jem is the protagonist because, at twelve, he's changed by the story's tragic events and displays remarkable chutzpah in the climactic scene while defending his sister.

A protagonist can be likable or unlikable, a hero or an antihero, but to carry a story, a protagonist must be compelling and memorable. The protagonist's main job is to create emotions in your reader. These emotions will be stirred because your protagonist will be reacting to a series of threatening changes—and if he cowers or cannot make up his mind, these falters must eventually be overcome because protagonists are proactive.

Hero or Zero?

Manuscripts that feature a wimp are easy to spot and, happily, easy to fix. Usually the writer simply doesn't realize that his character is a dishrag type because he modeled the character after a real person or he doesn't understand that fictional characters differ from us mere mortals.

Now, this doesn't mean that your male characters are all

testosterone-pumped musclemen, or your females are tough as nails, or over-the-top vixens. Think of Atticus Finch in *To Kill a Mockingbird*. Atticus is considered a static character because he doesn't change over the course of the story, but static doesn't mean wimpy. Instead he's *unforgettable*. As a mild-mannered Southern lawyer, he stands up to a gang of rednecks intent on hanging his client, racial injustice, and a rabid dog, teaching his children what a real hero is. Or take the character Joan Wilder, played by Kathleen Turner, in the film *Romancing the Stone*. In the beginning of the film romance writer Wilder is afraid of love, afraid of life, afraid of travel. But she *answers the call to adventure* because her sister is in trouble and arrives in a steamy jungle in Colombia in pumps, a down coat, and her hair twisted in a bun. Where she becomes embroiled with a mercenary in a treasure hunt for the ride of her life.

Let's talk about the difference between wimps and protagonists worth reading. For our purposes I call nonwimps heroes; in reality not all protagonists are heroes, but all protagonists are potent.

Wimps worry and fret and cannot make up their minds.

Heroes shoot off their mouths, shoot from the hip, and jump in feet first, even when bullets are flying.

Wimps sigh and retreat and try to blame other people for their problems.

Heroes take charge, take responsibility, and take risks.

Wimps avoid action and intimacy, and hedge their bets.

Heroes plunge in, kiss the guy or gal, and dare to be wrong.

Wimps don't know their minds and hearts, and often don't live by principles or beliefs.

Heroes know themselves and where they stand.

Wimps are forgettable.

Heroes are unforgettable.

Wimps crumble, hesitate, equivocate.

Heroes often seek out the dark manifestation of evil in order to save others.

Wimps cannot handle the pain, the pressure, the choices.

Heroes refuse to give up, admit defeat, or die.

Wimps are boring in life and more so in fiction.

Heroes are not found as often in life, but often star in fiction.

Do Nice Guys Finish Last?

As I've said, not every story needs a ninja warrior or an Uzi-toting, foul-mouthed mercenary to lead the story. Nor do stories need rapists, murderers, swindlers, and suicides in order to be dramatic and compelling. Stories can be headed by intellects and librarians, children, screwups, and young mothers. A protagonist can also be a schemer, like Emma Bovary, an iron-fisted Mafia head, like Don Corleone, or a lazy, good-natured womanizer, like Gus McCrae in *Lonesome Dove*. *But fictional characters venture into physical and emotional territory where most of us would fear to tread.* They venture into this territory for a variety of reasons—not simply because they're brave. A character might venture forth motivated by greed, desperation, loyalty, naiveté, or revenge. Your hero might be a thrill seeker or after glory or redemption.

It's simple, really. Fictional characters are bigger than life, bigger than death; they say what we dare not say in real life, jump

THE CASE OF THE ANTIHERO

Antiheroes are protagonists who are as flawed or more flawed than most people, who can disturb us with their weaknesses and make us empathize with their flaws. Antiheroes create a lot of tension in a story, and because they're protagonists, their personality flaws can cause problems for other cast members as well as for themselves.

An antihero usually lacks the traditional traits and qualities of a hero, such as honesty, dignity, and empathy. He can be rough around the edges or even criminal. He or she is always tarnished, is often not a role model but instead is motivated by self-interest, and often is a rebel. He can be leading an ordinary life and is pulled into the story, or he can be a fallen hero who needs to find himself.

We use antiheroes in stories because they bring a lot of heat to a plot and they are complex, complicated, and unpredictable. But mostly because they reflect realism that is so popular in contemporary fiction as well as film and television characters. Examples range from Geoffrey House in the House series, to Bridget Jones in *Bridget Jones's Diary,* Huckleberry Finn, and Stephanie Plum in Janet Evanovich's series.

higher, run faster, make love more often, and also usually mess up more than we do in the real world.

We read their stories because they are our knights chasing down a bad guy; the chick who takes a chance and loves the guy with the dark past when you married an accountant; the wronged woman who decides to get even when in real life you'd hire a good divorce attorney. We read fiction because characters are in over their heads and we need to find out how they solve the story problem.

The other thing to keep in mind is that characters are never perfect, are always flawed, and always have some crucial factor from their past or circumstances that complicates their success in the story.

Why Is the Key

Which leads to the why of fiction. If you do not know why your characters act as they do, you do not know your characters and, sadly, neither will your readers. If you've created characters who zip around in your story with the abandon of Ping-Pong balls, without a glimpse into the *why* of their behaviors, you'll only make your reader dizzy.

Similarly, if you're writing a memoir and have never questioned why other people in your personal drama acted as they did, your story might seem myopic and thin.

Motivation, based on a character's beliefs, family, and environmental and cultural background, provides a trajectory for characters to act and grow on. Motivations compel action, create goals in scenes, and drive characters to achieve goals. Thus motivations provide characters with credible reasons for their actions, and they should carry out those actions with plausible skills or acquire skills along the way. If readers cannot believe a character's actions, the story fails.

So you don't want your readers scratching their heads and asking why your character would run off with a grifter, or hop into bed with a psychopath, or head into the dark alley with a killer on the loose when he or she seems essentially sensible. Characters are much more consistent than real-life people, so if they break from their way of being in the story world, readers stop trusting the writer. Your characters are not your puppets—they're knowable and credible.

To help main characters remain consistent, build a profile for each. Decide on their physical characteristics and backstory, and most important, choose dominant and unforgettable traits as a foundation of personality. These traits will be showcased in the story events, will help him achieve his goals or fail, and will make the story person consistent. For example, Harry Potter's dominant traits are that he is loyal, brave, intelligent, especially able to think on his feet, stubborn, and impulsive. These traits are showcased in every story along with lesser traits and quirks that sometimes help him and sometimes land him in hot water. When Harry or any main character first appears in the story, he arrives with his dominant traits intact.

Not only must you know why your characters act as they do, you prove to readers that your characters want something and want it badly. Desire is the oh-so combustible fuel of storytelling. When story people want something, they want it so much they'll lie, cheat, steal, and murder. Harry Potter's motives change over the series, but he's always motivated to act for the good of others and to fight evil. Wimps don't want much—mostly to avoid the heat, avoid making decisions, avoid changing.

Deal Breakers

I've met a lot of fabulous characters in my clients' stories over the years, and I've also met a lot of duds. Here are some of the deal breakers that will doom a story:

Alpha-wannabe

I've worked on a number of thriller or action stories for clients and in many, the protagonist couldn't carry the story because he wasn't an alpha type. In the jungles of Africa or in Siberian forests, alpha males and females are necessary for the survival of the species. Likewise, in many genres, alphas are necessary for the survival of other characters in the story. In high-stakes novels readers identify with the hero's struggle to survive since it's usually a life-or-death situation.

It's especially important that the hero be bigger than life and take more risks. He always mixes it up, always retaliates, always is proactive. An alpha must go toe-to-toe throughout the story and cannot be burdened by his emotional needs. In one story I worked on the protagonist in a thriller often broke down and sobbed because his daddy never loved him and his wife didn't understand him. When he was fired from his job he skulked out the door with his tail between his legs, then ducked off to lick his wounds and fell apart, drunk and weeping. In another manuscript, whenever the going got tough, the alpha-wannabe wrote in his journal, when what he needed to do was kick his enemy in the groin.

So while an alpha can experience doubts, he's more heroic

than most of us ordinary folks walking around. The conflict usually forces him to draw on reserves of strength and depth of character. Sometimes in an action story the protagonist will become tougher or more cynical and sometimes he'll face a demon from his past—but the story typically isn't about a character arc, it's about solving a problem or saving the world.

Bimbo in Peril

This is my least favorite type of character and she usually stars in a horror or damsel-in-distress story. So here's the scenario: it's Halloween and twilight arrives early in a small Midwestern town nestled in the midst of vast cornfields and prairie. The moon is a mere sliver, winking occasionally as clouds hurtle across the sky. The trees are stripped naked, and the wind whistles through the isolated town with the ferocity of a freight train traveling down a mountainside, thrashing tree branches and sending leaves tumbling across lawns like ghosts playing hide-and-seek. However, the town is not completely isolated, because the main industry in the area, besides farming, is a high-security prison that houses the baddest of the badasses in the state.

After the last trick-or-treater has toddled off carrying his loot, Belinda Edwards, a lovely, straight-A student, locks the front door and heads to the den to finish her homework. She is home alone, and as Belinda studies for her algebra test, the lights begin to flicker, then go out. She gropes her way in the dark and finds a flashlight and candles. By candlelight and flashlight she keeps studying, as the wind grows louder and a storm starts pummeling the house with oversize raindrops.

Then she hears a crash, then the tinkle of glass coming from the back of the house. It seems like the sounds are coming from the basement. Next, instead of reaching for the phone and dialing 911, or running to a neighbor's home for safety, she grabs the flashlight and heads into the basement, where of course she's going to meet up with an escaped prisoner, a leering serial killer. The character is acting like a bimbo because the writer forces her to take foolish risks to place her in danger.

Make your characters smarter than this. A character should not trip blithely into situations she knows are dangerous unless she has a compelling reason to do so, such as to save another vulnerable character or her own sorry ass, or she's a cop packing a Colt .45. You want your reader worried, not exasperated. Also, the damsel-in-distress story line has been around for hundreds of years and in the past operated under the principle that the woman is helpless or in need of rescue. Today's readers are looking for spunky survivors. The world has changed, so make sure your characters have changed with it.

Clichéd

It's difficult but not impossible to invent freshly minted characters. Here are some of the clichéd characters that got on my last nerve as soon as I met them in my clients' stories and will cause your readers to immediately lose interest: men or women who are so astoundingly attractive that when they're around, other characters swoon, start peeling off their clothes, and lose their bearings. Evil dictators without any clue about why they became evil. Fanatical preachers who practically breathe fire and demand that their flock never question authority. The modest young man or woman who turns out to be the long-lost prince or princess.

The myopic scientist or inventor who refuses to acknowledge that his invention just might obliterate humankind. Generals with bloodlust who will sacrifice their troops for their blind ambition. Greedy corporate types who only care about the bottom line. The plain Jane who turns into a beauty after a makeover or falling in love. Then, of course, there are the strong, silent types (really, have you ever met one of these guys?), mysterious strangers, willowy blond virgins, noble savages, wicked stepmothers, and bitchy cheerleaders (also blond).

Goody-goody

Great characters stay with us, often because we recognize something of ourselves in them. This identification falls apart if your characters are goody-goodies. You see, fiction writers use tough love in creating characters because they're going to be punished. A lot. And they're always somehow flawed. On the page I've met protagonists who bake cakes for their enemies, who get tears in their eyes at the sight of a puppy or a baby, who only hang out with the elderly and infirm, who always turn the other cheek, and who literally help little old ladies cross the street. Some of the goody-goody types were fond of saying, "Oh dear Lord!" or "Oh my goodness!" and "Gee whillikers" when excited. This is to excitement what cornflakes is to food. They are often politically correct, holier-than-thou, unfailingly polite, and they never, ever cuss.

The trouble is main characters need fears, troubling traits, and dark sides. As a writer you sometimes need to plumb *your* shadow side and your darker feelings. When I interviewed Diana Gabaldon, who writes the Outlander series, I asked her about causing trauma and pain to her protagonists. Gabaldon said, "Well, you really can't be afraid when you write a book. If it's going to be a good story, the main thing about it is it needs to be emotionally honest. And that means that there will be things that are difficult to write or to deal with because people have a tendency to shy off from going to very dark places."

Limp Villains

Limp is a word with bad associations in our culture. Manufacturers of Viagra count on it. But when your villain is limp, the story is in real trouble. A villain is an antagonist who will cause the protagonist pain and has a deviant moral code.

His (or her) job in the story is to make our hearts beat a tango when he's around or make us dread his eventual appearance in the story like we dread the pain that comes with the onset of labor or a migraine.

Years ago, I was home on a Friday night and finished off a nice clam and pasta dish. Then, sipping a glass of wine, I started reading a suspense story. Within the first few pages the hair on my neck was prickly. At the end of chapter 3 I got up and poured another glass of wine. And while I was up, I checked to make sure the door at the bottom of the stairs was locked. (I was living in an attic at the time—a true writer's garret.) After about chapter 5, I rose again and double-checked the lower lock and engaged the upper lock with unnecessary force. And it was still light out. In fact, I had planned on going out for a walk, but decided it might be best to stay in for the night. Now that's a scary villain.

But some of the villains I've met in my clients' manuscripts are limp types: too shadowy so the reader never quite catches sight of them, lacking in complexity and daring, lacking in intelligence and cunning, or simply so vaguely drawn the reader never understands them.

I've read stories in which the villains don't do much—they are a vague threat, a distant possibility. But real villains are meddlers, connivers, and planners who imagine tortures and humiliations for their prey. In fact, villains typically are more focused on their goals than the protagonists are. They also take *extreme risks,* and the reader needs to know it.

Or, some villains I've met in my clients' stories seem conflicted about the pain they cause. The villain's job is to cause pain to vulnerable characters, not wring his hands because he's such a fiend. A fiend enjoys being a fiend because a true villain has some aspect of evil in his makeup. This means you need to understand your villain's psychology, justifications, and worldview so we come to understand how he can rape, maim, and kill without self-loathing, doubt, or remorse.

I've also read stories in which the villain makes stupid mistakes so the hero wins the day. One villain forgot his weapon, and another locked his keys in his car, which meant he couldn't get to his weapon. Another built a fantastical flying machine that was supposed to swoop down and snatch his victims, but then crashed the machine. But these ploys steal suspense because readers want a villain in top fighting shape and want the hero to defeat the villain, not the villain to screw up so the hero wins.

But what can be delicious in a story, and is often missing in my clients' manuscripts, is that the villain has some seriously kinky habits. Perhaps he hoards grisly souvenirs from his victims.

Perhaps he wears women's lace panties when he heads out on his nefarious deeds. Perhaps he collects torture devices from the Spanish Inquisition.

When interviewing Diana Gabaldon, I asked her why she believes that many writers get villains wrong, and fail to make them dark and complex. She replied: "Well, I would say that there are two things working there. First, there is a squeamishness that leads people to be superficial and stereotypical about their villains because they don't want to go deeply into these people. Yet they want them to be very bad, so they're picking out surface aspects which means it will never be convincing. The corollary to that, of course, is that they're not accepting of the villain as being a wholly human person. They're thinking that a villain is something *other.* And they're not." She laughed. "You do have to accept them as actual human beings and also as parts of yourself, which is where the emotional honesty comes in."

And finally, without confusing the issue, some villains are sympathetic. This doesn't mean they're fixer-uppers or can lead your kid's Scout troop or date your sister. This means readers can glimpse their humanity, can understand how and why they turned out bad, and can believe in their pasts and motives. Trouble is, sometimes writers make them too sympathetic, as when one of my clients created a villain who had such a tragic childhood that this background was supposed to explain his all-consuming bloodlust. This was just too far-fetched and inappropriate as motivation. On the other hand, even sympathetic villains are still potent, deadly, and paradoxically fascinating. And a story with a villain needs to place the reader smack in the middle of hell.

Just Too Wacky

Generally a wacky character is used in a story because he or she is a naive, possibly oblivious, and comic character who needs to learn the hard way.

Lots of authors have made it big by creating wacky, screwball characters. Janet Evanovich, Carl Hiaasen, and Elmore Leonard come to mind. These wack jobs create a lot of tension in a story because the reader never knows what he or she'll say next and what pile of doo-doo they'll step into. But if every word that pops out of your character's mouth is a one-liner or a double entendre, the story starts sinking under all the forced cleverness. Or if your character Violetta only wears purple, eats purple foods, writes with purple ink, drives a purple Mustang, and decorates every inch of her living space purple, this is called mental illness, not entertainment.

Also, if your character's behavior is *always* implausible, such as laughing off danger when most of us would be hiring a bodyguard—the villain has been leaving freaky, threatening notes warning that her days are numbered, but she still heads out at midnight to meet him in a lonely graveyard—well, readers lose trust. Likewise when the character's brakes are shaky and the roads are ice-slicked and the temperatures below zero, but she heads out wearing little more than a feather boa and skimpy miniskirt to see her favorite band that is playing at a club at the bottom of a twisty mountain road.

Martyrs and Victims

I once worked on a manuscript that had terrific potential and a fresh setting—an oil rig in the middle of the stormy North

Atlantic. Like her protagonist, the writer, an interesting and lovely Scottish woman, had firsthand experience working on a rig.

But like many manuscripts, this one suffered from several crucial problems and many of them stemmed from the fact that her protagonist was a victim. While she became a tad spunkier by the story's end, it came after the reader was weary of her cowering, saccharine tendencies and naiveté. It was especially difficult to witness the character being brutally raped and then hide her wounds and traumas—because she needed the job more than she needed dignity and safety. So she never reported the rape, and when she discovered she was pregnant—because many fictional characters are remarkably fertile—she slunk off to the Scottish highlands to have her baby, and then forgave her rapist. This was after her true love was killed by the villain-rapist and she was nursing another character through a fatal cancer while pregnant and deferring her dreams.

Call me a sadist, but at some point in the story she needed to belt somebody across the nose, slash the villain's tires, wail with grief, and plot a bit of revenge. In other words, the story needed a human and possibly over-the-top response from her, not long-suffering stoicism and irrational shame. The story needed anger or outrage, which is often a justifiable response to unfairness and abuse. Instead she hid out, kept quiet, baked bread, and fed the chickens. Remember, readers long to *bond* with characters, and victimhood, in all its guises, makes that impossible.

Not True to Type

As a writer you want to introduce readers to keenly etched characters or people they've never met before who will teach them something new. However, there are certain archetypes and conventions in fiction, especially in genre fiction, that are timeless foundations for stories. If a reader picks up a genre novel, he'll be assured that the general parameters of the story will be adhered to. In a horror story, in an atmosphere of dread and foreboding, the reader will get the bejesus scared out of him; in a Western the protagonist will win over the bad guys, bringing civilization to the frontier; in science fiction we often travel beyond the realms of the ordinary world and the story is based on scientific possibilities; in a suspense novel there is a crime, a search, and a solution; and in a romance the protagonists fall in and out of love, culminating in a happy ending.

Conventions in genres and subgenres keep the promise that the story makes to readers, a ready-made audience. If you're going to write in a genre, you need a deep understanding of the conventions and the character types most often found in the starring roles. If you haven't studied the best-selling books, the latest releases, and the classics in your genre, you're at a huge disadvantage. And while there are thousands of permutations, there are also some conventions that apply to characters that storytellers have been using for centuries. For example, in fantasy the protagonist often possesses some special attribute or power that he or she might be unaware of until faced with a threat. These powers might be magical, mystical, or innate, such as second sight. The protagonist often also shares the billing with a faithful pal, wise man or woman, or ally, although these might be a fairy or ghost.

So take risks with your characters but know the conventions. I've seen too many stories that seem written with no sense of the genre. A romance in which the female protagonist hates men. All men. For no discernible reason. A coming-of-age story in which the protagonist doesn't change because of story events. A spy novel in which the spy doesn't seem to know much about technology or the world around him. An astronaut who doesn't possess curiosity, along with a love of adventure and flying. A Western in which the hero doesn't dominate the story. A historical novel in which all the characters are freethinkers and feminists and seem totally out of sync with the beliefs and values of the times. In another historical novel the characters were mostly Michelangelo-genius types and I kept wondering where all the peasants, farmers, and blacksmiths went to.

Ordinary Joe

Since the beginning of storytelling there have been reluctant heroes and heroines, ordinary gals and guys who are thrust into a situation way over their heads. The late Alfred Hitchcock concocted some of his best films out of this scenario, as in *North by Northwest* when Roger Thornhill, played by Cary Grant, is mistaken for a government agent and lands in such a mess that he ends up scaling Lincoln's nose at Mount Rushmore. Or often in stories protagonists who are fairly ordinary have no choice but to take on a terrifying, cold-blooded killer or face adversity they never anticipated in their most horrific nightmares. As mentioned earlier, Joan Wilder in *Romancing the Stone* heads off to the jungles of Colombia to free her sister from kidnappers who are after a rare emerald. The thrill ride in these stories involves the mousy type finding her guts, her inner bad girl, her avenging angel.

Or take Juno, played by Ellen Page in the film of the same name, who is an Everygirl. Now, Juno is confident, funny, and intelligent, but she's no superstar, cheerleader, class president type. She's an authentic teen. So there is nothing wrong with an Everyman starring in a story because not every story can be headed by studs, superstars, and beauty queens.

However, wannabe-published writers often populate their stories with folks too ordinary, too normal, too complacent. They aren't a bundle of interesting or endearing quirks. They don't face their demons, they don't learn important truths, but most of all they don't fascinate or cause readers or viewers to ponder deeper issues and themes. The best ordinary types make us examine the human heart. Or ask us what it means to be authentic in an inauthentic world. If your character is simply ordinary, the result is a yawn.

Snivelers

We read fiction for many reasons, but in our intimate moments with a protagonist, we want that character to rise up to the challenges of the fictional world most of the time. Characters need to stumble and make mistakes, because the world of fiction erects obstacles and torments. But if your character hangs around sighing, weeping, or complaining, breaking down in her therapy sessions, or simply cannot take the pressure, readers will bail out quickly. One manuscript I worked on featured a character weeping throughout most of the scenes because her father was missing and never said good-bye. It wasn't sad, it was pathetic. Another featured a character who literally hid under the covers when the going got tough. And in yet another story the character always blamed other story people for his own missteps.

Instead, give your character a backbone (or have her grow a

backbone along the way) and use her pain, sadness, grief, remorse, and fatal flaw to *motivate her to act.* A character who's been wronged can seek revenge or understanding. Remember, too, that the threats in fiction exist to reveal how protagonists will react to adversity—and they need to act in surprising and interesting ways.

Superman Syndrome

Superman is a hero with few defects, although Kryptonite and a crush on Lois Lane do complicate his life. But in the twenty-first century Superman might seem like an overgrown Boy Scout, with too few flaws and hang-ups. Too often writers create iconic characters and magnify their good points and either don't endow them with flaws or rationalize their minor flaws. This invariably leads to melodrama because no matter how capable your character is, the reader wants him or her to survive the story travails but only by the skin of his teeth.

Storytelling needs conflict, which is caused by jeopardy, and also characters with psychological hang-ups, baggage, and secrets. So stir in flaws. Your super-tough, macho detective can be arrogant with a wicked temper or a weakness for scotch. Then have his best friend betray him and ruin his reputation and watch his life slide downhill.

I've read manuscripts in which an amateur sleuth has her life threatened three times in one day, but doesn't bat an eye or miss a wink of sleep. In another story the character, a kidnap victim, is as cool as a cucumber, even after being trapped in the trunk of a car. Call me neurotic, but I practically come down with claustrophobia when loading groceries into my trunk. And then there was the protagonist in the thriller whose wife was gang-raped and he kept on hunting down the bad guy he was after because he needed to solve the case, with barely a thought to her trauma; the story would have worked better if he'd hunted down the rapists and wasn't able to adequately chase down two sets of criminals at the same time. We feel empathy and sympathy with fictional characters because of their flaws and missteps, not because of their perfection.

Unfazed or Impervious

In a similar vein, it's also difficult to read about a character who zips through the story without a twitch, worry, or bruise. Fictional plots hurt characters, and readers want proof. I've read manuscripts in which the private investigator was whacked on the head with a two-by-four and then bounced to his feet grinning. In another story the character was knocked unconscious by a heavy door and woke up naked in a strange bed with no repercussions. Despite all the head wounds I've seen in manuscripts, they usually aren't accompanied by unconsciousness, concussions, headaches, dizziness, or a subdural hematoma. Another female character was beaten badly but in the following days went about life unfazed and unafraid, and other characters never mentioned her bruises and black eye. After a character is hurt in a story, the plot should show him weakened or changed in the following scenes.

While fictional characters are bigger than life, they bleed, vomit, and pass out from injuries and trauma. They also grieve, break down, freak out, and make fools of themselves. So make sure your characters react appropriately to avoid melodrama or silliness. And the more physical action and repercussions in your story, the more you'll need to rely on research and experts.

No More Wimps

There are many lessons to be learned here. Nonwimps generously share the spotlight with interesting co-stars. When a nonwimp is running the show, the action never stops. True, they sometimes panic, doubt, and worry, but they suck it up and plunge ahead. And take this one to the bank: nonwimps are motivated by their concern and love for others or have darn good reasons for why they do what they do. Nonwimps pursue goals, never give up, and determine outcomes that make fiction better than reality. They are as unlike wimps as Arnold Schwarzenegger is unlike Woody Allen.

Try This

1. Start with a story idea. Do you have a murder mystery, romance, or historical epic in mind?
2. Choose a main character to build your plot around. Decide what he or she wants and create a bio with these aspects:
    - A. a ruling passion, burning desire, or powerful goal he wants more than anything.
    - B. core traits that will be showcased by events in the story—tenacity, compassion, courage, generosity—and serve as the character's foundation.

- C. a flaw that gets in the way of achieving goals and possibly must be overcome, such as self-doubt, gullibility, bitterness, pride.
- D. emotional baggage and needs stemming from the main character's past. These needs, coupled with motivation, cause characters to act as they do.

Quick and Dirty Tips for Never Writing About Wimps

- Your main character must be in jeopardy in each act of the story.
- Imagine yourself in your character's shoes. Now force your character to do exactly what you're afraid to do.
- Any detail about a character must be so crucial the story would falter without it. Each detail and quirk must make the character come alive.
- Ask yourself what fascinates you about your character—a secret, a quick wit, a person unjustly accused, in over his head?
- Know what your protagonist fears and put the fear at risk in the story; then stir in his or her vulnerabilities to create complications.
- Orchestrate scenes to make your characters uncomfortable—overdressed or underdressed for an important event, cold or hot with no chance of relief, meeting unexpectedly hostile or nasty characters, craving a drink.
- To create fully realized characters, give them a whole

life from the beginning pages—including a past with memories, meaningful connections with other people, and dreams for the future.

- Motives are not something you *add* to a character, they're intrinsic and linked to the past.
- As you plan or outline the story, show increasing emotional intensity in your main characters.
- Endow your main character with a variety of emotional relationships with other characters. These relationships should reveal his or her complexity.
- Don't place too many emotional or action-packed scenes back to back. Pause from time to time so characters can reflect or experience moments of normalcy or lightness.
- Consider centering your story on a character blinded by a single-minded obsession, whose weakness is the flip side of her strength, and who gradually gains more perspective.
- Every impediment your protagonist faces should have the potential of being too great to be conquered.
- Fictional characters need to be out of sync with their surroundings. That's why fish-out-of-water stories naturally feature conflict. For example, in Hitchcock's film *The Birds,* Melanie Daniels, played by Tippi Hedren, blunders into a coastal town and tailspins into danger of being pecked to death by ravaging flocks of birds so shrill and realistic that many of us have been looking skyward ever since we saw the film.
- Control your entire cast. A fully realized main character will not be found living among stereotypes or faceless

nonentities, just as secondary characters will not be so fabulous as to overshadow the main characters.

- Ask yourself if all the other good characters in your story like, love, or support your protagonist at all times. I hope your answer is no.
- When your character has an arc—over the course of which he or she changes by the end of the story—from the opening pages the reader must witness the potential for this change. This might be reserves of strength, resiliency, or dignity.
- Villains are often the most interesting and motivated characters in a story.
- Your story loses emotional impact if readers do not believe the threats to your protagonist are real.
- An evil character with a heart of inky black can be as silly as a wimpy protagonist. If your villain's only motivation is avarice or he was simply born evil, he'll lack plausibility and your readers will yawn, then eventually nod off.

Resources

Breathing Life into Your Characters, Rachel Ballon, Ph.D.

Character, Emotion & Viewpoint: Techniques and Exercises for Crafting Dynamic Characters, Nancy Kress.

45 Master Characters, Victoria Lynn Schmidt

A Story Is a Promise, second edition, Bill Johnson

The Criminal Mind: A Writer's Guide to Forensic Psychology, Katherine Ramsland

Ten

Make a Scene: Writing the Building Blocks of Stories

> You don't build a story or a book of words and sentences and paragraphs—you build it of scenes, one piled on top of the next, each changing something that came before, all of them moving the story inexorably and relentlessly forward.
>
> —HOLLY LISLE, "Scenes That Move Your Story Forward," www.HollyLisle.com

You cannot write words without learning the alphabet; you cannot write sentences without words. And you cannot write fiction or memoir without scenes. Please don't underestimate this small gem of wisdom. Speaking of gems, here's a visual everyone can understand: when I imagine a story's structure, I picture a pearl necklace, with each scene a lustrous pearl. The string that holds the pearls, or scenes, together is exposition, description, or whatever necessary information readers need to understand the story world.

Like stories, scenes have a beginning, middle, and end. Scenes have many purposes: to enrich or reveal characters, to dramatize key moments, to provide information, to contribute to the theme, to push the plot forward, and to connect to what has come before or will come after. Scenes are the parts of fiction that are direct and dramatic and stage happenings in "real" time. Scenes are mini-containers for drama, the events where your characters go to work just as actors show up on a stage.

They give readers a penetrating reality, provide the bite in fiction and memoir, often contain confrontations and struggles, and propel the story forward. Scenes expose your characters at their most vulnerable and often portray life-changing moments. Scenes are the intimate moments in the story that create emotional involvement, forcing readers to empathize with characters.

So scenes are our main writing tool because they take place in the now and cause readers to worry. Scenes are those parts of your story where the excitement happens, where the protagonist struggles to move forward in his quest, where winning moves him closer to his story goal, or losing sets him back. And at the core of each scene is a simple but effective ingredient: change.

Contemporary fiction is highly visual because it competes with other visual media, especially film, television, and the Internet. So when writing fiction or memoir be sure to imagine yourself more like a playwright than a journalist. Fiction requires a series of divisions, a series of stops and starts, pauses, reversals, setbacks, and stumbles until we reach the concluding moments. All these dramatic units build and enrich the story, prolong the suspense, milk the tension, all the while keeping readers engrossed while events march toward the "prize"—the ending.

A scene can convey all sorts of information besides conflict: mood, a sense of time and place, anticipation, a reflection of what has gone before. Sometimes you might not fully understand what a scene's "job" is in the story until you actually write it.

Then you can edit and trim anything that confuses the reader and add elements to highlight that scene's particular role in enhancing the whole story. As you pen your final draft, you should be able to understand what each scene reveals and how it demonstrates characters evolving or leads to consequences.

Architecture of Scenes

Most scenes contain action, and action scenes are always based on change. They have a simple, three-part structure: a *problem, mission* or *goal;* a *conflict* or *obstacle* that makes the problem difficult to solve or the goal difficult to achieve; and an *outcome,* often a disaster. See how easy this is? In each scene your protagonist has a goal, and something or someone will stand in the way, creating conflict and leading to a disaster, success, or a draw.

Mission or Goal: In each scene your character wants something—to rob a bank, get laid, break up with her boyfriend, escape the villain. The goal must be specific and clearly defined and sets your character in motion. He's not hanging out waiting for fate to smack him alongside his head or hoping his therapist will phone and solve his problems. In the best fiction, characters are proactive, involved, motivated to survive. And the more desperately a character wants something, the more juice in the scene and the more your reader will identify with his goal.

Conflict or Opposition: As chapter 7 defines, conflict is the engine of storytelling. Each scene has its own built-in engine because it contains an obstacle slamming into your character's desire. Your character Jed screws up his courage and asks his boss for a raise. Trouble is, the boss just found out his wife is having an affair and couldn't care less that Jed deserves more pay and desperately needs more presidential flash cards or he'll lose *his* wife. I told you this was easy. If you've ever watched the Olympics or any high-stakes contest, you realize that victory is meaningless without sacrifice or struggle. So scenes are the struggles we all love to watch, just as we enjoy watching Olympic swimmers dive into the pool and race against competitors.

Outcome or Disaster: Most scenes end in a win, lose, or draw. Since this is easy-peasy, as often as possible end scenes with your character's failure. I know this sounds counterintuitive, but failures, calamities, an ass-kicking, a setback, a heartbreak all force characters to grow and change because we are all shaped most by failure. Winning feels good, but failure makes us human. Fiction is a long, harsh prison sentence for your characters. And odd as it sounds, there are few successes or wins in fiction because they're b-o-o-o-ring. Fiction is messy, a smackdown or battleground. Of course sometimes your protagonist wins, but then you'll prolong success until the last possible moment.

Parts of the Scene

Here is a quick list of the parts of a scene. Not every scene contains all these parts because many scenes are stripped down to essentials.

- Dialogue, including subtext or what cannot be expressed out loud
- Speech tags, as in "he said," "she said"
- Actions, reactions, gestures, and mannerisms

- Setting details
- A character's thoughts
- Observations or commentary by the narrator
- Transitions that move the reader in and out of the scene
- Exposition as needed

When to Write in Scenes

Readers want to experience and feel what your characters experience and feel. This cannot happen with summaries of underdeveloped characters—readers need to get to know them. If you're writing a romance, the reader has the illusion that she is falling in love. If you're writing a thriller, the reader feels the terrible danger the hero faces. If you're writing a fantasy, give the illusion that the reader is actually in another world where all is different and wonderful and magical. And so on for all the other genres.

Here are the moments in a story to capture in scenes or reasons to stage scenes:

- Inciting incidents
- Full flashbacks
- Showdowns
- Surprises, twists, complications
- Seductions/capitulations
- Crimes (especially the discovery of a corpse)
- Love scenes, especially when they prove characters have changed
- Fight scenes

- Struggles—sometimes choices or decisions, especially moral decisions
- Revenge acted out
- Deceptions, betrayals, misperceptions, misalliances, mistakes
- Chases
- Arguments/confrontations
- Disclosures/revelations
- Resolutions to important subplots
- Climaxes that answer the story question
- Plot points
- Turning points, particularly at midpoint

On the other hand, not every moment in fiction needs to be shaped into a scene. Transitions where you move characters around, mundane actions such as a character getting dressed, familiar actions like checking in at an airport, or a character's brief recollection or thread of thoughts. Another time not to write in a scene is when you embed necessary exposition, such as a character's or family's background. The trick to making exposition hold the reader's attention is to include specific sensory details.

In the list above, I include crimes, meaning a character can commit a crime or discover a crime, such as cops and detectives converging on a murder scene. However, in many stories there is an important scene that takes place offstage. Staging events away from the lens increases the mystery or suspense. These happenings typically occur in suspense or thrillers when a character is murdered, typically occur early in the story, and then the plot follows a character or characters tracking down the murderer or solving the mystery.

Deal Breakers

One of the big shockeroos of my career was realizing how many writers have no bloody idea how to write in scenes. Here are some of the most wincingly obvious scene problems I've run across:

Bellicose

When fixing individual scenes, look at all the places where characters are experiencing overdrawn emotions and where you're stating or reporting on emotions, as in *Jennifer was so scared she felt like she was going to faint*. Beware of writing about main characters who are always anguished, always unrestrained or explosive. Too much emotion, especially too early in the story, anesthetizes your readers. While fiction is a heightened reality, not all fictional characters are drama queens or crybabies. Neither should they always be stoic and heroic because that makes readers believe their part is improbable. The earlier the scene appears in the story, the more important it is to rein in emotions—save the tears, hysterics, and whacked-out, wild-eyed smackdowns for later in the story.

Bloodless

When an action scene is bloodless, the conflict needs to intensify into a clash between characters (or monsters, earthquakes, or a cancer diagnosis). In bloodless scenes a character is not threatened—he might be out of sorts, peeved, or, God forbid, bored.

The villain might be in the vicinity but somehow they don't collide. Now the threat doesn't need to be physical, after all, misunderstandings and betrayals can be extremely painful. Or a lie or an accusation can shift the story direction. But repeat after me: characters suffer and sometimes that requires blood.

Brooding

In a surprising number of manuscripts a too-large portion of the story focuses on a character alone brooding. The character's heart is broken, boo hoo, so she plops on the couch to sigh and gaze out at the pitiless world from her lonely studio apartment. Or the male protagonist cannot have the vixen of his dreams, cannot figure out how to kick his enemy's ass, so he sits around and frets. Tell the truth now: in your real life, do you like brooders? Nooooo thank you. Stories tap into our secret longings and fears. They give us an epic buzz and we wade into a swampland of emotions. Brooders are wearisome and stories with a character who spends too much time isolated from the rest of the cast are more like prison time than a thrill ride.

Dead Zones

A lot of the cell phone calls I receive from my friends seem to be interrupted by dead zones. You're chatting away . . . and then suddenly you're not. You're just left dangling there. In certain manuscripts I sometimes feel like I'm reading the dramatic equivalent of a dead zone. I'm reading along and then I'm sort of lost, or I realize I'm no longer engaged or, worse, that I'm not feeling anything. The best-written scenes help readers see the events and also experience them via their senses. If a character is slapped, we want to feel the sting of flesh on flesh, the quick, metallic taste of blood in the mouth, hear the whack of the palm landing. In a dead zone, the scene usually doesn't have enough sensory information filtered through a point of view character, and typically it goes on too long.

Flab

Sometimes readers need a certain amount of exposition or description to understand a scene, but these days readers don't want long, densely packed paragraphs explaining the world of the story or a certain situation. You are not a reporter or researcher, you're a storyteller. So generally (and this will depend on the type of story you're writing) give the barest amount of information you can get away with. The rest is flab and it sends the reader skipping ahead, searching for the good parts.

I've read exposition about the workings of a submarine that sank the story, and in a story about mysterious grave robberies, a scene bogged down into a history of cemeteries in Western civilization. When I'm in a submarine I want to feel claustrophobic and amazed at the gadgetry, and when I'm in a cemetery I want to feel scared or sad. Again, the solution is pretty simple: make choices and break up the information with action and dialogue.

Gatherings

Some writers gather characters around a dinner table, in a lawyer's office, or at a party or a business meeting, but then fail to explode the scene with emotion or revelations, or some kind of fireworks. Especially deadly are the oh-so-dull business meetings modeled on the ones we're forced to attend in the real world. Sometimes writers jumble together too many characters with too many agendas all gathered in one place and the result is confusion. But usually gathering scenes don't work because the writer hasn't figured out the opposition in the scene, and often the opposition doesn't pan out because the scene events serve only a single purpose.

Let me give an example: The Monroe family has gathered in a lawyer's conference room for the reading of Great-Uncle Duke's will but all that happens is his beloved golf clubs are bestowed on his favorite nephew, the family silver to his favorite niece, and various inheritances doled out. Everyone weeps and says nice things about the dearly departed. La-di-frickin'-da. Instead of tears and platitudes, the scene must serve several purposes and show crucial dynamics and tensions, such as backstabbing in the family. Mine the scene's potential: Duke's favoritism or heartlessness; how Alan, a ne'er-do-well nephew, is desperate for money to cover gambling debts; and how a marriage that is teetering might be saved by an infusion of cash. Or a ghost is watching the proceedings but only the most sensitive family member, eight-year-old Allison, can feel its presence and feels freakish and isolated by this knowledge. Will Allison become hysterical or frightened? Will the other family members think she's lost her marbles? Will Alan start plotting revenge because he feels shortchanged?

Talky

I've read manuscripts in which the characters rarely talk and others in which all the characters do is talk. It's hard to weigh in on which is more annoying. Some writers have a natural gift for dialogue or simply want their characters to jabber nonstop throughout the story. So their characters chat up a storm—yadda-yadda—and move and act little. These characters often have endless phone conversations and carry a ubiquitous cell phone, often attend meetings that are filled with prolonged strategies, and most cue-card conversations are crammed with reportage rather than drama. Mix it up, keep it brief, and home in on conflict.

Fizzling and Limp Scene Endings

Some scenes don't so much end as fizzle out. This is death to a story line. Scenes need to conclude, jump, or be cut off in the midst of excitement. They snap, crackle, and pop but never fizzle, even if the character is knocked unconscious. In fact, a near-coma could be just what a scene ending needs. On this note, do not take your characters to the supermarket to paw through the apples and avocados and conclude the scene by driving home planning a dinner menu. And don't depict your character Courtney tucked in an armchair reading, wondering if her fiancé, Thad, is going to call. Instead her best friend should call from a grooving club where she's just spotted Thad dirty-dancing with another chick. Courtney, whose biological clock is ticking toward midnight, is naturally threatened by a hot chick ten years younger than her. And please avoid putting your characters to bed, because it's a snore. A large portion of scene and chapter endings must contain surprises, cliff-hangers, failures, and other devices that force the reader to turn the page.

Lusterless Love

No matter how fabulous your own love life might be, translating emotions and action into a love scene ain't easy. Some writers try to prove their bedroom cred by writing scenes that are too graphic or technical and they focus on body parts and orchestrating gymnastic sexual marathons. Or the scene is rushed and before you know it the characters are melting into puddles of sweat and belting out orgasms. Or the scene is full of clichés and euphemisms, as in heaving bosoms and thrusting members.

But the best love scenes remind readers what it's like to fall in love and tease them with emotional foreplay and tension. Lots of tension. So forget play-by-play gyrations. You're keying into emotions, not mechanics, and the lovemaking should somehow be as individual as the characters, revealing the characters' inner worlds in ways we'll never see when their clothes are on. And if possible imbue it with conflict—this doesn't mean S and M but rather warring emotions.

Same-o

I have many secret and not-so-secret agendas in writing this book—the main one to point out the differences in stories that are rejected and those that are published. Near the top of my agenda list is to stress that not all moments in storytelling are created equal. If a novel never compresses action, never summarizes, but is always written in full-blown scenes with the same emotional temperature, the story soon grows monotonous. A shopping trip, or dressing for a date, or preparing dinner takes as long as a showdown. It's as if the writer doesn't know what is important and what's not and when to explode the drama and when to putter along.

Readers appreciate stories with variety in every aspect. Some scenes need to detonate, some should be quiet; some are short, others prolonged; some will be high velocity, some exist to build and prove the veracity of the story world; some scenes make us hold our breath, some resolve a conflict.

Vacuum

I read a lot of manuscripts that pause for endless weather reports and descriptions of dry, brown grass on an August day. Then they describe a picnic table sitting on the dry, brown grass. And then someone walks along the dry, brown grass. But perhaps most often I read scenes that take place in a white, empty room or some kind of weird vacuum. These scenes give me a sense of vertigo. The big clue here is that you need visual details on every page, in every scene, especially when you want to embed the most tension.

Zombies

I'm not fond of drama queens in my life—the older I get, the more I avoid these types because they suck the chi, or life force, out of people around them. They also suck the life out of fiction stories. But worse are zombie types—and I don't mean brain eaters. I mean characters that don't feel, react, or get outraged, pissed off or scared witless when they're dumped or slandered or chased by slavering rottweilers. When you create an action scene, render sensations fully so that readers cringe at the slap in the face, taste the blood from a cut lip, hear the whimper of pain, and feel your characters' rage and frustration. No fear or appropriate feelings in the characters, no feelings in the reader.

Types of Scenes

Action Scenes

Not all scenes are action scenes—some are used to set up scenes to come, some reveal characters or explain backstory, some explain the setting, and some move characters around in the story. Action scenes satisfy a longing in the reader for something dramatic to happen. However, action and movement are not the same thing because movement is brought to a crisis in an action scene. Use action scenes to create a hook in the opening of a story, to rejuvenate it in the middle, and to culminate a story with verve at the end.

Intense action scenes are structured like an inverted pyramid. Often, but not always, the opening of action scenes is where you introduce setting details and describe the physical characteristics of those involved. This means that the writer might want to linger in the opening, giving readers the lay of the land. Sometimes this includes fairly long descriptions, sentences, and paragraphs. Then, as the pace quickens and conflict intensifies, the sentences and paragraphs become shorter and the details are trimmed to essentials.

Quick-paced scenes such as fights, brawls, battles, car chases, confrontations, threats, and escapes are whittled down to clean, precise components. It's never possible to tell all, so choose carefully the most vital elements. Your aim is to set tension at the boiling point. Besides dialogue, these scenes are the parts of fiction with the fastest pace and often where the most heated drama occurs—you're focusing on one event, and you're isolating that event. Action reveals characters stripped of their defenses and pretensions. Action, when well crafted, can reveal hidden parts and expose strengths and weaknesses.

Once the action starts rolling, home in on the characters and keep it simple. Limit adjectives, adverbs, and qualifiers. If you're writing about a fight, the words should have clout and vibrancy and replicate the quickness of arms jabbing and fists flying. Sounds need to assault the reader's senses. Keep dialogue simple, intense, and focused around the conflict.

As the action intensifies, write in shorter paragraphs, then mostly short sentences, interspersed with fragments as things heat up. Dialogue also becomes shorter as the scene reaches the climax. If you read your scenes out loud, you should be able to hear the pace increasing.

In any action scene, especially a battle scene, choose the lens the reader will see it through. Will it be panoramic? Will it include inner thoughts, close-ups, crowds? If you shift the lens view, make certain that your shift in vantage is gracefully handled. Action scenes, especially battles, are best presented in chronological order and carefully choreographed and crafted.

Then there are action scenes that are not as fast-paced. In these scenes you want a sense of buildup and release, but at times you'll want to slow things down so that readers savor the events.

Lovemaking, epiphanies, even disasters and crimes are examples of these scenes. But while the pace can vary, keep in mind that action scenes are where the excitement boils and the pulse quickens. The pleasure of reading action scenes comes from their immediacy and feeling a stake in the outcome. They are not merely a sequence of events, but the character's pain, confusion, worry, and mistakes wrapped in the midst of it all.

Set Pieces

The big scenes in fiction in which the payoffs occur are called set pieces. A set piece is a scene that has the air of the inevitable. A reader can sense its approach like the onset of a thunderstorm before clouds begin scuttling across the darkening sky. These scenes *must* occur in a novel, *must* provide that delicious sense of anticipation (either hope or dread) that keeps us turning pages. When Tom murders Dickie Greenleaf so he can assume his identity in *The Talented Mr. Ripley*; the burning of Atlanta in *Gone with the Wind*; Halloween night when Jem is attacked in *To Kill a Mockingbird*. There is that necessary and delicious sense of buildup (Scout reluctantly dons the silly costume that ultimately protects her from her attacker) and a resolution (all hell breaks loose, the war is lost, someone is murdered, the murderer is revealed or apprehended).

Thus set pieces *deliver* emotion, provide a sigh of satisfaction when the storm passes, and usually raise the stakes for at least one character. Often when a novel fails, it is because it doesn't contain these big scenes, and without them the story never quite takes flight or provides the necessary drama that readers need to stay engaged. Set pieces contain intensity, and often minor scenes are used beforehand as the setup so that the big scenes needn't be interrupted.

Knowing when your set pieces occur helps enormously with plotting. If you know that on page 130 you're going to murder Conrad and he doesn't deserve to die, then create earlier scenes where you demonstrate his decency and goodness. Show his tender qualities and establish his relationships with other cast members. Establish that Conrad's death will be a tragic loss for many, but especially for his fiancée, Anna, who had lousy luck with men before she met him. And, of course, you can use his death to motivate a character—the detective or the grieving fiancée—to hunt down the murderer. And because most events in fiction cause something else to happen, perhaps Anna or the detective underestimates the murderer and the chase will unleash more danger.

Sometimes plots veer in new directions as we write, but identifying our major scenes helps us foreshadow and build the necessary tension leading up to them. The events staged in set pieces arise from your characters' core traits, values, and motivations and reveal the conflicts they're facing. Big scenes are also where you pull out all your tools—metaphor and imagery, carefully inserted setting details, dialogue, body language, and emotion-provoking sensory information.

SEQUEL

While scenes are about conflict, goals, and excitement, the sequel or follow-up to a scene is based on feeling and logic. The sequel is the aftermath; it demonstrates cause and effect. These segments are where your character responds emotionally and intellectually to the action, and then decides on his next step, thus creating another goal. Unlike scenes, sequels are not based on conflict, although they can demonstrate relationships such as when another character is sympathetic or serves as a sounding board.

Sometimes these reactions are immediate, sometimes they do not follow right after the action—there might be another scene or two in between the scene and the sequel. In real life, when we are hit by a terrible development, our first reaction is emotional. We weep or lose our temper, are filled with sadness or rage or dismay or humiliation. But whatever the reaction, it is emotional. Before rational thoughts take over, we go through a period of raw feeling when we are incapable of rational thinking.

At some point, we stop reeling emotionally and start trying to understand what has happened. We look back on what just occurred, try to grasp why it happened and what it means. Finally we reach a new decision and settle on a goal or an appropriate or inappropriate response.

Of course, not all scenes are followed by a sequel. In thrillers there are few sequels, while romance novels require a heavy sequel-to-scene ratio. Beginning writers often leave sequels out of a manuscript so it might be helpful to realize that they serve as a bridge, providing the reflection and introspection between scenes. However, unlike simple transitions, they cause further actions and help the reader understand the future. Sequels are also vital because they are an opportunity to reveal characters' deepest struggles.

A sequel can also serve as a convenient moment to introduce a flashback if it relates to the decision or goals. Using sequels in your story helps control pacing, creates the peaks and valleys necessary so that it doesn't drag or race ahead. Sequels, like scenes, should vary in length. Too many sequels are deadly; the story will bog down. If the sequels overshadow the story, build up the scenes to balance their aftermaths. Too few sequels indicates too few consequences for the actions in the story and can make them seem implausible.

Try This

Scenes often contain emotional reversal—a character is not the same at the end of the scene as he or she was at the beginning. Write a scene that takes place after a horrific or sad event—a fire, car wreck, earthquake, tornado, riot, or funeral. Use only limited flashbacks of the event; instead focus on how the characters are living and acting in the aftermath. Remember, too, that not all catastrophes are altogether tragic; there can also be chaos, humor, pathos, and confusion.

Quick and Dirty Tips for Writing Scenes

- The best scenes suggest more to follow and accomplish more than one purpose.
- Ask your readers if your scenes make them worry.
- Vary the length and intensity of your scenes. Some should be short and brisk, others longer and more complicated.
- Scenes are often the place where characters exchange power. One character has something that another wants and must somehow coax, coerce, or steal to attain it.
- Write a story so that the tension in the scenes is

cumulative—make the events tenser and tenser, darker and darker. Reveal your character becoming more and more desperate. Cut off options and escapes.

- If you can remove a scene without changing the outcome, clarity, and mood of the story, remove it.
- Scenes usually contain some form of reversal. Thus characters or some element in the scene are altered by the end of the scene.
- Analyze your story to determine if it contains what screenwriters call a touchstone scene. If your story was a screenplay, this would likely be the scene the movie poster depicts. An example of one is from the film *The Black Stallion* when the character Alec, played by Kelly Reno, and the high-spirited Arabian stallion, both marooned on an island after a ship capsizes in a storm, gradually become friends until Alec is riding the stallion, free and joyful at the end of the scene.
- The experiences in the scene should be shared. If you write a one-person scene, somehow the ramifications of the scene need to directly impact another character.
- Emotions are the heartbeat of scenes. These should be definable, compelling, and realistic. Most scenes contain emotional reversal. For example, if the scene is about a first date, perhaps the scene starts with anticipation and ends with disappointment. Or begins with dread and ends with yearning.
- Bring out your big guns for the opening and closing scenes. Before buying a book, many readers peruse the opening scene to make certain it kicks off the story. The best closing scenes not only conclude the plot and

tie up loose ends, they also demonstrate the reversals and changes that have happened to the characters and they *linger* in the reader's memory.

- In the first three-quarters (or so) of a novel, after an intense, action-packed, or emotional scene, make certain that the characters react appropriately. There should always be a balance between scene and sequel—action and reaction. (Scenes that occur near the end necessarily have more action, less reaction.) Also, after the most intense scenes, give the reader a pause, a few moments of respite or calm.
- Avoid introducing new developments or complications in the ending scenes—this dilutes the resolution of climax.
- Avoid using too many two-character scenes. They tend to box in the story. Two-person scenes work best in short stories, so add other characters from time to time, but only those essential for the scene's mission.
- Whenever possible use scenes to reveal secrets, revelations, or information that the reader didn't anticipate knowing.
- If possible, end some scenes with the outcome in doubt. Scene endings need not be tidy and tied up with a bow. While it might suggest more action or consequences, it should not feature a drop in energy. End with a twist, a question, or a push toward the next scene.
- If the plot warrants it, change your settings from time to time. Readers appreciate a story line that switches locales because it refreshes the story.
- Sex scenes are used mostly to develop characters, shift

or deepen relationships, and reveal characters' innermost desires. Used most effectively, the sexual interlude changes the characters somehow.

- Arrange natural breaks in some scenes, if possible—for example, the arrival of another character, a phone ringing, or the characters arriving at a new location.
- Action scenes must be carefully choreographed and crafted. One way to build intensity is for the paragraphs, sentences, and dialogue to become shorter and shorter as the scene reaches the climax.
- If you stage the death of a major character, make certain that the scene is explicit and prolonged.
- Quickie scenes—suddenly dumped into the story without foreshadowing or setup—are used sparingly and inserted chiefly for shock value or to intensify conflict.
- Begin as late as possible with minimal warm-up and leave as early as possible.
- If you choose to group scenes together in a chapter, it works best if there is a connection among them. It also works best if the chapter builds to a climactic moment.

Resources

Writing the Breakout Novel and *Writing the Breakout Novel Workbook*, Donald Maass

Scene & Sequel, Jack M. Bickham

Characters, Emotion & Viewpoint, Nancy Kress

http://hollylisle.com

http://johnaugust.com

Eleven

Find the Emotion: Writing with Emotional Potency

When there are no words, a glance is enough.

—GUSTAVE FLAUBERT, *The Selected Letters*

In fiction and memoir, the writer's main responsibilities are to write a thick, juicy steak of a story, and make the readers care, that is, bring us to tears or outrage or heart-thumping worry. Stories with emotional power engage the reader's intellect, senses, and emotions as he sees and hears the unfolding action. Since reading is an intimate and involving experience, stories must probe various parts of the reader's brain.

This means writers should be aware of the emotional triggers that spark the reader's emotions and capitalize on the human need to connect. The brain and emotions are products of evolution and were programmed to respond to things that affected our ancestors thousands of years ago. We all especially respond to fear, which is triggered by hormones flooding the body, signaling that danger is present. A reader who is feeling afraid or worried is a reader who is engaged.

The basic emotions are anger, disgust, sadness, contempt, happiness, fear, and surprise, with many variations of each. Emotions flood through us at differing intensities, some lasting a long time, some over quickly. Emotions trigger increased blood flow to the brain and flicker across the face, which was probably helpful in times past to signal dangers in the jungle when hunters were chasing down dinner.

While writing, make certain that you're working with these basic emotions and their variations. These emotions are on display by characters acting, deciding, choosing, and revealing values—in other words, through their emotional lives. However, emotions are individual and are what make people so fascinating and mimes so annoying (because those caricatures of emotions created by the person in whiteface are broad strokes and exaggerations).

Emotions also help propel a story forward, but it's not easy to strike the exact balance of emotions in each scene. No emotions in the people on the page, no emotions in the reader. Melodrama on the page and you inspire indifferences in the reader.

But how do you deliver emotion without going overboard? Beginning writers often fall into the trap of overdoing with shrillness or silliness. Their characters have hair-trigger tempers and are forever howling in fury, throwing tantrums, and issuing ultimatums. On the flip side, sometimes beginners pen a sob story of misty-eyed sentiments or a way-too-cheerful and saccharine, gee-whillikers tale.

On the other hand, how do you make sure your story doesn't leave readers feeling nothing besides shades of boredom? Some stories are half-baked because readers never care, never think ahead to what might happen. There must be a middle ground, a way of engaging readers without bludgeoning them into feelings.

Since emotions are embedded in the human condition, you need to find a way to portray jealousy, betrayal, grief, misery, rage—the whole gamut of strong emotions—with nuance yet believability. Start by observing your own life and everyone around you and understanding how emotions are evoked. Also take risks—write about feelings in your memoir or in your characters that make you anxious, sad, or scared. Writing is not a safe occupation and you often need to feel what you'd rather not feel. No feelings in the writer, no feelings in the reader.

Each of us experiences a range of emotions throughout the day with ups and downs and freak-outs and moments of calm. Likewise, on the page, emotions should veer from intensity to mellowness, anxiety to bliss, sadness to joy. But, of course, not every twitch or spike in blood pressure is captivating. And a character with wildly veering emotions makes a reader uncomfortable as opposed to empathetic.

When you write stories, every act and reaction stems from your characters' emotional core. This core will predispose the character to act and react in certain ways. And as your characters respond, so do your readers.

Intensify

Writers make many difficult choices as they practice their craft, deciding what to include and what to leave out. In fact, writing is a tightrope walk of guiding the reader to an experience and yet somehow staying out of his way.

Your first job as a writer is to come up with a plot idea or the bones of your memoir and to slap that first draft into shape. Once you've finished that draft (and nobody said it would be easy), then you can look for places in the story where you can intensify the emotions and give the reader reasons to feel what the character or real people feel. Some of these moments will be no-brainers—if your character gets dumped by her boyfriend, if a beloved friend dies, if someone is betrayed. Readers can empathize with loss, grief, betrayal, rejection. Also look for the places where the character's fortunes are reversed, where he's blindsided by fate, where he's physically threatened.

Then I want you to make sure your characters' desires are apparent in your scenes because desire drives the world. Protagonists want something badly in the story as well as in individual scenes. These desires propel fiction, and readers care about characters in proportion to how well they know them and their desires. Desire can be sublime, maddening, unruly, or enlivening. Desire can be about finding a truth or knowledge. It can be a longing for freedom or a need to escape. Imagine how desire can open a can of whup ass and drive emotions to create conflict.

In genre fiction there is often a desire to solve a problem—to capture a killer or criminal, stop a criminal plot, find a treasure, or solve a mystery. In horror stories you often see characters desiring (and struggling desperately) to stop something or someone because of the danger and horror that has been unleashed. No matter the story type, desire is staged amid difficult and inescapable circumstances.

If your characters possess deep levels of desire, longing, passion, or obsession, your story will stir a deeper level of emotion in the reader. Desire always stirs up problems and dilemmas, and so is linked to conflict because the obstacles to achieving it are mighty and crazy-making. Desire can also be used to comment on human nature. When desire is inappropriate or unrealistic, you can show the consequences. Desire can be heady, motivating, dangerous, deadly. When desire is forbidden, you're creating a combustible situation.

You'll need to analyze your character's desires and understand how they drive his actions, decisions, and choices, then orchestrate the fallout from these longings. While your characters might not analyze their desires, readers will instinctively understand their driving forces. So your task as a fiction writer is to reveal where these desires stem from, their importance to the character, and then thwart these desires. A reader longs to feel what a character feels; and a character's yearning for something vital to his happiness impacts readers.

Show, Don't Tell

When it comes to displaying emotions on the page, *show, don't tell* needs to be your mantra. In too many manuscripts writers make declarations about emotions that look like this:

Katherine felt a rush of anxiety and a rush of excitement at the same time.

Alan was outraged.

Kate felt warm and secure.

To Rhonda it felt like instant chemistry.

Suddenly she felt a wave of happiness flow through her.

She was excited to be heading to San Francisco to see her friends. She was happy and relieved to see their smiling faces.

Somehow Stacey found it very soothing to see the beautiful green tree limbs swaying in the breeze through the window.

She felt like a new person.

A flood of emotions ran through Martha, mostly negative.

Naturally, Jason was astonished.

Give me a break, dear writers. Let's think about this. Say that you've created a story about a character, Jennifer Travotti, who is being stalked by a crazed parking lot attendant. The clues have been mounting, and now Jennifer is certain that a series of incidents, including a car break-in, are not a coincidence but part of a threatening pattern. The final threat comes when she returns home and discovers that her apartment has been vandalized. She stands in the doorway and looks around at the savage disarray.

Beginning writers convey her emotions like this:

> Jennifer could hardly take it in. She was sure she'd never been more afraid, more confused. Why her, why now? she wondered. What had she done to deserve this? How was she going to make it through the day when she felt so scared, so vulnerable? Where could she turn?

Unfortunately, this kind of description litters the landscape of too many stories, and *litter* is the operative word here. When words such as afraid, scared, confused, and vulnerable appear on the page, the reader is not engaged. Emotions need life, not pronouncements. Instead use action, thoughts, and body language to suggest what lies behind the feelings. Perhaps Jennifer dials 911 but her hands are shaking so much it takes her three attempts to punch in the digits. During a dramatic moment the reader needs to feel what the character feels, to sweat and quiver and sob along with her.

To convey emotions on the page, try recalling your own intense feelings and get caught up in them as you write. I hope you've never been stalked, but certainly you've been frightened—by a near-collision on the freeway, when your toddler disappeared at the mall, when you heard bad news about a friend's diagnosis. You need to borrow from those events, recalling the quaky, shaky misery in all its detail.

Emotional Needs

Desires are often linked to emotional needs—unfinished business and wounds that have come about because of the hard knocks of life. Some characters want to be loved and some want to avoid love (and often these characters exist in the same story, or sometimes these contradictory desires occur within the same character). Some characters want acceptance or power or revenge. Some crave fame or love because of a lonely childhood; some want to be left alone in obscurity.

The trick to using emotional needs is that *they force characters to act in ways that place them at risk*. For example, perhaps a character that grew up in grinding poverty needs a fat bank account and a fancy home, believing wealth is the only security life offers, and goes to any lengths to acquire them. But because the character so desperately needs outward symbols of his worth, he might use nefarious means or focus only on his goals while his heart withers, as in the case of Ebenezer Scrooge. So *desire is always linked to backstory*, and is highly individualized and fulfills the prime directive of fiction: that characters always suffer.

One last point: always reveal a character's fears that he or she won't achieve his or her heart's desire and that this failure will have huge ramifications. This is an important point: *the failure of desire must be a looming and horrible possibility*. If a character desires true love, he meets a person who is absolutely perfect for him—in fact, so fabulous that life without her seems a wasteland. But, of course, this soul mate cannot be easily won or is already in love with another. Or a character might desire a big promotion not only because he's worked hard and earned it, but he needs the money it brings for a specific reason: he has elderly parents to support, his girlfriend will respect him more, it will put to rest long-held feelings of inferiority, or it will allow him to steer the company with creativity. Such is life, but better yet, such desires drive storytelling.

So now your characters have desires and fears, and these two forces drive them into actions, decisions, and choices, which in turn lead to failure, disasters, and sometimes successes, even though their responses and emotions are more intense than your own. When a character fails to come to life on the page, it is often because the writer hasn't breathed passion and robust emotions into him or her. You see, not only do fictional characters want things more than ordinary mortals, and not only are their fears often more hideous than those that haunt our everyday reality, they also have much grander, deeper, rawer, and scarier emotions than we do. It's not that you and your family and friends don't feel these emotions—if they weren't familiar and believable, the story wouldn't seem convincing. Most of us have experienced the freaky onslaught of adrenaline after being mugged , or losing our temper when our teenager skipped school, or sleepless nights waiting for the results of a scary medical test. Because we've all had deeply emotional experiences and feared and fretted, we can slip into our characters' shoes, feeling what they feel and weeping when they weep.

Deal Breakers

Writing about emotions takes finesse and restraint, and it also requires specific techniques that bring a reader into a scene and make us believe in the character's feelings or the story actions. The key is that you're prodding your reader's imagination, not doing the work for her. Let's examine a few ways that emotions on the page are a turnoff or have zero cred.

All the World's a Stage

In some stories characters occupy the stage as if every scene demands a Shakespearean soliloquy or declaration of robust passion. In these stories characters too often rhapsodize, emote, weep with joy, moan with pleasure, and declare their hearts with too much frequency and, um, vigor.

It looks like this:

"Marta, how could you leave me at a time like this?" Ted demanded, his face frozen in disbelief.

Wiping away tears, Marta declared, "After you gave me cheap chocolates for Valentine's Day, even though I'm allergic to chocolate, I realized I was a fool to hold out hope for us."

"But you know that I cannot resist a bargain. Isn't it more important that I cannot resist you"—he gazed longingly into her tear-stained countenance—"and your abundant charms?" With this, his eyes slid meaningfully to her plunging neckline.

Marta struggled with how to convey her outrage to this otherwise god of a man. "You've been my heart, my beacon of light, my reason for living these past months. But now I fear I—"

"Don't!" he shrieked, interrupting her declaration. "Don't say you're leaving!" Her shimmering eyes and tremulous mouth gave him courage. "I'll never buy chocolates again!"

Pass the freakin' popcorn. Over-the-top sentiments wear on readers because they feel manipulated. Drama, along with *suggestion,* makes storytelling go round because readers *interpret* what's happening on the page.

After you've written your first draft, make tough choices about which places in the story to underline with intensity and passion. These are usually places where characters are in the deepest trouble or you want to surprise the reader with information or emotions he isn't expecting. Whenever possible, place the most interesting and exciting parts of the scene near the end. However, remember, too, that storytelling needs rising and falling tension, so mix up the emotional temperature throughout your story.

When most of us begin writing we still don't have the discernment to understand what parts of our stories work and what parts are flat or overblown. While building your skills, ask patient readers to let you know when the emotions feel just right, when the characters seem numb, and where the characters are braying at the readers.

Bland

We all recognize bland writing when we read it; not only does the language never soar, but our emotions are never stirred, and the writing feels more like a memo than a story. I've noticed that beginning writers tend to overlook how transitions or small moments in their stories also need to intrigue the reader and convey emotion. Bland writing looks like this: Carl and Rosalie made a wonderful day of it. They left for downtown London at one on the dot. It was incredibly beautiful weather. The sun was bright and the temperature was warm. Carl was sweet and attentive to her, but for a long while during the bus ride into town and after arriving, they didn't talk much. Then they reached the festival, which was as gay and colorful as anything she'd ever seen.

Wake me when it's over.

Your job is to sear the reader's nerve endings. Every sentence needs to pack a punch. Again and again, with language, action, vivid description, meaningful events, and crackling conflict.

Readers deserve your best work, so here are tips for making writing less bland. First, if you have problems feeling emotions when you're writing, try playing different types of music while you write to evoke feelings. If you're able to feel emotions, it's easier to write them. As the music plays, try to think like your character. When he walks into the room and discovers his girlfriend has moved out, what would he feel and how would he react? Would he pound the wall? Pop open a PBR? Slip into denial?

Then employ a few style tricks: place the most emphatic (and emotion-provoking) word at the end of sentences: morgue, dead, dread, shattered, shroud, shrieked, slithered. Also make sure that you're writing in the active voice, and every verb is vivid and active and, if possible, contains onomatopoeia, such as smash, kerplunk, crash, bash, mumble, buzz, simmer, since the *sound* of these words communicates meaning. Another simple technique is to employ comparisons, especially through figurative language. Describing a basketball player as tall is bland; describing him as a human giraffe or a skyscraper gives the reader a little jolt.

Hallmark Cards

In these scenes writers depict sentimentality, not sentiment, trying to tug at our heartstrings but often failing miserably. Sentimentality often means that there is more emotion on the page than the situation warrants. Sentiment means the writers are honestly trying to convey complex emotions so we feel what the character feels. In Hallmark Card stories, scenes are often just too much of a tearjerker, as when a character sobs over her cat that was just squashed by the neighbor's SUV. Or a mother sings a lullaby to a baby with an incurable disease or a cherubic first-grader makes a valentine for her parents. Or characters meet and it's love at first sight instead of allowing their attraction to evolve over time. Sheesh.

Wield a fine brush, not a trowel. You can move readers without resorting to corny clichés, icky sentiment, and heavy-handed goop. Without realizing it, readers provide the missing pieces as they read. They use their imaginations. And later they remember that scene as being more impassioned than it actually was—a tiny glance, a raised eyebrow, a blush, a stammer, all could indicate the most volatile emotions, the deepest secrets. Never underestimate the power of understatement.

Inconsistent

What I often spot in manuscripts, but the writer has failed to see, is that characters come off as inconsistent or weirdly schizoid in their emotional responses. Intelligent characters fall apart with little pressure; high-strung characters are sometimes calm and clearheaded, sometimes so hysterical they can scarcely breathe; or a bitter cynic suddenly starts bestowing cheer and goodwill.

A character's beliefs, disposition, and personal philosophy create his attitudes and approach to life. Characters, like people, approach life with a sunny or sour disposition, and with many shades in between. A specific outlook can be cynical, realistic, pragmatic, prone to depression, or prone to blaming others. Your sunny character smiles and jokes a lot, and will likely be empathetic and calm. On the other hand, a dour or unhappy person might be curt or disapproving or condescending. Some people don't have great access to their emotions or it takes a loss or tragedy for them to feel at all. You need to decide on your character's basic personality and approach to life, then shape emotions within that framework.

In life people are inconsistent and unreliable. In fiction the *intensity*, *consistency*, and *authenticity* of the emotions are in sync with a character's background and traits.

Introspective

I know I've bitched about this before, but if a story takes place mostly inside a character's head, I quickly lose interest and cannot feel a thing. Using a lot of introspection is simply a cop-out. If your stories contain a large proportion of introspection, trim these segments in the final drafts. Readers become annoyed with a running commentary that goes on and on because it's simply too static. Stories in which characters spend a lot of time alone thinking become boxed in and lack conflict. *Flavor* stories with inner thoughts, but do not make them main ingredients.

Introspection is best used to convey motivation and a character's emotional state. His opinions about world affairs, or his neighbor's garden, doesn't interest readers. However, if you find you must delve inside your character's head at important moments, then ask yourself what emotions you want to convey. Are you showing your character's confusion, wonder, excitement? Is he or she responding to a major event, threat, or reversal, or just hanging around pondering his or her fate?

But most of the time, push your character out into the world and into the path of conflict.

Man-Child and Other Types That Leave the Reader Cold

Sometimes characters are so ill contrived, cardboard, or just plain wrong for the role they're playing in the story that they leave readers cold. Over years of working on manuscripts I've met lots of characters that didn't inspire any emotions in me besides despair—tough guys who were killing machines, women too dumb and masochistic to grow a spine, and plucky child geniuses. A few types are especially annoying—females that seem to have emerged from an eighteenth-century drawing room, complete with a case of the vapors and a tendency for frequent hysteria, and the man-child.

There are two subtypes of man-child. The first type jokes constantly about getting laid, shucking and jiving and carrying on as though he thinks only with his penis. Or he's the slacker type who is somehow supposed to be compelling although he is married to his bong, or spends his life playing video games in the dark or role-playing with other lonely sorts online. If the character is sixteen, these behaviors might be understandable, but most often these characters are in their thirties or forties and are trying to avoid intimacy and responsibility.

The second kind is a tough guy who jokes too much about wanting to kill people or swashbuckles through the story, often raging inappropriately as if suffering from testosterone poisoning. And stranger still is when writers depict both types as chick magnets, despite all evidence that he's a hormonal swamp of libido and childish instincts. I'm harping about the man-child type here because male writers who create them seem to think they're bewitching and deep and macho, but readers just cannot connect with them.

Sameness

In many of the memos I've sent to clients I've suggested that they strive for more variety and nuanced emotions. Typically characters react to every setback or crisis with tears or anger or lashing out. This quickly becomes boring. A wider range of emotions and reactions lends the ring of truth to stories. The longer the story, the more important this becomes.

Find eccentric or specialized ways people or characters can reveal emotions. Some people giggle when nervous, some pace, some lash out, some reach for potato chips. Remember, too, that emotions vary in intensity and have steps or stages. Most of us cannot stomp on the gas pedal and accelerate from zero to eighty mph when we hop in our cars, but we often feature story people who react as if this happens and at the smallest trigger erupt into over-the-top reactions. Emotions are also often a blend of several feelings. For example, grief is often tied in with guilt, rage, and feelings of helplessness.

Going for the Jugular

Writing about passionate or strong emotions is not easy. You want the person on the page to exhibit rage or heartbreak or regret but somehow they sound shrill, or there is jumping conflict, or it just doesn't ring true.

When the scene comes off as shrill, often characters are screaming bizarre threats or pleas or weirdness like, "I've always loved you but now I hate you."

In the case of jumping conflict, emotions skyrocket with little provocation. For example, a couple has an argument about which video to watch on Friday night and he screams, "You're a pain in the ass. Just get the hell out of my life!" She starts sobbing inconsolably because how can he call her names and threaten her just because she wants to watch a Julia Roberts flick? Someone pass a hankie.

A few suggestions might help you with this problem. First, make sure that the trigger for the emotion is appropriate. If your character is going postal over a video choice or a kid stepping in her flower bed, well, he or she just might be too high-strung. Second, make a list of all the ways your main characters might respond to events, especially a crisis in the story. This means you know your characters from the inside out—in a crisis will he be stoic, reserved, hot-tempered, or icy? Third, move your character through the *steps* of an emotion—after all, if all your characters are human cloudbursts, readers will lose trust in the story. So before a character becomes terrified, he might first be apprehensive, anxious, or panicky.

Finally, you need to make decisions about the emotional feel or tone of the story. While tone changes within a longer work such as a novel or memoir, generally there is an overall tone that pervades: creepiness, silliness, romance, terror, or the like. If you understand the larger effect you're trying to achieve, then displaying emotions in individual scenes becomes easier. You can also use subplots—such as a budding romance between married coworkers or a parent trying to cope with a rebellious teen—to highlight emotional intensity. After all, it is the people closest to us—our kids, lovers, parents—who push our buttons, so these moments can feature emotional fireworks to provide variety and heat in the story.

Try This

Stage a character looking out the window of a plane, train, kitchen, or high-rise. The character has just received some terrible news. Now write the scene but don't mention the bad news explicitly. The idea is to use meaningful details to bring the character's emotions into focus.

Quick and Dirty Tips for Creating Emotions

- Analyze how your favorite authors convey emotions, along with emotions on display in plays and films.
- Avoid using obvious imagery, like birds chirping when characters are happy and dark clouds threatening when characters are sad.
- Consider using a character's name to hint at his or her personality traits. For example, Richard Stark has a much different connotation than Richard Blossom. Ditto for Amanda Lovelace and Amanda Steele.
- The deepest or strongest emotions are the most difficult to render realistically so take the most care with them.
- Rendering emotions accurately requires that we write from experience, particularly recalling the moments of our worst humiliation, sorrow, and pain. If you cringe at the memory of a certain incident, all the better—find those emotions and explore them on the page.
- Much of nonverbal communication is conveyed in the face, so pay attention to facial expressions around you.
- Always know what your characters fear the most. Is it illness, poverty, loss of love, death? Is the fear rational? How do they avoid their fears? What will they do anything to avoid?
- Readers want to note *changes* in story people as they

move through their character arcs; these changes are signaled by emotions.

- Readers want to see emotions depicted in action and dialogue, but also in *subtext:* the subterranean river of emotions that exists beneath things. Remember that what is left unsaid is often more potent than what is expressed, and that subtext can also create a layer of symbolism and meaning in any story or scene.
- Emotions must build over the course of the story. Make certain the major scenes and the ending pack the biggest emotional wallop.
- Show a range of emotions. A variety of emotions lends the ring of authenticity to your story. The longer the story, the more important this becomes.
- Make the emotions significant and motivating. Greed, love, hate, jealousy, and, guilt cause things to happen.
- Writing advice from fiction author Antonya Nelson: "Feeling uncomfortable is a good thing. It means you are touching something raw and honest that has to do with feeling shame or inhibition."
- Give your characters emotional choices and have them regret these choices at times. Not taking action is also a choice with consequences.
- Show characters in a scene feeling contrasting emotions—one person can be upset in a scene while another is nonplussed.
- Use setting to underline the emotions of a scene. The natural world with its fog, wind, dusky gloom, and rain can be used effectively to stir feelings.

- Fictional characters often express surprising emotional reactions that we would not dare. And let's not forget their emotions are sometimes inappropriate and they simply make lots of mistakes and misjudgments. They are like your friend who blurts out the distressingly wrong sentiment at the funeral, the dreadful faux pas during the wedding toast after gulping down too much champagne, and giggling at the reading of the will. In life we've all known people who are not quite housebroken, who more often than not have their foot inserted firmly in their mouth.
- If you're writing fiction, be patient with the process. As in real life, it takes time to get to know a person and understand his emotional core.

Resources

Creating Character Emotions, Ann Hood

Characters, Emotions, & Viewpoint: Techniques for Crafting Dynamic Characters and Effective Emotions, Nancy Kress

The Art of Subtext: Beyond Plot, Charles Baxter

Creating Characters with Personality, Tom Bancroft

Creating Characters: A Writer's Reference to Personality Traits That Bring Fictional People to Life, Howard Lauther

Twelve

Tragedy Doesn't Equal Memoir: Writing Life Stories That Readers Cannot Put Down

> In most lives insight has been accidental. We wait for it as primitive man awaited lightning for a fire. But making mental connections is our most crucial learning tool, the essence of human intelligence; to forge links; to go beyond the given; to see patterns, relationship, context.
>
> —MARILYN FERGUSON, *The Aquarian Conspiracy*

I love going for walks at dusk, not only because it's a great way to unwind from the day, but also because marine air whooshes in from the Pacific and the sky turns into a vast, multihued Impressionist canvas. But I also have a not-so-secret motive for walking around the neighborhood at dusk: it's when my neighbors turn on their lights and I can peer into their homes as I stroll past. These lamp-lit scenarios depict the small vignettes of everyday life—a woman at the kitchen sink, a father pacing with a crying baby, a kid huddled over his homework, another playing a piano. The snoop in me loves these moments, and I sometimes make up little stories about the people I'm spying on, but mostly I feel strangely calmed by these glimpses of humanity.

Most of us are curious about other lives, and one of the best ways to satisfy our curiosity is in the pages of a well-written memoir. The interest in memoirs is fueled by many factors. We live in a world so complicated, uneasy, and rapidly changing that people have a special need to testify and reveal their experiences. Most important, memoirs have inherent drama because they are about true events. Breakout memoirs, such as *Angela's Ashes,* by Frank McCourt, and *The Liars' Club,* by Mary Karr, which were published more than a decade ago, paved the way and proved that memoirs can equal huge sales figures. Nonfiction best sellers like *The Perfect Storm* and *Into Thin Air* have also sparked interest in real lives. There is also a continued fascination with reality television and talk shows, with viewers hoping for but not always finding truths about humanity.

Recent megasellers like Elizabeth Gilbert's *Eat, Pray, Love* are also spurring the growth of this genre, and reading memoirs provides the ultimate comfort—if you're reading about the writer's troubles or dysfunctional family, it makes your troubles or family dynamics bearable. And memoir remains a viable opportunity for young and first-time writers. From a publisher's viewpoint, they're also fairly cheap to produce, since the advance for them is fairly modest unless you're a celebrity like Tina Fey or Laura Bush.

Often when I'm working on a memoir manuscript I do so with soul-sucking trepidation. I'm always afraid of what I'll find in the pages, and if I'll need to shatter the writer's ego, sense of self, or cherished view of reality. I'm afraid to tell the writer that her whacked-out family isn't particularly interesting and that, in fact, after reading about her losses and betrayals, I was mostly annoyed rather than sympathetic. While sometimes the writer has lived through genuinely fascinating events and circumstances, most people's lives, while they contain drama, don't necessarily guarantee a captivating tale.

And then there are large issues about the publishing landscape for memoirs that need sorting through. The memoir genre has been tarnished in recent years by bold lies and liars, but these scandals about authenticity haven't dimmed the public's interest or publishers' willingness to bring these stories to print.

But since memoirs have become such a controversial form, I'm always concerned about the veracity of events and viewpoints. After all, a number of writers have been busted for claiming fabricated, tempestuous lives that never happened or magnifying events so they look like badasses. Or they glue a happy ending on a tragedy, such as the man who wrote the fake account of meeting his wife while incarcerated in a German concentration camp. So I always approach memoirs with a bit of skepticism—I'd be naïve not to. We can cut through these brazen stunts with a simple reality check: memoir is the truth as best you know it.

What Makes a Memoir

So what is a memoir? It's always autobiographical writing about real events and people, but it is not an autobiography. The writing is artful and it's based on themes and as such focuses on influential moments in the writer's past. Memoirs typically spotlight a brief period of time or events. For example, Elizabeth McCracken's memoir *An Exact Replica of a Figment of My Imagination* focuses on a pregnancy, the birth of a stillborn baby, and the months of grieving following this birth.

Writing a publishable memoir requires top-notch writing skills, along with restraint, reflection, and analysis. The story in a memoir is as complicated and layered as a novel, creates a strong sense of place, and brings history alive. While a memoir tells a story, it lifts the story of lives beyond mere reporting. So memoir uses storytelling techniques borrowed from fiction writing: setting, character development, plot, dialogue, conflict, foreshadowing and flashbacks, imagery, and figurative language. Thus the story has a shape or structure and isn't a mere list of facts. The writer then stirs in his understanding or search for meaning in the events as seen in retrospect. *A compelling drive to make sense of events and memories drives memoir, as does the need to share truths and experiences.* In a memoir important questions are asked and answered about what it means to be human, to be alive, and to have survived a crisis. Finally, the subject of a memoir does not need to be glamorous to be fascinating.

Memoir writing requires what author Judith Barrington says is a unique blend of truth and art. But this is where things get tricky. In a memoir you can reorder events to make the whole more dramatic, and you can also approximate dialogue when you cannot recall every word spoken. After all, most of us don't go through life with a tape recorder in tow. You can also leave out details that complicate the story or make it dull. So although you can take liberties with some of the data, at its heart the story must capture the emotional truths and the essence of the interactions among the players. Memoirs aren't designed to report; they are about the writer mulling over and making sense of his or her world. Quite often these truths are painful, strange, or embarrassing.

Deal Breakers

Readers read memoirs to observe the shape of a life, uncover themes and meaning, and find directions in their own lives. The best memoirs transform our memories into what life means. Here are some ways that memoirs go astray.

Borg

I call this category of memoirs the Borg because these stories contain about as much originality, thoughtfulness, and depth as the cyborg freaks known as the Borg in the *Star Trek* series. In case you're not familiar with the Borg, they operate with a kind of hive mind where everyone who comes into contact with them is assimilated. The Borg stifles individual voices, and those assimilated become drones, working in concert for the survival of the hive.

In Borg-type memoirs the writer hasn't stepped outside the reality of his hometown, family values, cultural milieu, or religious upbringing to question, wonder, or, in fact, display any curiosity about what shaped him or her as a person or a writer. Typically the writer never questions the world around him, never thinks deeply about issues that would give most writers ulcers, and never arrives at any meaningful conclusions. A person writing a memoir needs to arrive at a fresh understanding of his past.

In a Borg-type memoir this doesn't happen, and the story has no depth, no themes, no wonder, and little meaning for people beyond the writer's circle.

In the *Star Trek* series the Borg are dangerous and feared because they erase a person's identity. But a Borg-type memoir lacks the dangerous moments of life because the writer doesn't understand that memoirs require drama and thinking deeply about the past, so the results are about as exciting as a trip to Kinko's. When I read a memoir, no matter if it's comedic or kitschy, I'm longing for a brilliant, layered story, heavy with insights, that pauses for thoughtful and life-changing moments and is woven with weighty images.

Mommy Dearest

One of the most loathsome memoirs I ever worked on was written by a woman who hated and blamed her mother with such relentless vehemence that while reading it, squirming the whole time, I would have preferred being eaten alive by mountain gorillas. You think I jest.

In this woe-is-me tale, the mother, the first female firefighter in Los Angeles, was always the Cruella De Vil of her childhood, while the writer was the innocent, fabulous wunderkind. But anyone with a smidgeon of common sense could read between the lines and discover that while the mother was far from perfect, the daughter's demonizing her was so over the top that the writer came off as pitiful and repugnant. And adding to the bizarreness of this sad tale, the writer merrily billed the memoir as lighthearted and humorous, although it was about as funny as a colonoscopy.

She also billed it as hopeful and suggested she was a role model for how to survive a childhood of abuse. That was like saying that the characters in *Pulp Fiction* are role models for sensitivity and restraint. In fact, the memoir was a deliberate attempt to inflict hurt and humiliation on a number of people. Just one example to make my point: the writer never referred to her mother as Mother, Mom, or by name, but instead called her "bitchface." Need I say more? Well, let me say a few more things. The story was also full of mean comments about her mother's appearance, clothing, and personal habits—all designed to embarrass her and paint the writer as superior.

Cruelty is not humor. The story also failed to delve into her relationship with her father, which to me seemed like the real story. Often writers of mommy dearest memoirs have such an ax to grind that they cannot see the reality right in front of them. If you're this creepily bitter and wounded, get your sad ass into therapy, *then* write the memoir. About ten years later.

Happy-Go-Lucky

When I hear from clients who are writing happy memoirs my heart always sinks a little. These memoirs can be as problematic as those written out of anger and revenge. Many of these clients are seniors and have no idea that drama stems from conflict. Now, there are some published memoirs that are lighthearted and comedic, but often there is an underlying edge or pathos to this humor. But the trouble is, most of the happy-go-lucky writers I encounter never bothered to read them.

Instead, they chirp along writing about gathering eggs at their grandparents' farm, trips to the big city, lemonade on the back porch, and their first kiss or marrying their high school sweetheart. They tend to be myopic and don't realize that nostalgia and sentimentality do not a memoir make. I often suggest that they read Homer Hickam's *Rocket Boys,* which the film *October Sky* is based on, about how the author grew up in a coal mining town and became a NASA engineer. It is a feel-good story because it is about determination and the human spirit. However, it is etched in conflict with his father, his refusal to submit to his destiny to become a coal miner, his bumpy road to winning a science fair that was his ticket to freedom, and how a mining town in West Virginia was dying. It also paints a compelling tapestry of living near a mine with its constant whistles and crises, a place where everyone is controlled by the mining company.

Journal Entries

Far too many writers believe they can transform their journal entries into publishable memoirs. This might have worked for May Sarton, but for most of us, our journals do not a story make. The ones I've read are particularly disappointing, because not only are they never written in scenes, they describe situations and don't tell a story. Instead, they are chronological yet random collections of data and memories and typically don't bring the other players in the story to life. There are often large gaps in a journal so it doesn't make sense to use it as your structure. But most writers haven't gone the extra step to analyze their younger self and draw fresh insights from their own history. A journal is a way to capture life's main events and emotions. A memoir is a much richer tapestry and includes impressions and re-creations of events and the gist of conversations, if not the precise language.

Missed Opportunities

Two manuscripts come to mind in this category. The first was written by an older man who grew up in Colorado in a middle-class family. He served in World War II and was at the Battle of the Bulge. However, instead of talking about how one of the most important battles in military history affected him, he commented offhandedly about seeing his first dead body. Then he went on to write chapters about his career in public relations, never reflecting on the influences in his life or a past era, never striving for potency and relevancy, which was a distinctly lost opportunity. The structure and approach was also autobiographical, anecdotal, and chronological, rather than memoir. A memoir is a search for the truth, especially emotional truth. Memoirs always have a shape; they are not scrapbooks or merely a list of facts or anecdotes, and they do not attempt to tell most incidents from birth to death.

The second manuscript that featured a missed opportunity was written by a man who ended up in a psych ward after having a schizophrenic breakdown when he was fifteen. While there were lots of interesting details leading up to his breakdown, it covered all sorts of mundane events such as his job as a busboy in a restaurant, his garage band, his ongoing rivalry with his sister, and his bitterness that his mental illness robbed him of his true calling—to be a jazz saxophonist. Why his illness robbed him was never explained.

However, I didn't give a darn about his busboy duties or that he didn't like his sister; I wanted to hang out in that psych ward. I wanted an intimate and up-close experience. I wanted to smell the place and eat the food and feel what it felt like to be locked up without a chance to escape. Because even on my crankiest days, when I feel like smacking someone, I know I'll never hit anyone (unless attacked by a mugger) and I'll never end up in a psych ward. So I want to travel there via someone else's experiences, and when the most interesting thing that happened to a person is not given its emotional and dramatic weight, I feel cheated. Stories are where human dramas take place.

Narcissist or Diva

Let's face it, there's a narcissist lurking in many writers—after all, if we were modest sorts we would use our word smarts to play Scrabble, not write books. The worst narcissist I ever worked with had modest success in the high-tech industry. But she, like many people, wanted to write about her horrible childhood, how downtrodden and misunderstood she was, the cruelty of nuns in her grade school, her evil father, and how she suffered through the most impoverished and torturous childhood in human history. What she missed in self-pitying missive was that she grew up in an extended Sicilian family that spent Sunday afternoons out in the country feasting, that she lived in an immigrant community, and that she was surrounded by the Mafia and an eccentric cast of characters. But she had no interest in their activities or in the rich culture around her.

Her stories included diatribes against any family member who had ever slighted her and focused venom on her son, who doesn't want to spend time with her. But despite obscuring reality, anyone able to tie her own shoes could see that this woman was so self-absorbed and held such a grandiose opinion of herself that it was just plain sad. When I met her for a (stomach-churning) conference, my impression was of her raging vanity and that she was the world's largest toddler. Bathed in tears of self-importance, she was flabbergasted when I tried to explain that her so-called memoir was far too focused on her interpretation of events, rather than on seeing the whole picture.

My impression of her was verified when she sent me a crazed six-page, single-spaced rant that outlined how brilliant she was and how inept I was. Her most fascinating accusation was that I didn't know the meaning of pain. Trouble was, after reading her tear-stained pages of prattle and self-importance, I knew pain all too well.

What Happens in Vegas Stays in Vegas

This problem is similar to missed opportunities. In these manuscripts the crucial family dynamic, such as sexual abuse, addiction, or mental illness, is glossed over or avoided. In one such story a woman wrote about growing up in a large Latino family. The story focused on her culture and the meals the family shared. But the five-hundred-pound gorilla in the corner was that her father was a brutal and violent alcoholic and his shadow lingered over every aspect of her family's lives.

Another writer wrote about her mother dying young from a tragic disease, but she was only seeing her mother through the gooey veil of childhood nostalgia. In this version her mother was a cookie-baking, party-throwing, loving goddess. But again, reading between the lines, her mother was also haunted by demons and suffered from terrible bouts of depression when she became nearly catatonic and locked herself in her bedroom for days. These events were the hidden keys to the story, and the writer avoided taking the reader to a deeper level and portraying her mother as a complicated person.

Another writer penned a memoir about the heartbreak of infertility, but skirted around key facts. It seemed that she harbored a lot of guilt about contracting STDs and worried that they'd contributed to her infertility, but she never explored those feelings. Instead, she dropped in the STDs and her sexual history in passing and seemed ambivalent about the details. If you're going to drop these sort of bombshells, they need explanations and a clear read on your feelings and regrets about your past.

Go for the gusto, people, or stick to Scrabble.

When Memory Calls Your Name

In the opening of *This Boy's Life,* memoirist and fiction writer Tobias Wolff writes: "This is a book of memory, and memory has its own story to tell." Memory always tugs at a writer and makes demands to be heard. Memory whispers of the past, yet spans two worlds—our feelings from our past and our perceptions based on now.

Memories have an insistent power; they demand to be heard, demand that we trace their shape, make sense of things. These memories are gold mines of images, events, people, and places. In these moments and images the power of detail, sensory information, and truth emerge to create a compelling narrative. Many memories hold emotion and naturally belong on the page, where these keenly felt events can be sorted through. And it is in this sorting process that the emotions from the past and the ones surfacing in the now meld into a powerful rendering of life.

There are many reasons why a writer should mine the past. In looking back, we discover and relive our childhood or young adulthood, and often those explorations invite surprise and wonder. The meaning of our lives resides in these memories; we connect to our younger self and to the world as it existed in earlier decades. Our memories hold a laser-like focus, an intensity and clarity that we can apply to our writing. For writers, remembrance, the tracking of your younger self, can unleash your natural voice and excavate truth, meaning, and imagination.

But sometimes we need a means of excavating those long-held stories, a way to track down those treasures, the jewels that hide in the dark recesses of memory. You cannot merely wander from forgetfulness to remembrance, or stumble onto the treasures of the past; you need tools to mine it.

When you track your memory, you're hunting the stuff of real life, the grit and sorrow, along with the laughter and good times. Whenever you're prompting or reviewing memories, approach the past with an open and questioning mind. Dust off the memory, but then examine all sides of it, using the lamplight of adult knowledge. Remove the filters and notice the emotions that arise from memory.

Search for the intricate connection of memory. If a memory slips in unbidden during the day, track its source. What were you doing or thinking when the memory came to light? In writing from memory, be selective. It's impossible to write about every event from birth to death. Choose significant moments, narrow your time frame.

Memory is a slippery thing. A distant scene will appear unbidden; a tragedy will refuse to leave our consciousness. We are sometimes haunted by our past and sometimes able to step into a distant time to relish life again. When mining the past, ask yourself what it means. So often we don't understand ourselves, our families, our tragedies until long after events unfold. So often we spend our lives puzzling, teasing over the meaning of things. While hunting down the past, don't overlook the gems found in the ordinary and everyday. Anna Quindlen once wrote that life is found in washing the dishes.

Getting Started

One helpful method for remembering is to create memory maps. The first map you'll draw is a floor plan of your childhood home, including the yard. The trick is to focus on details such as important pieces of furniture or architectural details. Sketch in the yard, including the lilac bush and towering maple, the flower garden, the swing set, doghouse, arbor, and hammock. Another tip for this technique is to use crayons—the waxy smell and familiar heft of a crayon will invoke the past.

Next, create a map of your immediate neighborhood. This map should be at least one square block, but, of course, you might want to extend the scope. On this map again create as many details as possible—the house where the neighborhood grouch lived, the tree house or hiding places, the businesses and landmarks. Include the names of neighbors who lived in surrounding houses, add street names, creeks, parks, playgrounds, shops, and restaurants.

Along with your neighborhood map, number a page one through ten. Now return to the map and recall ten events or memories that occurred in the neighborhood: the street corner where you played kick-the-can, the porch where you received your first kiss, the tree you fell out of and broke your arm.

If, like many of us, you've moved from your hometown, return to track your younger self. Look around and find the past, even when modernity encroaches on your memories.

Try following Frank McCourt's advice and create intricate lists designed to jog memory: write down the names of your third-grade classmates, all your teachers, your neighbors, street names, pets, cousins and shirttail relatives, and friends from different eras. Make lists of artifacts—favorite toys, books, clothes you loved over the years. Write about smells—riff on lavender beds, cinnamon-infused kitchens, the smells of the state fair.

Write about forbidden family topics—the shameful events or secrets that were never told or rarely whispered about. Write about conversations that you recall from your past. Write about the lies someone told to hide the truth. Write about your less-than-stellar moments—the times you acted like a fool but should have known better. Write about the times you were not proud of yourself.

Create a memory box stuffed with tokens of the past—ticket stubs, postcards, souvenirs, photos, letters. Spend time sorting through and touching these objects. Sift through old photographs and memorabilia—old report cards, childhood journals. Wear your childhood charm bracelet or old baseball mitt.

Take walks—research has shown that the left-right movement of your feet against the pavement stimulates memory and creativity. Page through old *Life, Look,* and *National Geographic* magazines from the era you're interested in. Watch movies set in the era you're interested in, listen to the era's music and review timeline books. Create your own timeline. In one column list your personal milestones from a particular decade; in the second column, list what was happening in the greater world.

Interview family members about their memories. Remember rituals and holidays and a specific day or evening. When you were a kid, what were Sunday nights like? Remember and play again the board games from your childhood—Monopoly, Clue, checkers. Recall the routes you traveled to school, to your best friend's house, to your grandparents' house. Write about "first times." The first time you wore a formal gown or tux, the first time you left home, the first time you attended a funeral. Reread some of your favorite childhood books.

Look around—reminders are everywhere. In memory's eye, you'll discover a source code for writing that you can use again and again.

Try This

To help you think about the meaning behind your memories, here are a series of prompts:

I was a girl/boy who worried about ___________________.

I grew up to realize ___________________.

The code of silence that enveloped my childhood meant that I learned (or never realized) that ___________________.

My family never talks about ____________________.

I have always wondered why my mother/father never ____________________.

When I was a girl/boy, I wanted to grow up to be ____________________.

When I was a girl/boy, I thought I was different from everyone else because ____________________.

When I was a girl/boy, I never understood why our family ____________________.

Quick and Dirty Tips for Writing a Memoir

- Ask yourself why you're writing—to discover the truth, to leave a legacy, to remember, to understand what happened to you? No matter the reason, analysis is required.
- A memoir has enough depth and information to create sixty thousand to eighty thousand words.
- Keep asking yourself what your memories mean.
- Linger, don't rush. You need time to mull over meanings and themes and to excavate memories.
- Read a variety of memoirs, noting especially structure and voice.
- Use lots of props and artifacts: letters, diaries, obituaries, photos, newspaper articles, etc.
- You might just not be as much of an expert on your own life story as you think, so interview people who were there to double-check your facts and dates.

- Memoir doesn't necessarily start at the beginning, but rather at a point where a question can be raised or intrigue created via a provocative opening.
- Like fiction, memoir is based on a structure that builds to a peak or climax, then descends. The climactic moment delivers emotional intensity and sometimes resolution.
- Create a timeline of the most important events of your life.
- Analyze your life to find connecting and recurring themes.
- Never invent facts, people, or events. The truth is too important to tamper with.
- Organize your material in a logical order, preferring dramatic to chronological.
- Use a structure that is easy to follow and look for patterns in your life that might suggest a structure.
- Populate your memoir with the care of a fiction writer, including physical descriptions and backstories for your cast.
- Avoid psychoanalyzing people unless this is your field of expertise.
- Avoid composites unless you're using them to avoid libel charges or the emotional fallout for the persons involved would be too great.
- Take care with crafting dialogue. Since most of us have not recorded real-life events, you'll be forced to recreate long-ago conversations. Do so with a strict adherence to accuracy.

- Write for others, not yourself, hoping to enrich your readers' lives with your insights.
- Write in a voice that is distinctive and in harmony with your roots.
- Ask other people from your past about *their* memories of your experiences.
- Take care with what you leave out—since memoir is not autobiography, what you leave out will be greater than what you include. However, take care that these omissions are not designed to slant the memoir in a specific direction.
- Don't write to show yourself in the most positive light.
- If the piece is emotionally difficult to write, allow it to cool between drafts.
- Use suspense techniques—delays and withholding information and tension, a sort of word-by-word force field—to compel readers to turn pages.
- Anchor a memoir with tangible objects from the past.
- Allow the reader to conjure up feelings of empathy without trying to solicit them.
- Work hard to sort out the interesting from the dull, the melodramatic from the dramatic.
- Strive to interpret the information and draw conclusions. However, when doing so, don't lecture; rather, elevate a life story beyond a report.
- Look for settings, dramatic world events, and personal crises that reveal people at their most elemental, when people are defined and changed.

- Make certain that the era when the events took place is also revealed and brought to life.
- Create character biographies of the main people in your life story.

Resources

Read widely—Frank McCourt's *Angela's Ashes; The Liars' Club,* by Mary Karr; *This Boy's Life,* by Tobias Wolff; *The Glass Castle*, by Jeannette Wells; *Don't Let's Go to the Dogs Tonight,* by Alexandra Fuller; *Are You Somebody?,* by Nuala O'Faolain; *The Tender Bar*, by J. R. Moehringer.

Finding Your Voice, Telling Your Story, Carol LaChapelle

Writing the Memoir, From Truth to Art, Judith Barrington

Inventing the Truth: The Art and Craft of Memoir, William Zinsser

Living to Tell the Tale: A Guide to Writing Memoir, Jane Taylor McDonnell

Thirteen

The Final Edit: Fixing Your Manuscript without Losing It

The conscious mind is the editor, and the subconscious mind is the writer. And the joy of writing, when you're writing from your subconscious, is beautiful—it's thrilling. When you're editing, which is your conscious mind, it's like torture.

—STEVE MARTIN, *The New York Times,* August 8, 1998

Revising a manuscript is a huge and often scary undertaking; in fact, it's such a gargantuan task, it probably makes you wonder whatever possessed you to write a story in the first place. Every writer has his or her own method of revision. For some writers, their system works great, but if my e-mail inbox is any indication, many run into problems with revising. Which really sucks because the true job of fiction and memoir writing lies in rewriting.

So in this chapter I'm going to pass along some methods and checklists to help you revise without losing it. Let's start here: the purpose of your first draft is to cling pitifully to life until you have the time, stamina, and insight to revise (or revive) it into a respectful rendition of itself.

While everyone has their own writing process, over the years of meeting and working with thousands of writers, I've noticed that people who write a first draft as fast as possible often have the most success. If you're a writer who tinkers endlessly with each sentence or fine-tunes every paragraph before you move on to the next one, your fresh and exciting idea often withers as you rewrite endlessly. Instead, begin each day's writing session by editing briefly what you wrote the previous day. You'll be fixing typos and small errors as you go along, but don't get bogged down in fix-it mode.

This also means you'll bypass the normal anxiety most of us feel when we sit down to write, and your first draft will actually resemble a second, fairly polished draft. Author Dennis Lehane has another approach. He writes his first draft longhand during the day and then transcribes the pages onto his computer each night, editing as he goes, so he ends up with a polished first draft without bogging down in constant rewrites.

The Steps of Revision

Here's an easy way to understand the revision process: Write the first draft. Age the manuscript a bit. Read the manuscript. Find the major mistakes, especially the big plot holes and places where the structure fails. Correct the mistakes to improve the story. Read the manuscript again and fine-tune the pacing and individual scenes. Finally, tighten and enhance the style. This means you'll be taking a strategic, practical approach and working from large to small.

Let's talk about reading that early draft. Many authors,

including Stephen King, who writes at such a maddening pace that his output leaves the rest of us mortals in the dust, insist that you need to take a break from your finished draft. If possible, leave the manuscript alone for at least two weeks, but probably not more than two months. This is because it is best to revise after you've achieved some psychic and emotional distance from the original draft.

Once time has elapsed, print out a copy of your manuscript—but print it in a font different from the one you wrote it in. I write early drafts in Comic or Trebuchet because they're friendly, and then switch to Times New Roman, which seems more official. This little trick helps you see the whole through new eyes and you'll catch more errors and typos.

It's especially important to work with a hard copy (ideally double-spaced so there is room for corrections). There are many mistakes you won't notice when reading it on a computer screen because you'll be habituated to ignore them and because scrolling through all those pages is hard on the eyeballs. You also want to view your work as an editor or agent will see it. And you want a document that lies corpse-like on the white page, its flaws revealed before you. If your story idea is solid, this draft will provide a decent foundation for your next draft. If your idea is half-formed, well then, pray it doesn't croak before resuscitation begins.

Next, set aside at least a few days to read through your draft. If possible, leave home—go far from your computer and normal work space. If you cannot leave town, move to another room, a friend's office, or a coffee shop. This, too, gives you editorial distance. It's also helpful to be in a location where you can go for long walks while you ponder whether your story is working or needs mouth-to-mouth. If you're lucky enough to be at a beach or a mountain cabin, bring along music, keep your coffee mug or teacup full, and turn off your cell phone or do whatever necessary to avoid distractions.

Read your completed draft when you're optimistic, sober, and alert. Reading it while you're tired, tipsy, hungover, or certain that the gods are mocking your paltry efforts is a recipe for doom.

Bring along a number of highlighter markers, colored pens, and notebooks and mark up your margins, take notes, track your thoughts. You may or may not choose to mark and make notes on the manuscript pages as you go along—some folks prefer to read it through before the red slashes appear on the pages. I can scarcely bear to read anything without a red pen in hand, but recently I received an e-mail from a student calling me a sadist. And she likes me. As you read and begin making notes on this draft, you're asking yourself some cold, sobering questions and you're tracking down consistency problems.

Project Bible

Based on these many hours bent over these corpses—uh, manuscripts—I've noticed that many writers need a better method to organize their materials. So as you read, if you haven't done so already, compile some kind of "bible" that establishes the facts and background of your story.

Writing a book-length manuscript is a long, long slog. A project bible helps you keep tabs on the many aspects of your story world or subject matter and works great for memoirs and nonfiction, too.

A project bible is a compilation of facts, research notes, scene locations, character backstories, characters' physical attributes, and scene order, to help you keep track of the morass of details that go into crafting long fiction. You might want to sketch family trees in your bible, include names of pets in the story, along with names of streets, buildings, bodies of water, and various flora and fauna you use to suggest a breathing, living world. You might also want to create mini-collages of your character's wardrobe or living room or a larger one of the whole plot.

Three-ring binders work well for project bibles but you can use almost any organizing tool. It works best not to assemble the bible on your computer. Your bible needs to be a compilation that you can carry with you, consulting while in a coffee shop or at your favorite writing retreat. Your bible should also hold some sort of outline or summary. In my bible I keep my book proposal and table of contents, stuck with about fifty Post-it notes. If you write fiction, perhaps you'll list the major plot points and the subplots. Maybe you want to muse about your characters' relationships, the conflict inherent in each relationship, and list all the secondary and minor characters. You might want to fashion one or two interesting physical attributes for your minor players.

If you're writing about the past, jot down notes about the era the book takes place in—if it's the eighties you might want to check out a few *Dallas* episodes, watch movies from that era, and make notes on hairstyles, fashion, music, food, trends, celebrities, slang, and the political climate.

Bibles are especially helpful to keep track of scenes, including the day, time, weather, and location of each scene along with the players in the scene. In your Bible you can also track deaths, accidents, and injuries. This means if your character is in a fight in scene six and suffers cracked ribs and a black eye, in the following scene he's still sore and his shiner is turning a sickly shade of green. It also means if your character Mira dies in scene eleven on a Monday, then an obituary appears on Wednesday, and on Saturday other characters attend the funeral.

The Bible also helps if you run out of steam while writing or need to put the manuscript down for a while, because it can keep you on track. It can also hold photocopied or scanned articles about craft or research, or farmer's almanac entries on weather or moon phases in your story. If your story contains the Eiffel Tower or a mountain range, find photos and add them to the Bible. Is your character going to cook a fabulous meal? Plan the meal so that when your character is mincing garlic or parsley or dropping a flaying lobster into a steaming pot, you'll have this figured out and the details will convince the reader.

The more organized you are, the more you'll be guaranteed that your redheaded character won't turn into a blonde in a later chapter (unless she visits her hairdresser) and a tall character will stoop when he enters the low-ceilinged cottage. It will help you track how many times you use a specific location, whether you're including weather in your story, and if your characters stay consistent. You can draw a diagram that illustrates the main characters' dominant traits. You can note how your character soothes herself when stressed out. Does she turn to a pint of Ben & Jerry's Cherry Garcia or a bubble bath or visit the corner bar? To get to know characters, make lists: what's in her closet, her glove compartment, refrigerator, junk drawer, and safe-deposit box. You can also track lies, secrets, infidelities, tarnished reputations, and losses.

First Major Revision

As you read your draft, look for consistency problems, but mostly focus on larger issues, scoping out the big picture—ask yourself if the plot hangs together and the architecture makes sense. The aim of your first pass-through is to analyze the overall coherence, structure, and plausibility. You'll be making your major revisions at this point, especially judging whether you need to change the beginning, ending, or viewpoint.

As you search for plot holes, pay attention to events or motives that are never explained. Note if there are too many dangling subplots or simply too many subplots. Often this draft is loose and sketchy, lacking in the narrative flow and glue that holds a piece together. Or it might be written in summary, missing the intimate details and moments that bring the story to life and you'll decide to change some summaries into scenes. You're noting the consistency of the viewpoint, evaluating the order of the scenes, and asking yourself if your story contains surprises, intrigue, and people or characters no one has met before.

In this reading make sure you need the first chapter or scene. Many stories are strengthened by a beheading because they start far before the first crucial actions. If it's a thriller, start with a crisis or disaster, not a tour of CIA headquarters. If it's a love story, collide the lovers as early as possible.

Checklist for the First Revision

- Is the plot clearly resolved?
- Is each scene necessary to tell the story? Can it be cut without affecting the main story?
- Does each action cause more actions and reactions?
- Evaluate the order of your scenes—is this the right time to include this action or should it wait?
- Is your timeline consistent?
- Do you need to add twists and complications to the plot if it bogs down, especially in the middle?
- Is description dispersed in small increments throughout and, if possible, coming through a character's viewpoint?
- Do you need to add flashbacks so the characters' motivations and goals make sense?
- Do the flashbacks contain action or are they mostly summary?
- Do you need to strengthen or add subplots?

If you find major problems, don't panic. Instead create coherent notes or a memo to yourself, as if you are an editor addressing a client. Chances are at this point you might need to expand or cut backstory, deepen main characters, cut or combine secondary characters, expand or cut subplots, reorder the scenes to heighten the tension, refine the middle so it contains a nice twist, and refine the ending so it concludes the plot. I repeat, don't panic.

Second Revision

Like a director creating a film, a good writer creates a seamless world on the page, knowing that sloppiness or gaps or pacing disasters jar the reader from the fictional world. The aim of a second pass-through is to make the story seamless and balanced. Analyze pacing, scene structure, setting, and character development. Now is the time to tinker with individual scenes with more attention than you did in the first pass-through. Also work on setting, exposition, and introspection, noting the proportions and appropriateness in individual scenes.

Your aim now is to create a story world that's so authentic that the page disappears and interesting lives rise into existence in its place. Be aware, too, that if the manuscript has too many interruptions, readers will feel a vague unease. Transform dull settings into backdrops that create a mood and add tension. If you're a left-brain type, this is also a good time to create a scene-by-scene outline or chart, noting the page length of scenes and chapters. You might notice that some days are too hectic and on other days not much happens. Or that chapter lengths vary too much. You might notice that many of your days start in the morning and end in the evening. Or that your protagonist is alone too often. You might observe that your scenes seem to wind down too often, that few cliff-hangers or surprises end scenes.

Checklist for Second Revision

- Does the story move fast enough to hold the reader's interest?

- If you haven't made the changes in the earlier draft, determine if summary sections need to become scenes or scenes would work better as summary.
- Do you need to add foreshadowing so that later major events have credibility and resonance?
- Do the actions and motivations of the characters make sense?
- Do you need to tighten and amp up conflict and emotion in dialogue?
- Does the reader always understand how much time has elapsed since the last scene?
- Are the transitions clear but unobtrusive?
- Do you need to trim flashbacks and transitions and omit digressions?
- Do you need to fine-tune and trim subplots?
- Does each scene have setting details?
- Are your secondary characters described briefly, and do they cause things to happen in the story?
- Do some of the scenes end with cliff-hangers or other devices that thrust the story forward?
- Does each scene raise the stakes (make the conflict more important or deepen suspense)? Does each scene have a mission along with a beginning, middle, and end?
- Are your characters consistent?
- Are there a series of unanswered questions embedded throughout?
- What is the proportion of inner thoughts to the whole? Can you trim these sections?

- Does the dialogue match the characters' vocabulary, intelligence, emotions, and knowledge in the scene?
- Is there subtext in some of the dialogue or is it mostly "on the nose" dialogue?
- Do you sometimes incorporate sequels to important or emotional scenes?
- Can the sequels be trimmed or eliminated?
- Are physical or emotional injuries to characters carried through?

Here's an example of a scene card you can use to track your scenes:

SCENE CARD

Chapter:
POV:
Major action:
Players:
Key Information:
Ending/Resolution:
Emotional content or emotional reversal:
Time span:
Pages:

Copyediting Revision

After you've fixed the major flaws, it is time to think like a copy editor, and your aim is to correct language, style, and hone in on details. You're also working on concision, clarity, resonance, and adding music to the language. This draft is also for making certain that there is enough tension throughout. Again, this should be undertaken with a new printout of the revised manuscript after you've taken a break for a few days, or better yet a week or two. Use a style manual and *The Synonym Finder* for this draft.

As you copyedit, one of the easiest ways to enhance the style is by pumping up weak verbs. Choose verbs that best convey action and emotion, attitude, or mood. Instead of *He sat in the chair: He sprawled in the chair* or *He slumped in the chair.*

Another easy trick is to trade verbs ending in "ing" for verbs ending in "ed." Instead of *He was sprinting for the wall: He sprinted for the wall.*

Weed out adverbs that end in "ly." *He walked slowly* becomes *He plodded.*

And please omit *suddenly* wherever it appears.

Checklist for Third Revision

- Scrutinize the opening for perfection—are the first paragraphs memorable?
- Does every word and every sentence have a purpose?
- Does the dialogue need tags so we know who's speaking?
- In the dialogue are characters' names repeated often?

- Is the dialogue written without any visual cues, such as gestures or expressions to help with context?
- Have you used figurative language to create layers of meaning?
- Have you repeated words, phrases, or images?
- Is there a mix of sentence lengths?
- Do your setting details, especially weather, create a mood?
- Have you used all the senses, including smell, throughout the story?
- Have you sometimes used short sentences and fragments for emphasis?
- Have you placed emphatic words at the end of sentences, paragraphs, and sections?
- Have you revamped dull verbs (get, got, look, see, walk, put), passive linking verbs (have, had, has, would, could, should, will, do, be, been, were, was), and passive structures?
- Have you spotted and corrected clichés, tired phrases, and overused phrases (black as night, each and every, above and beyond)?
- Can you justify each modifier, and have you trimmed unnecessary prepositional phrases?
- Is the dialogue punctuated correctly?
- Have you exchanged long, formal words for short, simple words?

These are your steps for revision—good luck and keep your spirits up!

Deal Breakers

Working on my clients' manuscripts sometimes I feel like a coroner performing an autopsy—I've got the corpse on the mortuary slab and I'm dissecting it, trying to determine the cause of death. As I've mentioned, most writers begin with great story concepts, but often don't have a handle on some aspect of craft. It might be pacing, or they've written a contrived ending, or inconsistent characters, or characters that don't quite come to life on the page. So with my scalpel, I push back an organ, peer into a body cavity, searching, always searching for the mysterious cause of death. Then somehow I need to help the writer resuscitate the mutilated corpse.

With a corpse—I mean draft—in mind, let's spell out deal breakers that editors spot without getting all *CSI*. In fact, these errors jump out by merely riffling through a few pages or without opening the chest cavity.

Chicken Tracks

I've received manuscripts in which there is about as much white space on the pages as there is print. Thus the chicken-tracks analogy. Paragraphs of description, setting, and backstory rarely exist, paragraphs are mostly one or two sentences, and the story has a high proportion of dialogue, mostly smart-aleck staccato that is more banter than revelation. Not even Robert Parker and Charlie Huston, maestros of fast-paced stories and clipped, sassy dialogue, write novels in which characters chat most of the time. So balance things out and write a story, not a comic book or a graphic novel minus the illustrations.

If your story has lots of white space, start analyzing the length of your paragraphs. You should only feature a handful of short paragraphs of one or two sentences in each chapter. Combine or lengthen the rest. Make sure there is a visual detail on every page and in every scene. Using a highlighter, mark one chapter with specific colors for dialogue, exposition, summary, and description. Is there a mix of colors?

Chronology Goofs

Chronology means the order the story is told in, but nowhere is it written that memoir or fiction needs to unfold in chronological order. However, if you're a beginning writer it's often best to keep the action straightforward with only a few excursions into the past. When leaping into backstory, create flashbacks and use transitions so readers are clued in and don't get lost. But the bigger issue is that every time you move your story in and out of time, you need to justify it. (This applies, too, to changing locations and viewpoints.) In too many beginning writers' stories it's too difficult to follow the time frame if it jumps back and forth between decades or centuries.

To salvage a story that moves around in time a lot, use a chart that's similar to the one found at the end of this chapter. After you've completed the chart, find a published novel that you particularly enjoy with a straightforward chronology, then one with a complicated chronology. Analyze how the authors made their structures work. Can you discern the logic behind the chronology they used? When did they employ scene cuts? When did they use transitions and how complex were the transitions? Did they use datelines or a device to signal a new time frame? Which structure would make the most sense for you to emulate?

Dumpola

When I receive this sort of manuscript, my heart always sinks and my eyes start to hurt because the pages contain little white space, and every part of the story, especially backstory, goes on for eight pages. Usually these stories contain too little dialogue, which causes readers to skip ahead in search of excitement. In these stories every person or character, interior, or change in the weather is dumped into the story in breathless, dense, overwhelming detail. It's all too rococo and the writers are also often guilty of parenthetical tendencies and allegorical portrayals. And typically information turns into a lecture when it should be dramatized. I always wonder if the writer is enamored of Henry James or other writers from an earlier era. No matter the reason for the excess, the story is too crowded and I feel like I'm being lectured to or I'm drowning in words.

To salvage this type of story, I remind writers again of the calendar year and that not all parts of storytelling are created equal—make choices and choose wisely and use white space. You might want to study what a paragraph should accomplish and how it needs to introduce and conclude an idea. Also, most paragraphs work best at about five or six sentences.

Dr. Strange

I'm afraid there is no politically correct way to describe this problem. I have worked with or taught more than my share of clients and students who were seriously mentally ill. Now, I understand that some of us are a bit wacky and that sadly, mental illness is a serious and dangerous health risk. I know the unbearable sorrow and heartache that mental illness can bring to a person and his or her family. Like all parts of the body, the brain sometimes doesn't work right. I also know several writers who describe themselves as crazy, but manage their illness and have brilliant writing careers.

That said, here's where I'm going to sound like a hard-hearted Nazi because these stories are rarely salvageable.

Storytelling emerges from lucid thoughts and analysis as much as it does from creativity. (And forget all you've heard about acid trips and writing, booze and writing, and most recreational drugs and writing—writing works best when you're clearheaded and rested.) Fiction manuscripts from people who are mentally unbalanced generally have an autobiographical whiff and, in the midst of abstractions and bizarre speculations about life after death, are most often written about a mystic-shaman who was sent to earth to save humankind. There is repeated mention of inner and outer minds, the inner being, purple skies, and mystic apprenticeships that take place in Mystic Villages. Characters are named Javalanta, Rogorshi, and Chaputa. And I love a great fantasy but these stories always really suck and make me want to pour myself a stiff drink. Make that two. And instead of feeling like I'm reading a story, I feel like I'm trying to decipher a mathematical formula written in Arabic or some language I'll never master.

Usually the character (or in the case of a memoir, the person) is persecuted and misunderstood, particularly by unimaginative family members. Usually the story line is nonexistent—in fact in the worst examples, sentences are also nonexistent, but tantric sex is, surprisingly, quite often present.

I'm no shrink, but it seems to me if you're having serious mental health problems that writing will not be the cure, and the rejection that will likely happen might exacerbate your problems. So seek medical help before you start writing. Write when you feel most focused and calm. Start small and master shorter forms—essays, articles, short stories.

Genre Guessing Game

Over the years I've received a number of e-mails from writers who could not figure out what genre they were writing in and wanted me to solve this problem for them without reading the manuscript. I've also read more than my share of manuscripts that were not mainstream, literary, or any discernible genre. Or the first chapters promised a romance (or political thriller, mystery, or the paranormal) but then morphed into science fiction by chapter 4. Now, there are many subgenres and cross-fertilization in fiction these days. But each genre operates under a set of strictures that meet readers' expectations.

You need to identify your audience and know the kind of story you're writing and why you're writing. Read widely and read interviews with authors talking about why they work in certain genres. Examine how libraries and bookstores divide books into categories. Talk to librarians and booksellers about various genres and generally seek out information about the guidelines for each. Many of the genres, such as romance, science fiction, and horror, operate websites and have online writing communities that gather information and review books, so seek them out.

Inconsistency

The longer your project, the more chances you have for inconsistencies. I mentioned in an earlier chapter that viewpoint inconsistencies are often apparent in beginning writers' manuscripts. However, lots of big and small inconsistencies also appear and are maddening to readers. Examples are a character who has blue eyes on page 12 has green eyes on page 60; a single-story ranch morphs into a bungalow; the landscape is flat and barren in the opening chapters, then mountainous and lush in a later chapter. Or, often the logic falls apart in small ways, as when characters are reading secret missives in the dark without moonlight, candlelight, or flashlight. To solve consistency problems, create a project bible, then find more than one reader to comb through your manuscript and give you feedback. If your story requires specialized knowledge, such as a legal procedural, you'd be wise to find someone connected with the field to give you feedback on accuracy.

Loose Threads

In a previous chapter I mentioned that I often write "sentimental" and "melodramatic" in my notes when I'm working on a manuscript. But often I scrawl "episodic" and am sometimes obliged to create a list of the loose threads or unconnected parts of the story. This especially happens when a writer pens a story that doesn't appear to be based on cause and effect, the foundation of storytelling, and when the story isn't unified by theme, language, and character motivation. Instead the story is like a series of one-night stands.

There is nothing wrong with a story in which each scene can stand on its own, dramatic and complete. But E. M. Forster once wrote: "'The king died then the queen died' is a story. 'The king died and then the queen died of grief' is a plot." Thus plotting, including in memoir writing, is about the *why* of things.

And speaking of one-night stands, in one manuscript a character went out and got fall-on-your-ass drunk and dragged home a stranger for a bout of unbridled, animal passion. In the next scene there was no mention of a hangover, or regrets, or sighs of contentment over the romp in the hay. Don't do this—forge connections, especially emotional connections, between actions, otherwise your story is merely a series of episodes.

As a solution, try creating scene cards described earlier in this chapter. Number and name all the scene cards, then note the scenes that each is connected to by jotting down their numbers on the cards. If you find scenes aren't connected to other events in the story, rewrite with cause and effect as your objective.

Mechanics

Too many mechanical and silly mistakes make me distrust or pity the writer. If within the first few pages I notice that the writer has not bothered to learn how to spell, punctuate, use recognizable and varied sentence structure, or properly format a manuscript, it's hard to take that person seriously in an extremely exacting business.

If grammar or punctuation isn't your forte, hire a proofreader to help you fix these problems. If you cannot afford a proofreader, bribe an English teacher.

Not Ready for Prime Time

For writers, the best words in the English language (or any language) are "the end." We long to be finished, we want the story out in the world. But you should never submit a rough draft to a critique group, developmental editor, book doctor, or any publishing professional. A rough draft will often garner a quick rejection or feedback with a too-long list of your failures and this can deflate your optimism and cloud your vision.

Sometimes I get the impression that writers believe their stories should be read simply because they wrote them—not because they wrote the best story they could. But you need to *earn* your readers, not assume you deserve them by virtue of typing words on a page. Some big clues that a story is not ready for prime time are if it begins with backstory, not a crisis; if it's preachy with an obvious, clunky moral; if it's wordy; if characters seem like stereotypes; if there is a hodgepodge of scenes and actions with no discernible reason for being; if the title is cutesy; and if the cover letter claims the writer's critique group or mother loved the story.

Find a few discerning readers to give you honest feedback. Make sure they are well read and familiar with the type of story you've written. Ask them bluntly if they think the story is ready to be mailed out. If their answer is no, go back to the drawing board, paying special attention to the checklist earlier in this chapter for analyzing your first draft.

Plotless

I once received a short story about a character who was vacuuming on a Sunday morning. That was it. There had been a dinner party the night before but the guest list and the dynamics of the party were never described, although it was noted that they'd eaten lasagna and garlic bread. The vacuuming clean freak was nameless and had no backstory. However, the day was described along with the spots and cat hair on the carpet as dust motes danced in the air and the scents of oregano and garlic lingered. Baffled, I searched for a plot, but alas there was none. A short story begins with a moment of change and charts the journey through this change and arrives at an outcome. Vignettes, small actions, and Martha Stewart moments do not a story make. If you don't have a real plot in mind when you start writing, you probably need to dump the project and start over. Also read books on craft, paying special attention to plotting and structure.

Sophisticate—Not

In many of the memos I write to clients I suggest that the story needs to be more sophisticated and nuanced. If it cannot pass my sophisticate test, it's not going to pass muster in publishing offices, either. Lack of sophistication and nuance can happen to most parts of a story. Foreshadowing that shrieks about what is to come instead of whispering. Too-obvious clues, like when a detective finds the murder victim's diary, which is full of her misgivings about her evil stepsister. Characters that overreact to every event with operatic flourishes. Too much weeping, shouting, and needless violence. Too many threats, speeches, and expository dialogue. Dorky stories written for young adults that seem like they were written in the Eisenhower administration.

There is no easy fix for this problem, but again, you need to find readers to help you see what is no longer visible to you. That's plural—one is not enough. Return their generosity with effusive thanks and by listening politely and not arguing your case. Also reward them with a good bottle of wine or booze, pans of brownies or lasagna (I recommend arriving at your meeting with the goodies still warm from the oven), or movie tickets or gift certificates to a bookstore for your young-adult readers.

Radioactive

In chapter 9, "Never Write About Wimps," I explain the importance of creating inventive and bold characters. However, when it comes to your cast, there can be too much of a good thing. This means not only is no one in the story employed, but the cast is a collection of freaks, pimps, perverts, gold diggers, con artists, lunatics looking for love, deranged felons, pedophile priests, and sociopaths of every stripe, including congressmen on the take (some heading for the crowbar hotel). You might be wondering what's wrong with assembling such a colorful cast of misfits. Or you might argue that Elmore Leonard has made a lucrative living out of assembling a radioactive cast, but he's Elmore Leonard and often what works for successful authors doesn't work for writers trying to break into the game. It doesn't hurt to include a few ordinary folks or at least one character the reader can identify with in the mix for ballast, empathy, and a reference point. When everyone in the cast is a nutter, the results are more like a fever dream than a story.

There is no easy fix here—start over and strive for balance and moments of normalcy dotted throughout the story.

Try This

Chart and analyze your manuscript using a graph.

CHAPTER	SCENE	TIME FRAME	CAST	ACTION/ PLOT POINTS	PAGES

CHAPTER	SCENE	TIME FRAME	CAST	ACTION/ PLOT POINTS	PAGES

Quick and Dirty Tips for Editing and Revision

- Write first, write fast. Conduct major revisions later, and don't be afraid to delete.
- Accept the reality that revision is the other half of writing.
- Always create a document labeled "extras" with everything you delete from your early drafts.
- For most story types, start with action and explain later.

If you start with description or exposition, the first scene must end with a question or a hook.

- Research is the most overlooked facet of writing a successful manuscript. Solid research creates genuine description and a credible story situation.
- Know your ending before you start writing.
- Save all versions of your drafts—number and/or date them.
- Seek at least one outside opinion.
- Always listen to feedback without being defensive. It's likely you won't agree with everything someone says about your manuscript, but most intelligent readers can be helpful with the major issues in a manuscript.
- Don't be afraid to cut ruthlessly, including whole scenes. If there are any redundant scenes or descriptions, take them out. Anything you cut can always be recycled and put to good use in another story.
- On the other hand, too much rewriting can drain the life right out of a piece. Don't strive for perfection; it doesn't exist.
- Don't trust your computer. Create printed backups.

Resources

Dictionary of American Slang, 4th edition, edited by Ann Kipfer, Ph.D., and Robert L. Chapman, Ph.D.

Common Errors in English Usage, Paul Brian

Self-Editing for Fiction Writers, Renni Browne and Dave King

Manuscript Makeover: Revision Techniques No Fiction Writer Can Afford to Ignore, Elizabeth Lyon

Novel Writing for Wanna-be's, Sam McCarver

The Complete Guide to Editing Your Fiction, Michael Seidman

The 38 Most Common Fiction Writing Mistakes (And How to Avoid Them), Jack M. Bickham

The 28 Biggest Writing Blunders (And How to Avoid Them), William Noble

The Art and Craft of Novel Writing, Oakley Hall

Fiction Writer's Workshop, Josip Novakovich

Revision: A Creative Approach to Writing and Rewriting Fiction, David Michael Kaplan

Fiction First Aid, Raymond Obstfeld

A Piece of Work: Five Writers Discuss Their Revisions, Jay Woodruff, editor

How to Grow a Novel: The Most Common Mistakes Writers Make and How to Overcome Them, Sol Stein

How to Be Your Own Script Doctor, Jennifer Keening

Fourteen

Driving an Editor Crazy: Goofs, Gaffes, and Howlers That Sink a Manuscript

The stupid believe that to be truthful is easy; only the artist knows how difficult it is.

—WILLA CATHER, *The Song of The Lark*

Someone once told me that we read fiction and memoir to be reminded that living is worth the pain. However, reading should not be painful, especially for an editor who might buy your manuscript. Now I realize that as an independent editor my tales of woe differ from those who toil in the field of publishing. But I've heard similar tales from editors and agents I've met over the years.

I have had dark days as an editor, days when I would rather have had a root canal than work on a manuscript, days when I longed to charge for pain and suffering because the story was a mess, days when I was weary of trying to explain how to write when it was clear the writer I was working with had given the whole enterprise little thought. There have been days when I needed to write a memo that I worried would break a writer's heart.

But even on my good days, when I loved the writer and the

manuscript I was working on, there have always been writerly habits that just drive me up the wall.

And don't even get me started on how some writers become miffed when I suggest that stream-of-consciousness journal entries do not a memoir make; that paragraphs shouldn't occupy four pages; or that you cannot stick bizarre punctuation onto each page as if scattering rose petals before a bride. But I'm jumping ahead of myself.

Deal Breakers

Throughout this book I've listed the deal breakers I spot most often in manuscripts. I hope that by the time you reach this chapter, you understand that these problems are really, really noticeable. Alas, there's no easy formula I can quote, but if you discover a few in your manuscript, it's salvageable. If you have five or ten, you probably need to start over or rethink your plot or overall strategy. More than ten and you might need to scrap the story, shelve it for a while, consult with a professional, or take a writing class.

So now I've got another list of faux pas and problems that might be invisible to you the writer, but are easily recognized by an editor. These problems don't fit neatly into the previous chapters, and while some might seem nitpicky, if you stack up enough of these gaffes, an editor might pass on your manuscript. Here's a little story about how small problems can add up (though if you jog fifteen miles a day or possess a highly functioning metabolism, you might not be able to relate): many years ago I was going through a particularly ugly divorce. I was miserable, I was lonely,

I felt misunderstood, and my future seemed shaky. In response I ate too much, drank too much, whined too much, and blamed too much. One day I was walking into a shopping center with my niece and nephew and spotted my reflection in a store window. I'd morphed from voluptuous to just plain fat.

Somehow I hadn't seen all the pounds pile on.

I started dieting the next day, but it was a "Holy shit, is that really me?" moment that woke me up. The deal breakers scattered throughout this book and the bad habits in this chapter are your "Holy shit, is that in my story?" moments. Like the deal breakers I've mentioned before, these problems are fixable, because writing is a craft and you're a worker. Some of the problems in this chapter aren't as grievous as the deal breakers you've read previously, some are especially grating, such as viewpoint screwups. But all steal from your credibility and diminish the reader's trust in your ability to tell a story. Here's my list of things I guarantee will drive an editor crazy or at least to shriek, "Amateur!" when she reads your pages.

Age Appropriate

Often writers run into problems making a character sound appropriate for his or her age. Young children are either geniuses or talk baby talk when they should have moved on to complete sentences. One writer created a series with a fifty-something protagonist. However, her character tended to sound geriatric, and she uttered a lot of pieties and outmoded phrases like "Jumping Jehoshaphat" and "knock me over with a feather." I reminded the writer, who is older than her character, that Boomers grew up with the Stones, Beatles, and Dylan. Another writer penned a series about a hip twenty-something protagonist who refers to males in the story as "gentlemen" when "dude" or something similar would be more likely. She also used words like "hence" and "perchance," which made the voice inauthentic, but mostly not age appropriate.

But It Really Happened

When it comes to fiction, the advice "write what you know" can usually be ignored. Even if your antics are more scandalous than those of Britney and Paris, or you're in more hot water than Russell Crowe, trust me, your life is rarely the stuff of fiction. Fiction is bigger than life and fictional characters are in a buttload of trouble—more trouble than you've faced unless you're writing from a cell or are in a government protection program. I've met a few exceptions to this over the years—writers whose life stories would make terrific fiction, but when I tried to explain that the main character must be significantly different from them, they were genuinely puzzled. It's simple, really: you are not the protagonist in your fiction. A make-believe person is, and he'll run faster, jump higher, and dodge more bullets than you.

There are other dangers, too—fiction readers often don't trust stories that stem from life as much as they trust stories born of creativity.

Now, I realize that autobiographical fiction has been written by the likes of Hemingway and Plath, but what works for most writers is to write about people they've never met having adventures and problems they'll never experience. Recalling the events of life is not the same as plotting, and the truth of a life is often constricting; it builds walls around our stories with real events and real people. Step outside those walls into a world where you'll choose for your companions story people you want to know better. When you write about yourself or real people, you also miss the magic that happens when a character takes shape in your daydreams and starts whispering her secrets, fears, and urges.

Also, real life is messy, and fiction, while complicated, needs to organize itself into three acts and resolve the main story question. Most often in life resolution is far from complete or tidy and venting does not equal storytelling. Instead of rehashing your own suffering, make your characters suffer. One last thing: if you disguise your life as fiction, it opens up a wasp's nest of other problems, such as the necessity of disguising names and identities so the real people in your story don't sue your ass.

Clichés

A developmental editor must sniff out faulty structures, underdeveloped characters, and plots that fizzle, but also note the overblown, generic, and clichéd. When I come across a writer who uses a lot of clichéd ideas, phrases, and trite expressions, my heart always hardens a bit toward him or her. I always circle the clichés in a manuscript and mention them in the memo because many writers are blind to them, although they're wincingly obvious to an editor.

Now, there are only so many original plot ideas in the world, but clichéd story lines don't have enough original elements or new twists on old standards. Thus a modern-day Cinderella tale seems too similar to the Disney version, or a remake of *Star Wars* includes a princess with a bizarre hairstyle. And while the world of storytelling contains many stock characters, I've encountered way too many done-to-death characters, like Irish cops with a broad brogue munching doughnuts and priests tippling the altar wine. Then there are falling-down drunks with hair-trigger tempers, and hard-bitten detectives with a steel will who are at their wit's end trying to solve a case although it's all in a day's work.

The trouble is that clichés have been used so much they're dead. Clichés that too often litter manuscripts are trite or weak expressions, like *blood red*, *each and every*, *leaves much to be desired*, *last but not least*, *to no avail*, *from bad to worse*, *short and sweet*, *vicious cycle*, and *uphill battle*. My red pen tears into these sorts of expressions like a vampire, and I'll spot more clichés, like *blessing in disguise*, *blind leading the blind*, *close call*, and *fall on deaf ears*. Others you can eliminate: *it's not rocket science*, *to be honest*, *thinking outside the box*, *in actual fact*, *the mind boggles*, *between a rock and a hard place*, *paradigm shift*, *cutting edge*, and *make no mistake*.

Don't go there. Oops.

Dialect

Dialect can be an important tool in a writer's arsenal, but it's one that can easily backfire. When used carefully it can reflect the education, status, sensibility, and locale of the speaker. However, dialect is often difficult to read, so a little goes a long way. Thus pepper dialect into conversation as a flavoring, not the main course. Accuracy is key, so make certain the dialect is specific to the character's region and class. Beginning writers tend to make all Brits sound alike when there are dozens of variations on Brit speak, including Cockney, a posh upper-crust variation, and the parlance spoken by people from Yorkshire or other regions. If you haven't visited the region you're writing about, you need to listen to actors in films, consult with an expert on the subject, or find some means to learn the intricacies of local speech patterns. Then make careful choices about what to include, choosing the most easily understood exchanges. Finally, when using dialect, focus on word choice, not the accent with which it is spoken.

Dippy and Oddball Names

I've run across a lot of problems having to do with character names. Sometimes protagonists have names that are too obvious or symbolic, such as Rose Petal Lamoure, Bryce Cannon for a cop, or Kandy for a young woman who is an airhead. Some names are just oddly matched to the character—a serial murderer named Felicity, a detective named Stoner, and a twenty-something named George who is supposed to be a hottie. Now I realize that George Clooney falls under the hottie category, but most people don't associate the name George with lust.

Sometimes a writer will pen a story in which five character names all begin with R, or feature names that are not appropriate for the era they were born in. One writer named contemporary teens Marilyn, Betty, Susan, Janice, and Ruth, when the top baby names for that year were Jessica, Ashley, Brittany, and the like. But I reserve my special ire for sci-fi writers who insist on giving their characters unpronounceable, alphabet-soup names, such as Sahrjhn, Lahndsr, Thyr Zxbryn, and Magruhl Shyi Drhzyxx.

Creepy Sex Scenes

Perhaps the, um, stickiest task I've encountered over the years is how to tell a writer that his or her sex scenes are creepy, inappropriate, overemphasized, or gross. Now, I know that one person's porn is another person's erotica, but as the saying goes, I know a bad sex scene when I read one. Or, as Isabel Allende said, "Erotica is using a feather, pornography is using the whole chicken." The basic advice is this: if your sex scene isn't directly related to the plot and not tossed in because you like leather and whips, leave it out unless you want an editor speculating about whether or not you're a sick puppy.

A few of these nasty lovefests come to mind. I recall a client who wrote a scene in which a couple visits a Wyoming ranch just in time to witness a stallion mounting a mare. This scene was told in graphic, horsy detail and resulted in the woman's becoming incredibly aroused. Eeww. Maybe horse sex is the (male) writer's idea of foreplay, but for most women it just isn't.

Another writer penned a novel about a suburban housewife's quest for sexual adventure. There were many problems with this particular manuscript but I was ready to join a convent after working on it, and I'm not Catholic. You see, it was mostly a catalog of sexual positions, random partners, sex clubs, creepy fetishes, and wild nights. The story line was nonexistent, even though the writer earnestly believed she was writing women's mainstream fiction. If you consider *Hustler* mainstream fiction, then maybe she had a point. But tell a story, tell a story, tell a story. A story is not thrusts, grunts, shrieks, and bare-assed freaks getting it on.

Dreams

Like many people, I dream nighttime fantasies of grand scope, drama, and adventure. My dreams fascinate me, and I sometimes tell my friends about them. But in fiction dreams rarely work, and frankly, they've been used so often that they've lost their appeal. And before you protest that Barbara Kingsolver uses them in *Animal Dreams* or cite other famous stories, just hear me out.

Dreams come from the land of sleepy mystery. They are crowded with symbols, irony, and metaphor. They often puzzle, trouble, or terrify the dreamer. On the other hand, the dreams I typically see in manuscripts are dull, vague, difficult to visualize, or too laden with meaning. I especially get bored with stories in which a character has the same dream night after night. Sometimes dreams can reveal trauma or hint at secrets, but often writers think they're shorthand for a mystical experience or deep-seated angst. Like other techniques in fiction, dreams need to be anchored by logic and clarity, and they need to define the dreamer.

Expressive

One tricky aspect of writing is nailing the nonverbal communication of characters or people in memoirs. In real life about 90 percent of what is said is communicated nonverbally. This obviously places writers at a disadvantage. Wordless communication happens via posture, facial expression, tone of voice, eye contact, and small gestures and movements. As with other parts of writing, you need to collect and pick up on the nonverbal cues around you. When a person is sad, worried, overwhelmed, or ecstatic, what do they sound and look like? How does the person use her hands?

Editors will be easily convinced your story is half-baked if your characters exhibit few, or repeat, expressions and gestures. I recall a manuscript in which the characters' eyes widened in about half the scenes, and another in which characters were constantly nodding. One writer featured characters who were always talking with their hands on their hips, sort of like a stationary square dance. Some writers make all their characters drama queens, with constant shrieking, emoting, and tearful outbursts. In one story the characters' voices were always cracking, and in too many stories I've read the characters are blushing, stammering, and wincing. My point here is to tone it down, mix it up, and make it accurate.

Fact Checker Breakdown

More than anything, factual errors remind me that I'm reading a manuscript and not a published work, especially when a story seems about as accurate as a Wikipedia entry written by a stoned teenager. In one story, set in 1962, JFK was not the president. In another, the writer of a novel that takes place in 1904 referred to single women as *Ms.* Trouble is, Ms. did not come into the vernacular until the 1970s. Another client's manuscript was set in Queens, a place he'd never visited, and his version was a suburban paradise with ranch homes, attached garages, leafy lawns, and mailboxes at the curb. Yikes!

I've read many confusing accounts of time and light, such as it being dark at 7 P.M. on an August night, or fireworks staged during daylight. Another fiction manuscript was set in the 1930s but referred to jeans, when back then trousers or dungarees covered the lower body. The manuscript also referred to high heels, a term that didn't really come into use until the 1950s.

Does this sound nitpicky? You bet—and if you aren't the type to pay attention to nits or other minute objects, you shouldn't write fiction.

Those small points aside, one of the biggest problems I notice is with crime, police, or legal procedures. For example, there is a corpse, but the police allow civilians, particularly the amateur sleuth, to mill around the crime scene, offering opinions and asking questions. In one story with an amateur sleuth, the police confided that the murder victim had been shot twice through the heart—and sadly this information came before the autopsy was performed. Did I mention it was nighttime when the body was discovered? In another story the toxicology results were available to a detective the same day the victim was murdered.

In yet another story the sleuth recalled being at a crime scene with her detective father when she was a child. Call me a skeptic, but I had a hard time imagining a detective allowing a six-year-old to gaze at a bloody corpse.

Along with legal and criminal procedures, I have a big bugaboo about weapons. (Once a character flung a knife across the yard and neatly toppled another character. Because this character wasn't a former circus performer, I found this act difficult to swallow.) Now, I am not a member of the NRA, nor have I ever fired a gun at anyone or anything, but even I can identify when weapons are misused, misidentified, or are outlandish additions to a story. What happens most often is that guns are incorrectly identified or appear to be weightless, and most characters are crack shots and hit the villains smack through the forehead or heart with a single shot. Find out if the cops in your story carry a Glock or a .38 Special or fire Tasers. Also know that in your frontier story, bullets from a six-shooter cannot rain from the weapon like hail.

So here's the tip: the further from your own life and expertise your story roams, the more authority you'll need to tell your story. If you're penning a techno-thriller, or writing about long-ago Ireland or a cattle drive in the 1800s, the reader needs to feel that you're as at home in the story world as you are in one that is happening outside your window.

Head Hopping and Other Viewpoint Issues

In fiction the viewpoint is the lens or focus through which the story is witnessed. Each type has advantages and disadvantages, and you want your viewpoint to be lifelike and practical. I read a manuscript written in the first person (I) and the character died at the end of the story, so the whole seemed contrived. The most common viewpoint problems happen when, in the midst of a scene, the viewpoint lens shifts and jumps around, thereby disorienting and confusing the reader. In these stories the writer leaps among the characters' thoughts and slips two or three viewpoints into a single scene. Now, as writers, there is a tendency to want to access everyone's thoughts and feelings. But this doesn't need to happen via viewpoint—dialogue, action, gestures, description, and subtext can all hint at a character's inner world. Also, in a short story it rarely works to introduce a second viewpoint; a short story needs to be focused and poignant.

Another problem is when a beginning writer chooses an omniscient viewpoint, thinking this will lend the story a vast tapestry of experience. What usually happens, however, is that the story is muddled and lacks nuance, and readers are never allowed intimate access to at least one character they can care about. As in real life, it's not always necessary to know what everyone is thinking and doing.

If you're writing fiction, you need a solid understanding of viewpoint because it helps the reader develop empathy. Choose your viewpoint by asking yourself *why* the person is telling the story, what this character has at stake, and how intimate the story will be.

I want to mention another one of my peeves. When you write in the first person, or the third, it can become awkward to constantly train the camera lens (viewpoint) through that character. Be careful of writing *I could see*, *I saw*, *I looked, then I ran*, etc. Ditto for *Ahead Mary spotted the train in the distance* or *Jack noticed that the sky was becoming dark*. Simply state facts instead of always explaining that you're filtering sightings through a character's vision. Write *The sky was clear,* as opposed to *I saw the sky was clear.*

Inconsistent Voice

In fiction, voice varies depending on who is telling the story, but it must be engaging and consistent. We all have a range of language and diction that we use in different situations, but I've read stories with a twenty-something character who at times sounded like a physics professor, then a few pages later like a bimbo. Now, a professor will sound more formal in front of a lecture hall than she does while having a beer with her colleagues afterward, or later in bed with her lover. But you need to make choices about your characters' vocabulary, word use, and general approach to life. Is the professor laid-back, or does she prefer to keep her distance from people? Her vocabulary will help impart this.

In one story a nineteen-year-old protagonist who describes

another woman as a "brick shit house" (a dated phrase) and says "crapola" but uses words like "misanthrope" and "obsequious" sounds inconsistent. If you're writing historical fiction, you especially want to focus on each main character's idiolect, or specific vocabulary, imparting his level of education and life experience.

Injured Party

Many writers struggle with injuries, accidents, and other physical ailments that befall characters. A character is whacked in the forehead, but no one comments on the big lump on her face. Bruises and injuries must not only cause distress, they should change over time. When an injury is serious enough to knock a character off his feet or leave a mark, the injury should linger for at least a few days, reminding the reader that the character is in danger or vulnerable. So when characters are injured, make certain that the pain, soreness, stiffness, and visible signs of the assault follow. Also make certain that you know exactly what an injury looks like as it heals.

The same goes for illnesses. If a character is undergoing chemo, she needs to exhibit side effects from the treatment. In one story I read, the character never became nauseated or lost her hair. So skip the miraculous and research the illness you're writing about.

Melodrama and Sentimentality

If there is one deadly word that shows up in my working notes most often, it's *melodrama*. A term applied when a writer dumps in implausible events or sensational action for effect. Usually this means writers are employing outrageous plot devices in an attempt to elicit obvious emotions. Characters tend to be stereotypical and hysterical, and harrowing scenarios reign with child snatchers and puppy dropkickers littering the story world. Death, suicide, tragic illnesses and injuries, broken hearts and dreams, unnecessary violence, and impossibly ecstatic sex are also the norm. Now, all these topics can be infinitely fascinating and fertile territory for writing, but not all need be used to graphically illustrate the human condition.

Here's another big truth about writing: it must contain emotional and intellectual complexity, which is the opposite of melodrama.

Melodrama spells out situations in broad, obvious, and unimaginative strokes, as when nice people die in stories and bad people get away with nefarious schemes or strangers fall madly in love within moments of meeting on the train. Or it just tries too hard, as a school bus teeters on a cliff with the birthday girl—who just received her first kiss—on board. And then she's miraculously saved but her adorable and fluffy kitten (her birthday gift from her new beau) dies and the boyfriend ends up in a coma. One story comes to mind about a dancer trying out for a Vegas review who is a Tonya Harding type (the Olympic figure skater who had her nemesis's knees whacked, in case you forgot). The dancer drugs her competitor, but as the ambulance carries off the near-comatose, blue-faced victim, she finally realizes that winning isn't everything and she should strive to be a better person. Which she tells the victim in a tearful hospital scene.

Like melodrama, I'm afraid sentimentality in all its forms makes me pissy. Now, sentimentality has been the rage in storytelling going back many centuries and was especially present in eighteenth- and nineteenth-century fiction—James Fenimore Cooper comes to mind. It happens when writers try to induce strong emotions in the reader that exceed what the situation warrants. It also happens when characters' emotions are reported on instead of shown, via drama. I find it in manuscripts when a startling number of single tears slip down a character's cheek as he clutches his dead or maimed (fill in the blank) lover, beloved golden retriever, mother, father, wife, child. Or when the aforementioned golden retriever rescues the toddler from a fire. Sentimentality cons readers into feeling emotions in situations that are corny—stray dogs in the pound, or when battered children are featured in a story.

Beware, too, that when language tends toward sentimentality, it's usually florid and weighted down with modifiers. Clichés, simplistic and overused expressions, overwrought emotions, and stock responses are key ingredients of sentimentality in fiction.

Mind Matters

References to the mind, thoughts, mental processes, and the ways people think drive me crazy. Readers understand that thinking is going on without being told that the wheels of the brain go round and round. Examples: *My mind raced. I searched my mind for a memory of the last time I saw Dave. Ann's thoughts skipped at the possibilities of winning the prize.* Forget, too, about: *racing thoughts, my thoughts stretched back to that long-ago day,* and *her thoughts were whirling like a Tilt-A-Whirl.* It often works best to simply drop into a character's thoughts without announcing you're doing so. And please do not place quotation marks around thoughts.

Nameless in Seattle

I once met a writer who proudly announced that he'd written an entire novel without giving any characters names. Yawn. When I asked him why, he sputtered some oddball excuse about how names were for the unimaginative. Oh contraire—names anchor characters in the reader's imagination. Only Cormac McCarthy can get away with this ploy—trust me on this one.

Over-the-Top Symbolism

In my not-so-humble opinion, often the best images and symbolism in writing appear organically in a story. They are not deliberate or labored or elaborate or saccharine confections. They emerge like mushrooms after a spring rain. Wild mushrooms are not planted, and it seems to me that symbols and allegories should not be, either. This means you don't compare your character to a sturdy oak or a Greek goddess. Nor do you feature a character gazing for hours at an ant farm and comment on how the insects are a microcosm of humankind. Don't try this hard.

The other problem is that writers sometimes get the symbols wrong or their choices are simply odd. One writer I worked with used azaleas as a central image in a story of a torrid love triangle. Now, there's nothing wrong with azaleas. Where I live in Portland, they dot many lawns with vibrant pink blooms come April or May. And nothing says romance like flowers. But azaleas are woody shrubs, more appropriate to a landscape gardener's repertoire than the central image of a story. They are not romantic, aromatic (as was incorrectly reported in the manuscript), or evocative. So choose wisely and pay attention to the images that swim your way via your intuition, and don't use the writer's version of a jackhammer when creating them.

Protagonist with a Bizarre Downward Arc (or, To Hell with Happy Endings)

At the heart of most stories is character growth, called the arc, and the plot is the means for readers to observe the character's arc. But not all characters become wiser or stronger because some, such as the heroic types (think John Wayne playing them in films) remain fairly unchanged as they fight bad guys. Then we need to recognize that the world is full of tragedy, and so is fiction. Typically when you write a tragedy (think *Hamlet*), it means that the complicated protagonist or antihero, who has flaws, strengths, and likable traits, suffers and then dies or is ruined to conclude the plot. Not every story that ends with the protagonist's death or ruin is a tragedy. A tragedy happens most often when the protagonist's fate is avoidable, as in *Romeo and Juliet,* or his flaws are his undoing. Tragedies typically have dark themes or are a dark study of the soul. So if you want to write a tragedy, I say, go for it. After all, not every story needs a happy ending.

However, if you're writing a story in which your protagonist loses his marbles, kills himself, or wallows in mediocrity and apathy, and there is no backstory or motivation that justifies these behaviors, I can guarantee you'll drive an editor crazy. A good example of a bizarre downward arc in a film is *Leaving Las Vegas,* in which the main character, played by Nicolas Cage, decides to drink himself to death. The film contains little backstory that explains why he is ready to check out or finds life so impossible.

I hated the movie, although I'm aware that many critics didn't agree with me.

We read fiction to watch people change in ways that have some inherent logic. Now, this logic might not be *our* logic. But if your character's wife asks for a divorce and then he goes out and splatters the subway with bullets before killing himself, ask yourself if this makes sense or you're merely saying to hell with happy endings.

Punctuation Blunders

The English language has about a gazillion rules about punctuation, many of them slippery and difficult to grasp. I believe there are about forty uses for commas. But when you approach punctuation like a drunk weaving home from a bar, I guarantee you'll look stupid or at least careless. I've read three-hundred-page manuscripts that contained no commas, manuscripts that splattered hyphens across the page without any regard for what a hyphen is supposed to accomplish, and have worked with a surprising number of writers who had no idea how to punctuate dialogue. Or writers who don't know the difference between a hyphen and a dash. One easy tip is to remember that hyphens join and dashes separate.

If you're grammatically or punctuation challenged, find a good reference book and use the *Chicago Manual of Style* as your reference for numerals, titles, and other tricky issues. Especially be careful of starting dialogue or a sentence with a numeral—it just isn't done. Also, it is *percent*, not % and *plus*, not +. Beware of using too many asides in parentheses—they're best avoided because you want the reader's eyes to sail through your paragraphs.

Avoid quotation marks for emphasis or to highlight words, punctuation marks outside quotations, and apostrophes for plurals. Also leave out exclamation marks, and especially don't add two or three for the heck of it because they make you look like you're eight years old!!!

Sentence Issues

Our tools are so humble—words strung together to create meaningful sentences. But of course sometimes sentences fizzle and/or run amok. A large number of writers craft stories in which there is a deadly sameness to their sentences. All are about the same length, all in the same noun-verb-object pattern. Dullsville, baby. I happen to love run-on sentences, but only in the hands of a writer who is making a deliberate choice to strap on a galaxy of words, not someone who doesn't know when to stop a thought.

Be especially careful of using too many short sentences in a row (it's like driving over speed bumps) or using a lot of extremely short paragraphs. The manuscript will look like this:

> Belle heard a noise and turned around.
>
> Jason stood in the narrow hallway.
>
> Silence stretched between them.
>
> "How've you been, Belle?" he asked.
>
> She gazed at him.
>
> "I thought I'd never see you again."

Can you see what's going on here? Not only is the writer struggling to inject drama via sentence structure, but the whole turns out choppy. So vary your sentence length and structure. Ditto for paragraphs.

Soul

I break out in hives anytime a writer mentions *soul*, as in *soul-shattering* or *she felt his passion in the depths of her soul* or *my soul died a little the day he left me* or *my soul sang with each touch of his hands on my skin* or *soul mate*. I don't care how many best-selling authors use *soul* in their stories, it is cringe-worthy prose that hurts my eyes.

Unnecessary Prologues

A prologue is introductory material set apart in time, space, or viewpoint (or all three) from the main story and creates intrigue for upcoming events. To qualify as a prologue, the information or events must exist outside the framework of the main story.

I've read prologues that happen the day before the story begins and prologues that have almost nothing to do with the story, and a prologue that was repeated word for word in a later chapter. Prologues must illuminate all that follows and create unease and curiosity. Since you're essentially starting the story twice, you need to be able to justify this choice.

The Unresolved Ending

Open-ended endings sometimes work in short fiction, but in a novel-length story I want to know if your protagonist wins, loses, or draws, who the murderer is, and who will pay the price for the story events. Endings that leave me thinking about the world of the story and its inhabitants are fine; endings that leave me guessing are annoying. Again, this is my preference and a number of novels with ambiguous endings have been published. I often find that writers go this route because they can't quite make up their minds how to end things. But the more ambiguous the ending, the more clues about the character's nature need to be scattered throughout the earlier chapters.

Vague References

Vagueness in all its forms spikes my blood pressure. Instead of writing about a "very large crowd," write that the crowd numbered fifty thousand. Instead of mentioning that your character is tall, write that he's six-foot-seven. Instead of tall buildings or little houses, write about skyscrapers and cottages. Instead of dogs and flowers, write about poodles and gardenias.

Word Territory

Many writers, even great writers, don't respect word territory. This means that the same words or expressions appear again and again in the story, often in close proximity. The more unusual the word, as in a manuscript that uses *verdant* about thirty times to describe Kentucky in springtime, the bigger the violation.

Resources

The Synonym Finder, J. I. Rodale

Writing the Blockbuster Novel, Albert Zuckerman

Eats, Shoots & Leaves: The Zero Tolerance Approach to Punctuation, Lynne Truss

Sin & Syntax: How to Craft Wickedly Effective Prose, Constance Hale

The New Well-Tempered Sentence and *The Deluxe Transitive Vampire*, Karen Elizabeth Gordon

Making a Good Script Great, Linda Seger

Epilogue: Living the Writing Life

How we spend our days is, of course, how we spend our lives. —ANNIE DILLARD, *The Writing Life*

In previous chapters we covered the mistakes I've seen most often in my career and how you can avoid them. Sometimes it seems like all writing advice boils down to: be bold, be brave, and don't suck. The previous chapters covered the "don't suck" part of this advice, so now let's talk about adjusting your head and habits so you can be bold and brave.

Toughen Up

The first thing you need to do is *toughen up*. I'm talking alligator hide, babe. This business is about as gentle as the main drag in Deadwood in 1876. When I hear my students and clients whine about receiving negative feedback, I worry that they're not tough enough to be writers. Now I realize that sometimes there are creeps and sadists in the publishing world or writing workshops, and I've heard horror stories about criticisms so cruel that they could wither a redwood. But most people like me are pussycats licking cream from our whiskers compared to what happens in the acquisition meetings held at individual publishing houses. In these meetings, the editor who is championing the manuscript tries to sell it to the marketing and art departments. They all must agree on its sales potential. If this group cannot imagine your story will make a profit, they pass. A lot of what you do as a writer is to push your manuscript into those meetings and give it a fighting chance to survive.

Don't Lose It

Along with my advice to toughen up, I also warn you: *don't lose it*. By *it* I'm referring to your sanity. We all know that Hemingway offed himself and Sylvia Plath stuck her head in the oven and turned on the gas and how a whole slew of writers drank themselves to death or just freakin' lost it. These stories add much to the myth that writers are crazy or at best children in adult bodies. You and I are going to work hard at *not* losing it or giving in to anxiety, depression, and self-destructive tendencies.

Here's a little story for you. A few years ago I was teaching at a West Coast conference and ended up having dinner with an agent who had flown in from New York. Most of the people who take part in writing conferences are pretty much worked to death, especially the conference coordinator and committee. Most conferences are held in large hotels near airports, and most agents and editors spend three days locked in a room listening to pitches.

So this agent and I were both thrilled to breathe fresh air, walk around in a charming Portland neighborhood, and eat at a restaurant far from the hotel. As we walked we chatted about making a first impression on an agent or editor. And she said, "The main thing I want to know is that you're not a crazy person."

I've never forgotten her comment, especially since that day I'd spotted a few less-than-sane types wandering around the conference. It seems that every conference has them, and they often wear bizarre outfits more suitable for a Halloween party, or scuttle around, eyes on the floor, muttering to themselves. They radiate a scary vibe and write strange stuff about a serial-killer cannibal who believes he's a born-again Aztec god.

Now, I'm not a therapist or a shrink, but I can advise that if you're depressed or anxious before you start writing, you should get some help because writing just might make your symptoms worse. Writing is a long, hard slog and your brain needs to be in tip-top shape. You don't want to show up at your computer every morning jittery or tired and hungover. You want to feel rested and clearheaded and excited about your story.

So please don't use writing as an excuse to go off the deep end—no binges, no all-nighters, no cutting yourself off from your friends, no dwelling on the bitter truths about the publishing industry. The successful authors that I meet seem like a pretty healthy, hearty, and happy bunch. Most pros are passionate about their work, are in loving and stable marriages, have children and outside interests, and have found ways to balance the hours of working at a computer.

Read Like a Writer

My next suggestion is that you need to *read like a writer.* In Stephen King's *On Writing* he mentions that "Reading is the creative center of a writer's life." Reading enters into your many layers of consciousness and teaches you the rhythms of language and narrative structure. It illustrates when a flashback works best and how sequels can help with pacing.

Recently I taught a memoir workshop at a conference and asked the fifty or so participants how many were writing memoirs. They all raised their hands. Then I asked how many had read ten or more memoirs. About ten writers raised their hands. Then I asked how many had read twenty or more memoirs. No one raised a hand.

Later, I met with writers whose manuscripts I'd critiqued as part of the conference. Two of them were writing young adult (YA) fiction, and when I told them their chapters indicated that they weren't reading contemporary YA, they were both surprised at my observation. One, who was toiling away on his fourth draft, hadn't read this genre since he was a kid. He was then retired. When I suggested he needed to read at least forty or fifty of the best YA novels, he visibly blanched.

Reading is your job. If you don't read the genre you're writing in, your unconscious will never absorb the techniques and structure needed. If you're writing a memoir, read every memoir you can get your hands on, and also read fiction and notice how authors handle scenes and themes. If you're writing mainstream fiction, by all means read the classics and the latest breakout novels, but also read genre fiction. For example, pick up a few Carl Hiaasen novels and notice how quickly he gets in and out of scenes and his rapid-fire dialogue. Or if you're writing genre fiction, familiarize yourself with the best authors of your story type, and also read mainstream fiction and pay attention to language and how authors handle inner conflict.

Unlearn What You Already Know

This suggestion might sound harsh: *unlearn much of what you know about writing.* Forget term papers, annual reports, and memos. Forget corporate style and technical style, jargon and all the other writerly habits of the corporate world. If you've been writing software manuals or claim reports for the past twenty years, you might want to rent a forty-foot sailboat and head out into the Pacific until the wind, waves, and emptiness vanquish all your habits and all you can see are the many lavender shades of sunset and blue water and you come to recognize the songs of dolphins and cries of pelicans, or some indication that you are no longer a drone, uh, I mean a corporate writer.

While this unlearning transpires, toss out your multisyllabic words and obscure references because you need to construct clean sentences powered by vivid verbs. Your modifiers need to sparkle and perform a job that nouns can't manage, and metaphors and images need to trill as memorably as a chorus of bagpipes at a funeral. It's especially important that each sentence hits just the right notes.

Study the Craft

Next, *devour books on craft and attend classes* taught by true experts. Now, some writers have three children under six, so attending a writing class is impossible, but we can all learn from books on craft and online courses. Pay special attention to the blueprint aspects of writing, such as scene structure, but also garner every morsel of information like a pioneer family storing up food for a long, harsh winter.

Almost all professions require a degree or advanced degree, training, apprenticeship, or some aspect of paying your dues. You don't want a dentist digging around in your mouth with sharp objects unless he or she has graduated from dental school, and when you break your arm or develop kidney disease you want to visit someone with a diploma on the wall. Like other pros, put in the time, hit the books, and refine your skills via an apprenticeship. Most of us don't get paid for this apprenticeship and that pretty much sucks, but it seems to me that it beats racking up thousands in loans for attending medical school.

Read Poetry

Read poetry and, if you're smart, write poetry, also. Yep, I said poetry. Nothing instructs a writer about metaphor, imagery, and the potency of language more than poetry. Also nothing teaches the "less is more" truism better than poetry. Your poems don't need to be fancy, just toss out a few lines when a particular slant of light reminds you of a long-ago moment. Or write when an incident in the supermarket line starts you musing about things other than slapping together dinner and herding your family through another evening of homework and bedtime routines.

Writing and reading poetry brings us deeper into the vast sea of language because trying to convey an idea in a few lines teaches us depths of language we'd never find on our own. An easy way to read a poem a day is to subscribe to Garrison Keillor's "The Writer's Almanac." It's a brief radio program broadcast by National Public Radio stations but you can also order it delivered to your e-mail box by signing up for the almanac at http://writersalmanac.publicradio.org.

Have Fun

Writing mojo comes from having fun. After you learn the basics, play with writing. Experiment, brainstorm, and dabble. Writing starts from creativity, not anxiety—it is a great joy, so splash around and don't worry about making a mess in your early attempts.

Writers, unlike, say, tax lawyers, indulge the opinionated, naughty, silly, and unfettered aspects of their personalities. The writing self doesn't drive to work and sit in a cube for nine hours a day, five days a week while worrying about the stock market and going bald. The writing self remembers what it feels like to climb trees and bodysurf in the Atlantic and watch clouds. So yes, write smart and know what you're doing in your story and why, but also take risks and try to create with trust and abandon. Think grade-school science experiments. Stay loose and enjoy the writer's equivalent of mud and finger paints and clown hats.

Juggle

Along with this advice, *juggle several projects at once.* I know this might sound counterintuitive, but if you plod along writing only one project at a time, you won't have anything to work on if the project bogs down or you temporarily run out of steam. Sometimes we need to step away from a big project for a while as we figure out a solution to a particularly tricky difficulty. When this happens it can be refreshing to dabble in a smaller project. This sort of tinkering refreshes the imagination, creates small successes, and boosts confidence.

Write Your Heart Out

Write your heart out. When writers ask me how to approach a first draft, I advise them to write fast, as if their pants are on fire, and stay close to your story. Don't write in stops and starts, don't put it away for days, weeks, or months, allowing it to wither until it's more convenient to write. You need to put writing first in your life and keep plugging away; carry it around with you. The more often you visit with your characters, the more likely they'll whisper their truths and heartbreaks. Or if you're writing an essay or an article, get those first inspirations down while they're blazing hot and keep tinkering with your concept and structure. Once the project is done, whatever the heck that means, because a draft often doesn't feel like it's *ever* done, set it aside a bit to cool off before you start revising.

Keep a Word List

Keep a word list. A few years ago while fine-tuning a manuscript I realized with some embarrassment that I was using the same words again and again, particularly *dazzle*, *simmer*, and *whisper*. You see, all writers need to observe word territory—the same word cannot appear near its twin or appear too often. And my territory looked more like a slum in Calcutta than a wind-swept moor.

So after this project was over I created a word list. It's a simple Word document and the list is alphabetized. I constantly add to my list, especially looking for words with sparkle and oomph. Some of the words I've collected are: *silvered, slough, besieging, languor, cleaved, bluster, churr, roil, drubbing,* and *scalawag.* And keeping a word list makes reading more fun because you're always on the lookout for new additions for your list.

Use Music as Your Lodestone

After *Mystic River* was published and soared to the top of the best-seller list, I interviewed Dennis Lehane. I've never forgotten some of his advice for writers and I never forgot that he writes his first draft by hand, then types the pages into his computer each evening, editing as he goes. But I was especially fascinated when Lehane talked about how he uses particular albums or musical moods to help him through the writing process.

If you like classical or Springsteen or Pavarotti, find the tunes that soothe you when you need to be soothed, lift you when you need to be lifted, and lull you with background sounds that allow your brain to both focus and roam.

Emulate

Research, then emulate, the lives and habits of successful writers. When I talk with unpublished writers I get the impression that they think published writers are somehow different from other humans or that we've tapped into some special vat of magic. But published authors have the same quirks and neuroses as the rest of the population but have found tricks for focusing their lives on writing. Find out how your favorite writers accomplish this via researching on the Internet, reading, listening to or watching interviews, attending book signings, or watching authors on C-SPAN.

Take It Easy

Take it easy on yourself. One thing I've noticed in all the years of teaching writers is that writers are often hard on themselves—full of recriminations and I-should-know-better reproaches. Writing is a lifelong and sometimes lonely apprenticeship. Sign up for it and then realize that sometimes you're going to be the geekiest, dorkiest new kid in class. So what? Somebody's got to be the geek in the crowd. My hope in writing this book is not only that you'll make fewer mistakes, but maybe you'll laugh a bit when you discover that you screwed up.

No matter what level you've achieved with your writing,

watch how you handle your missteps. And especially listen for your inner critic. You can tell if your inner critic is running the show by the *tone* of the voice in your head. If you're calling yourself names, focusing on your mistakes, and recalling past mistakes, this means your inner critic rather than your inner editor is whispering in your ear. Your inner editor is clear-eyed, helpful, and sane. Your inner critic is sneaky, undermining, and nutty.

So here are some questions to ask yourself: What if I decide to kick the habit of self-criticism and take control of my thoughts? What if instead of listening to my inner critic, well, uncritically, that I begin engaging it in a dialogue? What if instead of always noticing my mistakes, I start focusing on what I'm doing right? What would happen if I surround myself with people who focus on my strengths? Think about it.

Find Readers

Find sophisticated and possibly coldhearted readers. Although I've just advised you to be kinder to yourself, I'm afraid I need to advise you to find not-so-kind readers. Most writers need to turn over their first manuscript to readers for feedback. Some writers can use their spouse as their trusted or first reader, but that doesn't mean this will necessarily work for you. You might want to join a critique group or beg a friend who always has his nose in a book to give you feedback. Most beginning writers just don't have the objectivity needed to see the mistakes in their early drafts, so find these angels and buy them a beautiful bottle of wine or dinner for their efforts.

Inspiration Notebook

Keep an inspiration notebook. Since we never know when inspiration will strike, and cannot rely on our memory, the first discipline of writing is to carry a writer's notebook at all times. A writer's notebook is a tool, a companion, and a treasure of ideas and dreams.

Use this inspiration notebook to remember and notice everything. See how the world is gold all around you and press these images onto the pages.

But remember, this is not a diary or a confessional. It's a place to gather, to begin stories, essays, novels, and songs that derive from your own meaning and understanding. It's a place where you hone your awareness, turning your writer's eye toward your life and your past and sorting it out. You're arranging your ideas into a format for readers, while you learn about what moves you.

Notice everything.

Walk Alone

Walk alone. The late Brenda Ueland was famous for her nine-mile rambles and advised writers to do the same in her book *If You Want to Write.* "My explanation of it," wrote Ueland, "is that when I walk in a carefree way, without straining to get to my destination, then I am living in the present. And it is only then that the creative power flourishes." Since Ueland first wrote this advice research has shown that while walking, the left-right movement stimulates creativity and right-brain activity. In *The Vein of Gold,* Julia Cameron suggests walking as a tool for creative renewal. She points out that "We speak of 'food for thought' but seldom realize that as artists we need *thought* for food. Walking, with its constant inflow of new images, gives us new thoughts that nourish us. It replenishes our overtapped creative well and gives us a sense of . . . well, wellness."

I particularly like to go for walks when I feel wrung-out by writing or when I'm struggling to articulate what is wrong with a client's manuscript. During these problem-solving walks, sometimes the missing elements and answers become apparent. At other times, I glimpse only a portion of a solution and need to keep circling it with patience. I cannot tell you how many solutions and ideas occur to me while walking and how it adds to my writing routine.

Plan B

Create a Plan B. We all need a Plan B for when the manuscript or article doesn't sell, when our plot never seems to take shape, when our day job becomes more demanding. Be flexible in your approach and keep noticing how other writers make big shifts in their careers.

Writing as Practice

Make writing your practice. I need to get woo-woo on you now because the word *practice* has an Eastern connotation, usually used by Buddhists or people describing a spiritual practice, yoga, or meditation. The idea is that your healthy habits become a central part of daily life and affect all you do. Your practice becomes deliberate, sustaining, and strengthening. My practice is writing, and I want to suggest you choose it, too. From this bedrock I capture the world I encounter and it teaches me to be more reflective and aware and centered. Like meditation, it forces me to train my mind, particularly to stay focused on a single task, for me as difficult as climbing in the Himalayas, not that you'll ever find me huffing behind a Sherpa guide. Also, and I don't quite know how to explain this, but instead of searching the world for a source of joy, my writing becomes my source of joy.

It seems that in meditation (I suck at it so can only speculate here) you watch your thoughts emerge and swim across the mind's inner screen and then release them. Writing might take an opposite approach—a way to *capture* what enters the mind as well as all that shows up in daily life. It's a way of listening in, of allowing inspiration to arrive, like opening the door to friends arriving for a dinner party.

And writing as a practice seems the opposite of straining, striving, fighting, and fretting over every idea or word. It's more of an immersion based on trust rather than wrestling words onto the page. So here is the real mojo: it helps you gain conscious control of your mind. It makes the world and your cares disappear. It helps place worries and problems in perspective. It trains you to live with a great deal of awareness and see a story everywhere you look. Writing as practice opens a door to the huge world of knowing within. Translating what you know, what prickles your skin or makes you weep, isn't easy. But with practice your translations come to life through language and the emotions you can stir with it. And that comes from ever deepening, always thinking about what you're seeing, and always questioning, always remaining open.

Resources

On Writing: A Memoir of the Craft, Stephen King

Reading Like a Writer: A Guide for People Who Love Books and for Those Who Want to Write Them, Francine Prose

The War of Art: Break Through the Blocks and Win Your Inner Creative Battles, Steven Pressfield

Page After Page: Discover the Confidence & Passion You Need to Start Writing & Keep Writing (No Matter What!), Heather Sellers

http://rejecter.blogspot.com

www.authorlink.com

Acknowledgments

If you're reading this, I probably don't need to tell you that writing isn't easy. Sometimes it's especially difficult. In the midst of writing this book, while I was stopped in traffic on a July morning of enormous beauty, a young woman searching for her ringing cell phone crashed into me when she should have been braking. Since that moment of loud impact I've been recovering from various injuries—I won't bore you with the details, but trust me, they've made writing especially not easy. I want to thank the many medical professionals who have been putting me back together, especially Glen Zielinski, whom I have designated as my genius in residence; the warm and oh-so-smart Athena Paradise; Charles Goldberg, who sees the whole person; and Joseph Goldfedder, one of the loveliest people I've ever met. I also want to acknowledge my good pal Stacey Pearo, who called often and listened and cared even when I was in pain and cranky and whiny. Thanks, too, for friends and students who kept me going and to the Willamette Writers for their support. Many thanks to Tarcher for believing in this project and the art department who designed this oh-so-fun cover, and of course, big thanks to the special talents of my smart, savvy, and easy-to-work-with editor, Gabrielle Moss. And finally, outsized thanks to the many writers I've worked with over the years. I know that this book is filled with smack talk and that I'm letting out the smart-ass, bitchy, and opinionated editor within. But please know (and I fear I sound a bit woo-woo and out of character here) that you are the mountains and sky and birdsong in my life. No matter the phase of your writing career, I recognize that you're magnificent, important, brave, and powerful. I love you and appreciate your stories, your belief in me, and your belief in the power of telling stories.

The Lingo of Fiction

Action: Events or moments in the fiction world that readers can witness, including dialogue. An action scene is a scene where the movement escalates to a crisis.

Antagonist: The character or force in the story that opposes the protagonist.

Archetype: Character type, image, or plot that is found repeatedly in storytelling, such as wise old woman, shaman, innocent child, dark forest, or road trip/journey of discovery.

Author intrusion: When the author provides information that is not known to the characters or narrator, or exists beyond the scope of the story. Usually a commentary or editorial about some aspect of the story.

Backstory: History of a character or events that took place before the story events.

Caricature: Characters that are drawn with a single, dominant trait or an exaggerated trait.

Catharsis: Describes how after the buildup of emotions (worry, fear, dread, pity), the reader feels a release at the end of a story, particularly a tragedy.

Character: A story person who is brought to life via action, attitudes, dialogue, description, thoughts, and the impressions and reactions of fellow characters. A character is also revealed through comments from the narrator, setting, choices, and decisions.

Character arc: The changes, evolution, or degradation that happens to characters over the course of the story or series. This transformation, often a lesson learned, takes fiction beyond a mere series of events and reveals changes in behaviors, views, and motivations.

Character development: The means used to develop and reveal characters, including appearance, traits, thoughts, emotions, manners, gestures, actions, backstory, and dialogue.

Cliff-hanger: When the outcome of an event, scene, or story is unknown or in doubt.

Climax: The major turning point in the story that culminates the conflict and resolves the story question, staged toward the end.

Complication: Intensifying the conflict; usually the protagonist meets an unforeseen obstacle.

Conflict: An opposing force that impedes the protagonist's progress toward his goals.

Crucible or cauldron: A locale or situation that embroils and holds together characters as the conflict in the story heats up. The characters' motivations to remain within the crucible are greater than their desire to escape it.

Denouement: The resolution of a story. Unraveling or untying the knots in a story's ending by sorting out the details and solving the questions and issues raised.

Deus ex machina: Latin for "a god from a machine." Borrowed from Greek drama in which a god descended or arrived onto the stage to resolve problems.

Dialect: In broadest terms, dialect is speech outside the norm. It illustrates a character's differences and influences stemming from culture, class, region, education, age, ethnic origin. It is rarely written exactly as it is heard; instead it imparts its essence.

Diction: A writer's or character's choice of words.

Dramatic summary: A quick means of summarizing the key point of a scene, event, or necessary information rather than providing a play-by-play depiction of action.

Dynamic characters: Characters who change as the result of events in the story. This change usually involves their worldview, beliefs, and values.

Epilogue: A device used to tell readers what happens after the story is over.

Epiphany: A key moment or revelation in the story when a character reaches a profound realization or insight, usually a reversal of his original understanding.

Episodic fiction: A story that is told in parts, where one event happens after another without a sense of overall linkage, cause and effect, or connection to a theme.

Exposition: Data necessary for understanding the story world and characters.

Falling action: The action that follows the climax and moves the story toward its resolution.

Flashback: An interruption of the front story by inserting an event or scene that happened before the story began.

Flat character: A character that is not developed or complex, or is depicted as a stereotype. Sometimes used purposely, as in minor or walk-on characters.

Foil: A character that is used to reveal qualities in the protagonist by holding the opposite qualities.

Foreshadowing: Introducing clues or hints to suggest later developments.

Frame story: A story structure where the time line is not chronological, but instead begins with the present or immediate past, then travels back in time to a more distant past, before returning to the time of the opening.

Front story: The events and forward progression of a story after the inciting incident.

Hook: An effective opening that creates a question or suggests conflict to come, and piques a reader's curiosity, demanding that he or she keep reading.

In medias res: In the middle of things, starting a story or scene in the midst of ongoing action.

Inciting incident: The precipitating event that sets the story in motion, disrupts the status quo, and threatens the protagonist.

Inner conflict: A character's confusion, resistance, or doubts about his goals and direction.

Interior dialogue or monologue: Revealing a character's thoughts.

Melodrama: Using or exploiting implausible, sensational, sentimental, or emotionally charged aspects in a story to create drama.

Motivation: A character's drive that builds throughout a story and provides plausible explanations for actions and goals.

Multiple viewpoint: A story that rotates the point of view, with the reader going into the thoughts of more than one character. Best used to illustrate maximum character contrast.

Narrative: The story, or what happens in fiction and nonfiction.

Narrative distance: The degree of access that the reader is granted to the characters' thoughts, perceptions, and knowledge.

Narrator: The voice and implied speaker in fiction who tells the story—this is not the writer. The narrator can be an insider in the story—a major character, a first-person character, or a minor character.

Novelette: Stories of about eight thousand to twenty thousand words.

Novella: Fiction generally considered between twenty thousand and forty thousand words, but can vary.

Pace: The speed at which the story unfolds.

Plot: A unified, designed structure or arrangement of events. This series of causally related events emerges from a series of ever-intensifying conflicts, reveals characters, and forces them to take action and push toward a climactic conclusion.

Plot line: The series of events that push a story ahead.

Plot point: Crucial events in fiction from which there is no turning back and which crank up tension and introduce new elements and complications.

Point of view (viewpoint): Perspective, vantage point, or filtering consciousness from which the story is presented.

Premise: The takeaway message of the story, proven as a result of the story ending. For example, *Love conquers all* or *Humankind is essentially good.*

Protagonist: The main character in fiction that the reader comes to know intimately, and who is most changed and hurt by the events of the plot.

Recognition: The moment in a story when a character (usually the protagonist) understands the truth of his or her situation.

Resolution: The ending in the story after the climax when the situation is sorted out.

Reversal: The moment in a story when an unexpected event occurs, changing the plot direction.

Rising action: The events, conflicts, and crises that happen in the story leading up to the climax.

Round character: A character who is developed to the point that a reader comes to understand him and his worldview.

Scene: A structural unit in fiction, set in a precise time and location and made up of action, description, and sometimes exposition. A scene is an event that is essential to the plot, is based around a goal or purpose, meeting some form of opposition, and usually contains some form of emotional reversal.

Secondary characters: The supporting cast in fiction who help develop the plot, subplots, and major characters. True secondary characters know or come into contact with the protagonist and are developed more fully.

Sequel: A section that follows a scene where a character reacts to events.

Setting: Time and place of a story, including weather, interiors, geography, region, lighting, and other factors that establish credibility and context.

Short short: Fiction story that is under one thousand words.

Short story: Fiction story that is under ten thousand words but is often much shorter.

Speech tag, dialogue tag, or tagline: Information that accompanies dialogue and briefly introduces who is talking, as in "he said" or "she asked." In general, speech tags should be invisible and exist only to prevent confusion.

Static: A term that describes a scene or story element that lacks action, dialogue, and tension and doesn't serve to push the story forward.

Static character: A character who remains unchanged throughout the story. Static is not necessarily a negative connotation.

Stock characters: Minor characters who occupy traditional roles, such as nosy neighbor, sassy waitress, cynical cop, etc.

Story line: The series of linked events that follows a protagonist pursuing the story goal toward a resolution and fulfills the story's promise, thus making it emotionally satisfying.

Style: How a writer uses language to communicate ideas or a story. Includes voice, syntax, diction, sentence length and structure, and figurative language.

Subplot: A subordinate story line or series of minor events that coexist and weave through the main story line, such as a romance brewing within a suspense story.

Subtext: The river of emotion that lies beneath scenes. Usually what is unspoken during dialogue, often because it is too dangerous to speak of.

Suspense: Creating curiosity, worry, and involvement by withholding and delaying information and resolutions.

Symbol: An object, action, or image imbued with meaning; it stands for something beyond itself.

Telling: Can refer to relating information that happens offstage or a habit of summarizing rather than dramatizing action, emotions, and information.

Theme: Central idea and concern in the story. It is often a fairly simple concept, such as pride, patriotism, greed, or justice. Theme is not the moral of the story; it unifies the story, providing a foundation and boundaries.

Timeline: The amount of time that elapses between the first and final event.

Tone: The writer's attitude or implied attitude toward the material and sometimes the reader, expressed through word choice and imagery.

Transition: Words, phrases, and sentences that move readers through time and space and indicate a change of mood or emotion.

Unreliable narrator: A narrator who intentionally or unintentionally misleads the reader. Often has a hidden agenda, secret, or specific reason for misleading the reader.

Voice: The distinct and memorable sound of the writer, narrator, or character.

Wraparound structure: A story that begins near the climax, then returns to the opening scene or inciting incident and proceeds toward the end.

The Lingo of Publishing

Advance: Money paid to an author in anticipation of royalty earnings.

Advance copies: The first copies of the book from the printer sent out early for publicity mailings.

Advance reader's copies (ARCs): Are usually bound galleys sent out to bookstores and media several months ahead of publication.

Agent: A person who represents the author's manuscript to the publisher, negotiates contracts, and acts as a liaison between the author and publisher.

Backlist: Books still in print but not recently published.

Back matter: The sections after the main body of a book, such as appendix, index, endnotes, bibliography, author biography.

Book doctor: A professional who provides an editorial service for a specified fee.

Clips: Photocopies of a writer's published writing samples.

Distributor: A company that buys books from publishers and resells them to retail accounts.

Earn out: The point where a writer sells enough books to earn the advance payment, after which royalties can be paid on subsequent sales.

Front matter: The pages, such as table of contents, dedication, and epigraph, that appear before the main body of a book.
Galley: Early version of typeset pages in prepublication stage. Often used by author and copy editor to proof before publication. A galley copy can also be bound and sent to reviewers before publication.
Genre or category fiction: Categories of books designed to appeal to a specific market, meaning readers. Genres include westerns, thrillers, mysteries, male adventure, romance, science fiction, fantasy, and historical. Genre can also refer to nonfiction, as in how-to, memoir, and self-help. Within the major genres are subgenres.
Graphics: The parts of a book that are not writing, such as photographs, graphs, illustrations, charts, etc., used to enhance and explain the text.
Handle: A brief description of a book designed to generate interest.
House or publishing house: A book publishing firm. Can also refer to an imprint or division within a large publishing company.
Imprint: A specific line of books published by a publishing house.
ISBN: International Standard Book Number—the identifying code assigned to books.
Line space: Four blank lines inserted into a double-spaced manuscript.
Mainstream fiction: The opposite of genre fiction.
Market: The readers of a particular type of writing.
Mass market paperbacks: The inexpensive, small paperbacks sold in a wide range of retail outlets, including grocery stores as well as bookstores.
Mid-list: An author or title that has respectable sales but has not become a best seller.
Multiple submission: Copies of the same manuscript sent to more than one market, publishing house, or agent.
Out of print: A title no longer stored in the publisher's inventory or listed in its catalog.
Platform: Industry buzzword for the author's or would-be author's visibility in the marketplace and ability to reach an audience via various media.
Preface: Introductory materials that explain why the book was written.
Press kit: Information provided to reviewers, journalists, and bookstores

about a new book. It includes a press release, author bio, copy of the book cover, testimonials, etc.

Print run: The total number of copies a publishing house will print in the first printing. This number is arrived at by considering the author's previous sales history, copies that have been presold, and similar books that exist in the marketplace.

Proposal: A summary of information about a proposed nonfiction book, complete with an overview of the contents, marketing research, and competition analysis.

Remaindered: The excess stock of unsold books that can be sold at discounted prices.

Return: Copies of a book that have not been sold and are returned to the publisher by the bookstore or wholesaler.

Royalties: The amount paid to the author by the publishing house per book sold. Royalty percentages vary and are based on a percentage of the cover price.

Slush pile: The unsolicited manuscripts held by a publisher waiting to be read/reviewed.

Small press: Small-scale publisher—usually publishes fewer than twenty-five titles per year.

Submission guidelines: A publishing house's specific guidelines for how they want a manuscript formatted. Also a publisher's guidelines for submitting queries, proposals, and manuscripts.

Subsidiary rights: Additional rights; other means for a published work to generate income, such as audio, or selling a portion to a magazine or selling the rights to an overseas publisher.

Synopsis: A detailed summary that outlines the key events, plot points, and characters in a manuscript.

Tip sheet: Guidelines created by a publisher to clarify how to write for a specific line of books.

Trade paperbacks: Large and more expensively produced paperbacks sold chiefly in bookstores.

Unagented submission: Proposal for book or manuscript that is sent to publishing houses without an agent's representation.

Unsolicited manuscript: A manuscript, proposal, or article that an editor did not ask for.

Word length: Length of a novel or nonfiction work, expressed in the number of words.

Index

About the Author

Jessica Page Morrell is the author of *Bullies, Bastards & Bitches: How to Write the Bad Guys in Fiction; The Writer's I Ching: Wisdom for the Creative Life; Voices from the Street; Between the Lines: Master the Subtle Elements of Fiction Writing;* and *Writing Out the Storm*. She works as a developmental editor and teaches writers in workshops in the Northwest, at writing conferences throughout North America, and at Evergreen College, in Olympia, Washington. She began teaching writers in 1991 and was formerly the writing expert at iVillage.com. She hosts a website at www.writing-life.com, and has written a monthly column on topics related to writing since 1998, currently running in *The Willamette Writer*. She also contributes to *The Writer* and *Writer's Digest* magazines, and writes a monthly e-mail newsletter, "The Writing Life," as well as a Web log at http://thewritinglifetoo.blogspot.com. Jessica will never take part in a reality TV show where you need to cohabit or compete with backstabbing strangers, because she's not perky or conniving, but she is smart-alecky and rabidly opinionated about most things, especially politics. She lives in Portland, Oregon, where she is surrounded by writers.

NEW ACCENTS

General Editor: TERENCE HAWKES

Dialogism

IN THE SAME SERIES

The Empire Writes Back: Theory and practice in post-colonial literatures *Bill Ashcroft, Gareth Griffiths, and Helen Tiffin*
Literature, Politics and Theory: Papers from the Essex Conference 1976–84 ed. *Francis Barker, Peter Hulme, Margaret Iversen, and Diana Loxley*
Translation Studies *Susan Bassnett-McGuire*
Rewriting English: Cultural politics of gender and class *Janet Batsleer, Tony Davies, Rebecca O'Rourke, and Chris Weedon*
Critical Practice *Catherine Belsey*
Formalism and Marxism *Tony Bennett*
Dialogue and Difference: English for the nineties ed. *Peter Brooker and Peter Humm*
Telling Stories: A theoretical analysis of narrative fiction *Steven Cohan and Linda M. Shires*
Alternative Shakespeares ed. *John Drakakis*
Poetry as Discourse *Antony Easthope*
The Semiotics of Theatre and Drama *Keir Elam*
Reading Television *John Fiske and John Hartley*
Literature and Propaganda *A.P. Foulkes*
Linguistics and the Novel *Roger Fowler*
The Return of the Reader: Reader-response criticism *Elizabeth Freund*
Making a Difference: Feminist literary criticism ed. *Gayle Green and Coppellia Kahn*
Superstructuralism: The philosophy of structuralism and post-structuralism *Richard Harland*
Structuralism and Semiotics *Terence Hawkes*
Subculture: The meaning of style *Dick Hebdige*
Reception Theory: A critical introduction *Robert C. Holub*
Popular Fictions: Essays in Literature and History ed. *Peter Humm, Paul Stigant, and Peter Widdowson*
The Politics of Postmodernism *Linda Hutcheon*
Fantasy: The literature of subversion *Rosemary Jackson*
Sexual/Textual Politics: Feminist literary theory *Toril Moi*
Deconstruction: Theory and practice *Christopher Norris*
Orality and Literacy: The technologizing of the word *Walter J. Ong*
Science Fiction: Its criticism and teaching *Patrick Parrinder*
The Unusable Past: Theory and the study of American literature *Russell J. Reising*
Narrative Fiction: Contemporary poetics *Shlomith Rimmon-Kenan*
Criticism in Society *Imre Salusinszky*
Metafiction: The theory and practice of self-conscious fiction *Patricia Waugh*
Psychoanalytic Criticism: Theory in practice *Elizabeth Wright*